Family Traditions

Family Traditions

Celebrations for Holidays and Everyday

by Elizabeth Berg

Illustrations by Robert Roth

The Reader's Digest Association, Inc.
Pleasantville, N.Y./ Montreal

Acknowledgments

My thanks to Elisabeth Crow, former editor at *Parents* magazine, who got me started; to Deborah DeFord, who edited this book with incredible patience, skill, and sensitivity; to James Wagenvoord, who knows how to make a writer feel believed in; and to Alison Brown Cerier, who thought of this book in the first place. Thanks as well to all the friends and strangers who shared their ideas with me—their names would fill another book, and I would happily read it.

We thank Joseph Bruchac III for permitting the inclusion of his poem, "Birdfoot's Grandpa," copyright© 1976 by Joseph Bruchac III.

Illustrations by Robert Roth
Book and jacket design by Janet Wertsching Kanca
Cover calligraphy by Elaine Dillard

A Reader's Digest book.

Produced by The Reader's Digest Association, Inc., in association with Alison Brown Cerier Book Development, Inc.
Copyright © 1992 Alison Brown Cerier Book Development, Inc., and Elizabeth Berg.

Library of Congress Cataloging in Publication Data

Berg, Elizabeth.
    Family traditions: celebrations for holidays and everyday/by Elizabeth Berg.
        p.   cm.
    Includes index.
    ISBN 0-89577-456-9
    1. Family festivals.   2. Holidays.   I. Title.
GT2400.B47 1992
394.2—dc20   92-23896

Printed in the United States of America

This book is dedicated to my family: Howard, Julie, and Jennifer, without whom I would have not much.

Contents

Today's Family

We live in an age in which it is hard to spend time together as a family. We are inordinately busy, for one thing, whether primary wage earners or elementary school pupils. Also, the definition of family has changed. We are dealing with new and complicated ways of living together. Some of us have nuclear families. Some of us are divorced and single parents; some of us are remarried; and some of us have remarried more than once, creating a rather confusing assemblage of members who aren't entirely sure where on the family tree they belong. Some of us may choose to live our lives alone, but may still be close enough to some friends to consider them more family than family.

Whatever our circumstances, many of us honestly don't know how to celebrate together. We may even see "tradition" as something stultifying and old and rigid, nothing that has any meaning for or application to us personally.

What all of this means is that we can no longer simply follow the examples of old; it is up to us to create new family traditions and celebrations.

The celebrating part is not so hard. We know all about celebrating, and we have some ways of doing it; the only challenge is to find new ways—probably some ideas you have not tried before. The most important thing is that we understand the need for celebration: It lifts days away from other days, gives us something to look forward to, makes a formal statement that life is full of things to be grateful for.

The notion of honoring tradition is a little harder. We understand that we need something to add a sense of order and stability to our lives. But we are not so sure about how to create our own traditions. We seem to think that they must be heavy and complex ideas that have been around for hundreds of years and intend to hang around for a couple hundred more. As far as I'm concerned, nothing could be further from the truth. I believe a tradition is something that you do once and it feels right; and so you do it again and again. It is a ritual dressed up in evening clothes, its chest inflated, its home in your heart. And it need not be big or heavy or religious or difficult at all.

For example, every morning my husband makes coffee and puts out two cups: his and mine. I rely on this. If I had to reach into the cupboard to get my own cup, something would be wrong. As it is, I get up, I come into the kitchen, I see my cup sitting there, and I know I'm me, in my house, ready to start the morning; and I feel a little happy. Similarly, I sleep every night with a greatly damaged pillow that really should be thrown away but for which I have an enduring fondness. When I lay my head on it, I know I am me, at night, in my bed, ready for sleep; and I am comforted. Every Saturday night, my husband makes dinner while I lie on the sofa reading a good book and listening to the pleasant clangs and bangs of someone else making a meal. On Sunday, our family goes out for Chinese food. These small things are some of our traditions. They identify us like a fingerprint. They anchor us. If we did not have these particular traditions, we would have others. That is because traditions insist upon themselves: Look around, and you will see them trying to exist everywhere, in everyone's life. Clearly, we need them.

I know of a man who is very important in his job, works long hours, and is almost never home for dinner. Except on Friday. Then he leaves the office at four o'clock, no matter what is going on. His family knows that they can depend on this, and they celebrate with a fancy dinner at home every Friday night.

My friends Jeff and Dan have a house that has both a living room and a family room. I have never seen them—or evidence of them—in their living room. Once I admired its beautiful decoration and said, "But you never use it, do you?" "Oh, yes!" they said. "Every Sunday, we read the paper in here."

My neighbor decorates the rear side windows of her van for the season: Valentines, snowflakes, pumpkins and fireworks are drawn by her children and taped into place. I think of her car as a mobile cheer-spreader.

My friend Keith tells his son Adam "Bellybutton Stories." Every night at seven-thirty, another episode is delivered. If Keith is out of town, as he often must be, he calls—from a plane, if necessary. It is hard to tell who gets more out of this.

All of these things are traditions, inventions of people who mean to routinely put love and comfort and meaning into their lives, and into the lives of those they live with.

THE FAMILY WE CREATE

It used to be obvious what "family" meant. You could find it clearly represented everywhere, from first-grade readers to television screens, and it was always the same: a bread-winner, work-away-from-home father, a stay-at-home, cookie-baking mother, and apple-cheeked children who aspired to not much more than emulating their parents. This notion has not entirely left us: We may view the past with humor and even horror, but we also view it with a mix of guilt and powerful nostalgia. Something about that bygone framework worked. Something about it made family members feel not so desperate and empty. But something about it also did not work, or we would not have changed so much.

I believe that "family" can mean a group of two or more people who care about each other and want to spend time together. I believe that single people can be part of families, by being "adopted," or by "borrowing." I know, for example, of a single man who annually invites his friends' children to help him make Christmas cookies; and there are old people taken into families from nursing homes. Finally, there are people who live alone and feel no need for family involvement of any kind, but who enjoy creating and observing traditions of their own, all by themselves or with a changing array of co-celebrators. I believe that all of these people can find new and meaning-ful traditions that help to shape and express their lives.

THE STUFF OF TRADITIONS

Where do traditions come from? Sometimes they get started because of a unique experience shared—by you and your family alone—and then purposefully re-created. Sometimes they are suggested by holidays, special events, momentous occasions. They can be what "everyone else" does (like eat turkey on Thanksgiving); or there can be a twist that is all your own (my family enjoys "Thanksgiving, Part Two" dinners).

Consider history as inspiration—your family's, your country's, your religion's. I find history often beautiful and always interesting and helpful in providing perspective. It has a way of marking our place in the larger sense. It can give us a feeling like we get when we lie on our backs looking at the stars.

Let me set up a situation for you that will probably not happen: You will find an idea that makes you very excited. You will want to share it with your family, implement it right away. You will tell them about it. They will be very excited, too. You will instantly put it into practice. You will enjoy it very much, even more than you thought you would, and you will continue to do it forevermore. This sounds great, right? Why won't it happen? Well, because people are slow to adopt new ideas. They are suspicious about them. They are resistant to them. And sometimes, when one member of the family is greatly enthusiastic about something, other members feel obliged to rain on the parade a little. Teenagers have a reputation, deserved or not, for hating everything parents come up with. Women typically are more interested in making changes and improvements than men. And so on and so on.

My advice is to forget about these stereotypes, and forge ahead with enthusiasm. No matter who you are or what your place in your family is, if you discover an idea and you want to try it, do! And then try it again. Give it a few times before you decide whether it's working or not.

On the other hand, don't be afraid to reject things that don't work. If something appealed to you, but then didn't go over, maybe you can make changes that make sense for your own unique group of people. Or maybe you can try something else altogether that didn't seem like it would work, but in fact does.

Above all, remember that the object here is to have fun as well as to create something special and meaningful for people who mean a lot to you. Any effort directed to that end is energy well spent.

Every Day Is Special

We don't need a preordained date on the calendar to have a reason for celebration. Our lives are rich with events and relationships that are worthy of marking, of building traditions around, when and where we say.

We have ways of being that define us, become necessary to us. We like to go to sleep and wake up in a certain way. We like wearing certain things for certain reasons; going certain places at certain times. Of such things are our own traditions made.

If no special holiday is coming up on the calendar, we can put it there. We can let our imaginations soar; insist on Christmas when we're ready for it in July; eat Thanksgiving dinner all over again, three days after Thanksgiving.

Just setting aside time for the family to play together can give us both a reminder and permission to have fun together. A mundane Tuesday becomes something special, just because we say so.

We can work harder to understand each other: decree a time and a place where we will make every effort to work cooperatively together, to appreciate and understand each other's point of view, to make plans together.

So much about us is up to us! We have a lot to do with our happiness, our contentment, our level of involvement in the lives we live together. Every move we make toward a happier family life is a move toward making us happier individuals. Every day really can be special, just because we decide to make it so.

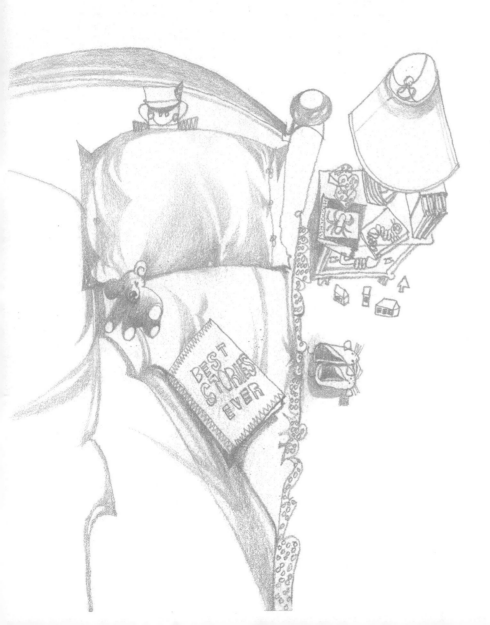

Everyday Rituals

*I have an old gray cardigan sweater
that should have been thrown out long ago.
But it is comfortable and familiar, and I
wear it nearly every day when the weather is
cold. "Well, summer's over now," my
neighbor says when she sees me in it for
the first time each fall. My sweater has, in
that way, become a marker for both of us,
a way of showing where we are in the
cycle of seasons and of our lives. It has
become a ritual.*

"I t's always the little things" holds particularly true when we consider the value of everyday rituals. For it is these small practices, these recurring and unique habits, that provide the color and comfort and richness in our lives. They are in large measure what define us. They also do a lot for making us feel secure. In a world unstable and frightening, it is a relief to have predictability in your daily life. Thus it is that many of us have our favorite coffee cups we drink from each morning, and our own unvarying routine for preparing for bed at night.

Where do these rituals come from? Some come from the families we grew up in, or from our religious backgrounds or practice. Some we make up, because of our particular likes and dislikes and because of our needs. Some, though, we see someone else doing and think to ourselves, Hey! I'd like to do that, too!

I hereby present all manner of rituals to you, many that can be done daily, in hopes that you will find some to enrich your own life. Don't wear a sweater as disreputable as mine, though. Your family will never stop giving you grief about it. (My family has even been known to hide my sweater. I suppose that is one of their rituals. But one of mine is that I always find it.)

AT MEALTIMES

Dinnertime is often the only time for a family to be together. It seems important that at least once a day all members sit down together and relax, find out what everybody is up to. A little effort put into making each meal special goes a long way. Also, these rituals provide a sense of wholeness, even if members must occasionally be

missing: older children coming and going; a parent on a business trip. The stability of the rituals helps make for continuity when changes are made within a family as well as when a new family member is introduced.

SAYING GRACE   A mealtime prayer can be something traditional and familiar, something that's been said in your family for years. It can also be a more spontaneous and general offering up of thanks—perhaps for something nice that happened today. Rotate turns for being the one to say grace, or say it all together, perhaps by singing it. It is a good thing, before diving into your meal, to stop for a moment to appreciate the presence of the food, the labor of the cook, the satisfaction of being hungry and knowing that relief is before you.

ROTATE ROOMS   Although it is certainly convenient to eat in the kitchen or the dining room, no one says you have to. It can be fun once a week to eat elsewhere: outside in the summer, before a blazing fireplace in the winter, in someone's bedroom just for kicks. (The person whose room it is can make it his or her "restaurant" for the night— decorate accordingly, greet the clientele at the door with menus, provide specially chosen music.) On Sunday night, you might get in pajamas early, order out for Chinese food, and watch a family movie together as you eat.

ETHNIC NIGHTS   Make a Mexican meal complete with colorful napkins, authentic condiments, and a piñata. I once went to a Chinese grocery store for the ingredients for a chicken dish, and ended up bringing home the "right" soup spoons and bowls, and chopsticks, too. Dinner was more fun that night, and now we regularly use those dishes when we eat Chinese food. In summer, try an Asian picnic under Chinese paper lanterns. Don't forget to celebrate your own ethnic background, too!

NAPKINS Disposable table products come in astounding varieties. It's fun to go to a party store and buy a large variety, so that the dinner table always looks different. Cloth napkins are great to use, too—they feel more elegant, do a better job, and are reusable.

CANDLES Light them one night a week for a special reason: hope for world peace, the recuperation of a loved one from illness, the recovery of the environment.

FAMILY BULLETIN BOARDS These can be used to hold magazine clippings, photographs, notices about upcoming events, this week's favorite comic strip, and letters. The board can be cleared each evening, and the material brought to the table for discussion.

CENTERPIECES Table arrangements can be much more than a bouquet of flowers. Perhaps a toddler would like a beloved teddy bear to occupy the place of honor at the dinner table. Perhaps Dad bought a new objet d'art that he'd like everyone to view and appreciate before putting it in its permanent place. When the leaves are gorgeous in the fall, they make a wonderful centerpiece. (Careful, though. One city mom newly transplanted to the country decorated her table beautifully from what she found outside—poison ivy!) Centerpieces, in short, are limited only by your imagination and the space allotted to them.

Picnic from the Far East

FROM THE GRILL
Skewered Spicy Jumbo Shrimp
Sweet and Sour Chicken Wings
Mushroom Caps Stuffed With
Water Chestnuts

FROM THE GARDEN
Julienned Vegetable Sticks
(carrots, celery, zucchini, green
peppers, spring onions, sweet
red peppers)

FROM THE KITCHEN
Cold Rice Salad
(with snow peas, mandarin
orange, and sesame dressing)
Fried Wontons
Fortune Cookies

One-of-a-Kind Napkin Rings

Spend an evening together making a family collection of napkin rings.

- Start with large wooden curtain rings or plain store-bought napkin rings.
- Paint on colors, designs and/or names; or glue on ribbon, dried nuts, beans or seeds, macaroni, buttons, or braid; or wrap tightly with hemp twine, string, or yarn and tie it off when you've completely covered the ring.
- Use several coats of a good polyurethane varnish to finish off your creation for a longer-lasting treasure.

AFTER-BREAKFAST CIRCLE If you're one of the rare families that eat breakfast together, consider adopting the tradition of holding hands together to observe a full minute of silence before you start your day. It is a peaceful beginning, a kind of deep breath before the onslaught.

MAXIMIZING TIME TOGETHER

For most of us, there is never enough time to do all that we want to do. Sometimes the things we care most about get the least of us. Parents worry that children are not getting enough time with them, and they are often right. One of the ways to work against that is to include your children as much as possible in daily activities.

DINNERTIME HELP Contrary to popular opinion, children do like to help. Assign your children jobs they can handle, from folding or illustrating with crayons the paper napkins you'll use on the table, to making the salad. Being in the kitchen together lets you spend time conversing, bumping affectionately into each other, sharing in the business of being a family. It may not be as fast as one person working efficiently, alone, but it's a lot friendlier.

THE LAUNDRY BRIGADE When you go to sort the laundry, bring a kid or two. Have them find all the towels and put them in a pile for you. Or sit them on the dryer to swing their legs and tell you about what they did in art today while you sort the towels. When kids get older, they are able to take on more responsibilities in the laundry room, of course. Then you can work side by side, enjoying conversation about your son's latest basketball game while you both fold the socks. Make sure you don't send your child off to college without knowing how to do laundry!

WARDROBE DUTY Help each other lay out clothes for tomorrow. Sometimes your children will come up with new combinations for you that you'd never have thought of. (Sometimes you or your children will need to exercise a great deal of tact. The words "interesting" and "someday" come into play here. Last time I suggested an outfit for one of my daughters, that's exactly what she said: "Oh! Well, uh, that's interesting. Maybe someday.")

THE DAILY CLEAN-UP Tidying up can be made more interesting by trading messes. You clean up the Lincoln Logs or make headway through the pile of clothes and CDs on the floor; your child puts away the shoes you left in the living room, gathers together your work papers.

MAKING LUNCHES Do it together, assembly-line fashion. Once in a while, include a "surprise" of some sort: a picture from a magazine, a cartoon, or simply a note saying the person is terrific.

KEEPING IN TOUCH Once a week, try sitting at the kitchen table together after dinner and writing a postcard apiece to someone special: Grandma and Grandpa, a special friend, even a famous person you admire. The postcard size assures that this will not take long. This task might be accomplished by your children while you are paying bills—you drop a "note" to the electric company, and your child sends greetings to Aunt Vicki.

MORNING WISH   Each day, before dividing up for your respective "jobs," have each family member make a wish for the day. This can be for a promotion, a good grade on a test, even for a sunny day. Have a recording secretary write the wishes down. That night at dinner, see if anyone's wish came true.

DAILY LEISURE TIME   Relaxing together is important, even if you can only fit in fifteen minutes at a stretch. You can break up a movie into a mini series—watch a little each night. Spend time with the family pets. Go for a walk. Make sure that you get in a little pleasure in the middle of all your obligations.

SPECIAL TIMES

Luckily, there are times when the family is not rushed and stressed and fragmented; you can be together in a more leisurely way. Perhaps that is on a weekend. Perhaps it is during the rehabilitative phase of an illness. It may be a rainy day, or a snowy one. Sometimes when one parent is out of town, the other takes a more laid-back approach to family routines. All of these are opportunities to share special times and to create new habits.

THE FAMILY-ACTIVITIES JAR   It's important that the family do something together for at least a couple of hours a week. The jar is a place for family members to make suggestions for what they would like: visiting the zoo or the art museum, going to a movie, and going roller skating are just a few possibilities. The person making the suggestion signs her or his name, and activities are chosen on a rotating basis. Every family member may not enjoy what every other member likes to do, but one of the reasons for this practice is to learn appreciation for others' points of view. I, for example, who usually prefer art museums and plays and concerts for activities, have become a bit of a "motor head," like my husband. I now actually enjoy looking at Corvettes, and I have spent several hours at a racing park. (OK, I brought a novel with me, but I went.)

THE IN-HOME CONCERT Find out about different composers by renting tapes or CDs from the library. Then have a living room concert. You may want to preface it by reading aloud some information you've gathered about the composer you're playing. (It's always more interesting to listen to music when you know a little about the person who created it.) Try classical, jazz, country and western, opera. When you find something you like, you might want to buy it to start building up a music library. You can also have family recitals, where everyone contributes, whether by a sophisticated piano sonata or free-form kazoo.

TURNABOUT MEALS On weekends, let the kids decide what's for breakfast, and make it, then call the parents to the table. Or, even better, let the one who usually prepares breakfast stay in bed, and be served a beautiful breakfast there. A close relative to this idea is for the parent who doesn't usually cook to do so one evening a week.

BAKING DAY One father loves to make bread with his preschoolers. Every Saturday, he puts up some fancy coffee, plays his favorite old rock and roll, outfits himself and his children in "professional" aprons, and gets going on white bread, or whole wheat, or herb; or croissants, bagels, even pretzels. If bread-making seems too big an undertaking, remember that making cookies takes very little time—and there's nothing like eating chocolate chip

Anytime Drop-in Biscuits

This is a quick and easy bread to make that can add a nice touch to any meal and add fun to kitchen time together.

2 c. flour	2/3 c. shortening
3 T. sugar	1 large egg
4 t. baking powder	1 c. milk
1/2 t. salt	

Mix dry ingredients together. Cut in shortening. Mix egg and milk, then add to flour-shortening mixture, and stir just till moist. Drop by heaping tablespoonsful on greased baking sheet. Bake at 425° F for 10 - 12 minutes. For breakfast: Make a well in top of unbaked biscuit and fill with teaspoon of fruit preserves. For lunch: Add 1/2 c. of grated cheese to dry ingredients. For dinner: Add 1/2 c. currants and 1/4 c. chopped walnuts. OR: Make them pure and simple and eat with butter, gravy, honey, or absolutely no topping at all!

cookies straight from the oven, accompanied by a big glass of cold milk. Look through a cookbook together for inspiration. There's no age limit on interest in this idea, and there's no end of recipes to try!

PET NIGHT   Pick a night of the week to be devoted to the family pet. Take your dog for a long walk or brush him; treat your cat to a new toy; buy your fish a new plant. It's really fun to go "shopping" at a pet store! And whatever type of pet you have, he deserves it—he gets along with everybody, never complains, and helps relieve stress.

ONE ON ONE   To rediscover your children, separate them. Make an arrangement where there is a one-to-one ratio. Or leave all your children but one home with a babysitter, and let that child have one or both parents to himself. One family does this on each child's birthday, but it can be done on a rotating basis anytime.

OUT-OF TOWN SPECIALS   One parent or the other may have to travel out of town frequently. Why not make up some traditions for when this happens? For example, the night before you go, write a goodbye note and tuck it under family members' pillows. Call home at a certain time each night, preferably close to bedtime. Bring back gifts for all, of the silliest things you can find. For those who stay home, let this be a time for things that aren't usually allowed: eating junk food for dinner one night, or having a huge sleep-over party. When my husband goes out of town, I declare myself free of cooking, and my kids and I eat out every night.

RAINY-DAY-CLOSET   Buy things throughout the year that will make for a rainy-day activity: board games, drawing

supplies, clay and paints, books, paper dolls, squirt guns, sewing cards, jigsaw puzzles. Wrap these things like presents. On a day when you have to stay in because of the weather, let your children select something, grab-bag style. The key is not to offer too much. My mother once entertained my children for two days straight building card houses with them. Adults in the family like surprises, too: a new CD, a bottle of fine wine, or a volume of essays.

CRAFT TIME There is no one who can't make something! Many craft ideas take only a couple of minutes: sewing a fancy appliqué onto socks, for example, or making a tiny cottonball "snowman" for outside a dollhouse. You can paint a shirt with fabric paint, make a wall hanging out of felt. Back a favorite photograph with cardboard, then cut it up for a puzzle. Teenagers might want custom-made furniture for their rooms, such as beanbag chairs made from fabric they select, or shelving that they help to anchor to their bedroom wall. Wander through any crafts store for many more ideas. Remember that a long-term project is fun to work on together a little at a time. My younger daughter worked for a long while with her father in his basement workshop, eventually producing a toy box for our dog. We proudly display it in the living room, and the dog really uses it! (Of course, he's much better at taking things out of it than putting them away in it.) We've also made dolls and stuffed animals that took forever, but that are held in higher regard than the store-bought guys.

SICK DAYS Unfortunately, these days do happen. Some of the misery can be alleviated by comfort you unfailingly provide. For example, present meals, even if it's only Jell-O

Make a Book for Family Memories

- Start with your pick of photo album or scrapbook.
- Inscribe your family name and year(s) included on the front and spine (use permanent marker, or white ink, or make a paper or cloth inset to glue on).
- Make a title page: This should include a current photo of each family member, and/or a group photo, as well as a picture of each family pet; the starting date of your book; your current address and phone number.
- Create collages for each special time: Special times can include celebrations, big days, vacations, parties, performances, holidays, or special visits from out-of-town. To make the collages, glue into the book ticket stubs, rail passes, programs, postcards, dried flowers from a boutonniere or corsage, photographs, menus, matchbox covers, or anything else that will help you remember that special time together.

and broth, to the sick person on a tray made beautiful with doilies and a flower—fresh, dried, or drawn—in a vase. A cool washcloth laid across a forehead is something that's always done in our house for a fever. The sick person is allowed to have stacks of movies and books and magazines. He or she may also expect a gift when the working parent returns home. My children usually camp out in my bed when they're ill—something about being close to Mom and Dad, I suppose, comforts them. Also, our double bed is big enough for the caretaker to lie down with them to watch movies, read, play games, or simply rest. When a lot of tissues are being used, I draw an open-mouthed person or creature on a large grocery bag. The mouth is the hole through which the tissues are tossed. This bag does wonders for keeping used tissues in one place. Remember that parents deserve pampering when they're sick, too!

CELEBRATION DISHES   Every so often, something happens worth celebrating that has nothing to do with calendar holidays. Someone got rid of braces or aced a difficult exam. Someone got a raise, a new office, a new job. Grandpa sailed through his open-heart surgery. Someone special has come to visit. Every time something special happens to a family member, or to the whole family, the celebration dishes come out. They may be just a dimestore cup and saucer, or a whole place setting of elegant china. But they always make the special event official, and they are never used for anything else. You may want to add a homemade crown for the special person's head, or a glittery star to put beside the plate.

THE CELEBRATION-OF-FAMILY DINNER Make this once a year or seasonal. Pick a Sunday, and dress up for a very special dinner featuring all the family favorites, even if they don't "go together" (there is no law that says tacos and prime rib can't be on the table at the same time). Have everyone write down three appreciative statements about being in the family, and read them at dessert time. Also, have each person bring to the table an object that symbolizes something important. Use these objects as a centerpiece, and during dinner let each member talk about why they are important.

WRAPPING CENTER Some special occasions call for a family wrap session. Here's where your wrapping center, which you attend to all year, comes into play. Keep wrapping paper and ribbon together in one special place. Remember that you can get really good buys on things after their season has passed. Also remember that you don't have to stop at paper and ribbons—encourage all family members to add other beautiful objects to decorate your gifts.

BEDTIME RITUALS

MAKE-UP TIME The world is imperfect; families fight. But it really is a good idea not to go to bed mad. Try to make sure that wrongs between family members are righted before everyone goes to sleep. Talk together about what went wrong and what might help. If you don't feel you can say it, write a note to apologize, or make a gesture that clearly says you want to start over. If the bad feelings have to do

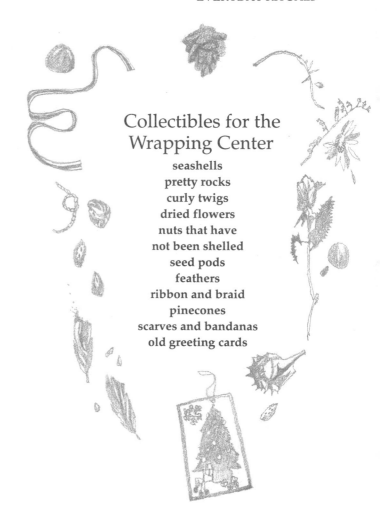

Collectibles for the Wrapping Center

seashells
pretty rocks
curly twigs
dried flowers
nuts that have
not been shelled
seed pods
feathers
ribbon and braid
pinecones
scarves and bandanas
old greeting cards

with someone not present, it may help to talk out loud, to say what's in your heart and on your mind, as though the person were there.

REVERSE TUCK-INS Who says the adult must tuck the child in? At our house, my ten-year-old tucks me in, then goes to wait in her bed for her father to tuck her in. He, in turn, is ready for sleep when our teenage daughter comes down to bid goodnight to both of us. Our dogs accompany her to her bedroom for a canine tuck-in.

READING Make the most out of a time-honored before-bed activity. It can be made more special by having a "story blanket" you lie under for this event only. Use special bookmarks—those you buy or make, or a beautiful piece of ribbon. You can have a special technique for reading: you read one page, your child reads the next; a chapter a night, etc. I know a man who tells his son a "made-up" story each night, part of an on-going adventure story. When the man is out of town, which is often, he telephones his son to deliver the daily installment. It's not being there in person, it's true, but the telephone story provides consistency, reliability, and fun—and much love.

BATHING Any bath can be jazzed up by using bubble bath, candlelight, or a new water toy. Thin slices of lemon can float in the water, colorful nuggets of bath oil can be dissolved in it. There are all kinds of soaps—different shapes, different colors, different smells—that can be hidden and presented now and then as small surprises. One's own towel and washcloth make bathing seem special, especially if one's name or some favorite design is on those towels. My daughters used to like to hear a story while they bathed, thus killing two birds with one stone.

NO-BEDTIME NIGHT   Once your children learn how to sleep late, you can institute the stay-up-as-late-as-you-want-to night. In our house, that's Friday, since the kids then have a couple of nights to recover before school starts again. If kids know there is one night of the week they can stay up really late, they are often more cooperative about going to bed other nights. And guess what? I've found that they don't stay up so late after all—they just love the idea that they can if they want to. Older kids may appreciate a parent pulling an "all-nighter" with them. This is a time when it's easy to be silly, to feel like peers.

TAPES BEFORE BED   Who says children don't enjoy Mozart? Try a little with them before bedtime. Or listen to music they select, or a story, even a meditation tape. (I once received some as a gift and my children loved them.) It is a soothing experience to lie quietly in the darkness with sounds coming to you both at the same time.

BEDTIME TALKS   It is my husband's practice to lie on the floor of our daughters' rooms each evening for a little chat. They tell him what they did that day, or talk about something that's troubling them, or something they want to do. This is a very relaxed time of day when they know that the rush of the day is finally over, and they can take their time saying what it is they want to say. There's something about being in pajamas and smelling of soap that brings out the dreamer, the storyteller, the philosopher in both parent and child. It's a privilege and a delight to be together.

NIGHTTIME PRAYERS   Prayer can take whatever form you're comfortable with. It can be as simple as a moment of quiet meditation—of lying back, closing your eyes, and slowing yourself down in order to listen to what is inside

Nighttime Serenades

- To know one another better: take turns listening to one another's favorite musical pieces
- To remember that you are part of something bigger than yourselves: try a tape of nature sounds (the sea, bird song from different habitats, the wind blowing over prairie grasses)
- To build a shared "vocabulary" of experiences: go to the library and pick out a tape of music, stories, or poetry that's new to everyone
- To learn together: choose a classical piece and listen to it every night for a week; then enjoy the satisfaction of recognizing it forever

you. It behooves all of us to review our days before we sleep, to make sure we're on track, and to offer up thanks for the good that's happened.

SAVING MEMORIES

We tend to think that we will remember things forever. But we don't. Any effort made toward recording family life—from special events to what life was like when our now-six-feet-tall teenager was 14 months old—will be appreciated later.

FAMILY JOURNAL   When my first daughter began to talk, I had a long list of her phrases I hung up for my babysitter, so that she could understand my daughter. How I wish I'd saved that list—all I can remember now is that "undies" was orange juice! A family journal would have been just the place. Consider keeping one for recording such things as they happen—your three-year-old saying, at sunset, "The sky's coming down"; your husband sending you a huge bouquet for no reason—record the date and describe the bouquet, as well as the way you feel.

The family journal also can be used as a daily diary. Have everyone make a short entry every night after dinner about what they did/thought that day. Children who are too young to write can dictate their little stories. Those too young to speak can be represented by a photo a week. These journals become a wonderful way to document the evolution of your child's learning to write—first the leggy printing, then the excruciatingly careful cursive. Write down what your new junior-high schooler said about her first day in class, your sixteen-year-old's first words after she gets her driver's license. These daily entries are also a

Passing Along the Memories

If you have photos, scrapbooks, or other records of your childhood (or the lives of your parents or grandparents), share them with your children. Build a family library devoted to preserving and enjoying the heritage you have in common.

way for a parent who's out of town to see what he missed. The key to keeping up with this is to remember that the entries can be very, very short.

THE FAMILY MUSEUM   Set aside some shelves somewhere for keeping family treasures. When you go on trips and bring back souvenirs, this is the place to display them. When your son is in the school play, frame the program and keep it here. Add family collections of seashells, rocks, stamps, china figures (our family loves pigs), even toys from fast food restaurants.

PHOTO-ALBUM UPKEEP   Once a month, sit around the kitchen table working on the family album. Make repairs, add, savor again the memories those photos represent.

HOME-MOVIE NIGHT   In this day of the video camera, you might want to spend a night every six months or so watching family movies. We find that we document a lot, but rarely sit down together to watch the film. Circle a day on the calendar to do that, then make some popcorn and sit down to watch yourselves.

The Family Conference

I was about four years old, sitting at the kitchen table with my nine-year-old sister, when I heard my mother ask her, "What should we put in the Jell-O tonight— bananas or fruit cocktail?" My eyes widened. I stopped breathing. What would my sister say? She twisted her braid in her fingers for a moment, thinking it over. Then, "Ummmmm...bananas!" she said. And, unbelievably, I thought, my mother said, "OK, bananas it is." I went into my bedroom to think about what I'd just witnessed. My sister had decided something to have for dinner! Just like that! What I really wanted to concentrate on, though, was: when would it be my turn? When would I get asked to make such an important decision?

I can see my mother, my sister, and me in that kitchen of nearly 40 years ago as clearly as I can see the teacup I now have at my side. I always thought my childlike longing to be included in decision- making was something unique, even something to be embarrassed about, until quite recently when a man who is my contemporary told me, "Boy, when I was a kid I used to just long for a kind of family meeting, you know, where everybody would sit down together, and where what I said would be listened to and taken seriously." He leaned back in his chair, staring into space, probably feeling like a little kid again. "I just thought it would be great!" he said.

It seems all children have a need to be taken seriously in this way. But within the confines of normal family life, it hardly ever happens. Children tend to get listened to with one ear by their busy parents, who are also making dinner or doing laundry or working on papers they brought home from the office. It isn't often that children contribute in making decisions beyond what flavor of ice cream they'd like. The parent who cooks decides what's for dinner. Chores are assigned by the parent. When conflicts arise in the family, they are usually handled on the spot by a parent or surrogate parent. When vacation plans are made, children are rarely consulted. Yet the truth is, even really young children have important things to say, creative ideas to suggest, and a real need to feel that their opinion (and their person) counts.

One way to count everyone in is to have a regular family conference, during which all members of the family have an opportunity to hold forth equally. In addition to

Everyone Counts
Family members with special needs may not contribute exactly as other members do, but they surely belong at—and enhance by their presence—family meetings.

35

In Single Parent Homes
Family conferences deal with matters outside children's relationship to the absent parent. Those issues are dealt with at other times and places.

meeting some of the needs of children, family conferences are gratifying for parents, too. They get a chance to ventilate, to be heard by everyone all at once. In addition to that, when parents make time and space to really listen to their children, they find out a lot about them. They can discover that their children are bright, capable, creative, aware, flexible, and quite charming. Even in troubled family situations, where a parent would, at least for the time being, be hard pressed to see any glowing qualities in his child, he can still recognize the need for all family members to feel important.

Some families have conferences only when things go wrong, when there are serious issues to be resolved. It's better to have a regular time set aside, a weekly meeting if possible, that is not only for conflict resolution but also for simply checking in with each other. It's easy enough to say that our schedules are so busy we just don't have time for such meetings. But I believe that it's precisely because we're so busy that we need these meetings. They benefit virtually any kind of family group—single parent, "blended," those with younger children, and those with older children. It is never too early (or too late) to start having them.

WHAT A FAMILY CONFERENCE IS (AND IS NOT)
A family conference is a regularly occurring meeting of all members of the family who live together. It is a place to be heard. It is to plan things to do together, to distribute chores, to establish rules, to express complaints, and to

settle conflicts. It is also a place to share good feelings about each other, and it goes a long way toward helping family members learn not to take each other for granted.

The family conference is not a gripe session, a place to bad-mouth each other, to make accusatory statements, or to otherwise attack each other. Nor is it a place for any one person to dominate, though it must be acknowledged that the parent is the CEO-equivalent, the place where the buck stops, and the one ultimately in control. Adults do, after all, have more knowledge and experience, as well as more responsibilities.

The goal of family conferences is a feeling of individual self-worth and of connection to other family members. This makes for more peaceful living in your house. It also makes for more peaceful living in the world at large: Once you've learned successful conflict resolution at your kitchen table, you can, and undoubtedly will, use it in many other places.

Another goal of the family conference is to teach communication skills, good judgment, a sense of responsibility, and self-discipline. Teenagers who "get into trouble" lack precisely those qualities. Family meetings can help reinforce the notion that rights and privileges must be earned through appropriate and responsible behavior.

Finally, the goal of the conference is to understand that as a family you are all in this together. Everyone has certain obligations. And everyone, despite age or role, deserves respect and individual attention.

Some Things to Discuss at a Family Meeting

- Things that have gone right: acknowledgments and thanks

- Things that have gone wrong: Who's fighting too much about what? What can be done about it? Are people honoring bedtimes, promises they made? Is homework being done? How about chores?

- Requests for changes in family protocol: Does someone want a later bedtime? How about meals— anyone want to try a hand at cooking this week? Or at shopping? Any great ideas for menus?

- What can you enjoy together as a family this week, this summer?

- Neighborhood news: What's happening? If a neighbor is ill or housebound, is there any way you can help?

- Looking at the world together: Any concerns? Any suggestions for things to do as a family, such as write a congressman, help clean up a park, learn where certain countries are, understand what the top stories mean?

Tips On Choosing a Leader

1. Have a parent be the leader at the first meeting, and model what will be the usual procedure.

2. Rotate the chair on a monthly basis (or more often, if desired) to anyone school age and up who will take the role seriously. You might want to start a tradition that as soon as someone gets two digits in age (turns 10), he or she is eligible to chair a meeting. You can pick new leaders by age (say, youngest first); or by sex (boy–girl–boy–girl); or by drawing names (make sure you take out the name of the person who chairs each week so it doesn't get drawn again the following week).

3. Provide a gavel to the leader, and/or a special hat.

HOW FAMILY CONFERENCES WORK

Family conferences are conducted much like business meetings: there is a leader, a recording secretary, a specific agenda, and a certain order to follow. Say your meetings are scheduled for every Wednesday evening at 7:30. Have everyone meet at a pre-ordained place. Perhaps it is the kitchen table. Or perhaps it is on the living room floor, with everyone lying against big pillows. The value in floor meetings, by the way, is that the older people do not loom over the younger ones in the way that they usually do. (It's been proven that children open up more when an adult's head is lower than theirs!)

WHEN THEY SAY "NO" If some family members refuse to participate, have conferences without them. They may change their mind when they see that policies get made that affect them.

A POSITIVE BEGINNING Before the meeting officially begins, try to set an upbeat tone. You can go around and have each person compliment another member of the family: "Julie, I really appreciated the way you pitched in and helped me do the laundry the other day." "Dan, I appreciate your calling me to ask if there was anything you could pick up for me on the way home from work the other night." "Linda, it felt good when you told me I looked nice the other day." You might also, or instead, have everyone share a joke they've heard that week, or share an amusing anecdote about something that happened to them. The point is to start the meeting in as positive a way as possible.

CREATING THE ATMOSPHERE OF SAFETY It is very important that the family conference feel like a safe place for putting things forth. Brainstorming, for example, is a wonderful way to come up with creative ideas and solutions, but not if people are afraid they'll be dismissed or made fun of. The idea in brainstorming is that you say anything and everything that occurs to you, no matter how wild it may seem. Sometimes the idea that seems most unlikely at first ends up being the idea that works best.

That feeling that "anything goes" must also be present for other issues. For example, a fourth-grader may be having problems with schoolwork and feel very much pressured, which makes him crabby and hard to get along with at home. When he expresses feeling overwhelmed by schoolwork, it is not helpful for his tenth-grade sister to say, "Oh, fourth grade! You don't get any hard work in fourth grade! Wait till you get to tenth grade!"

OLD BUSINESS The leader asks the secretary to read the minutes from the last meeting. After that, any "old business" is discussed. For example, if you decided last time that everyone had to knock before entering 11-year-old Mary's room because she'd been feeling she had no privacy, you would ask Mary if she's been satisfied with everyone's behavior. If you decided you'd like to start thinking about the family summer vacation, ask if anyone's had any ideas yet about where to go. Old business can also be a time to reexamine things like curfews, bedtimes, other rules. Do they still make sense? Families grow and change all the time, especially children. Things that make sense one day may not be appropriate six weeks later.

How to Be a Good Leader

- Make sure the meeting starts and ends on time.
- Make sure everyone gets a chance to be heard.
- Don't interfere unless absolutely necessary.
- Keep track of the time—move things along so that you can finish in the allotted time.
- Be aware of how everyone's doing—try to make sure no one is left out or feeling attacked.
- Keep members focused on the issue at hand.

Some Rules

- No sarcasm.
- No ridicule.
- One person at a time talks.
- Each new speaker recognizes what the speaker before him said by restating it.
- Complaints are voiced only with the understanding that the speaker is interested in focusing on finding a solution.
- Set an hourglass sand timer in the center of the group when you need to time things, but make certain that people mainly watch the speaker, not the timer.

In order to keep adults from taking over, try to let children make suggestions first. If they are appropriate, adults should refrain from adding more.

NEW BUSINESS   Next, move on to new business. Everyone should be given a chance to say whatever is on his or her mind. These issues can be spontaneous or they can come from a container, such as a large jar, chosen especially to hold notes concerning issues people want addressed. If you have such a container, keep it in a common area, perhaps the kitchen, and have an agreement that no one is allowed to read the slips of paper until meeting time. In the interest of fair representation, these slips of paper should be signed; if Suzy has put in only one item, it's not fair to take up the entire meeting time with seven of her brother Fred's.

In working toward solutions to problems, work for consensus and refrain from voting. If you vote, you create winners and losers. Instead, agree that a solution must be acceptable to everybody, and everybody must accept the consequences of not honoring the agreement. If you cannot reach a consensus, two things can be done. You can table the issue and bring it up at the next meeting, or you can take turns trying different suggestions and then evaluate at the next meeting what seemed to work best.

A POSITIVE FINISH   When you have dealt with all the new business, it is time for the leader to sum up the meeting, perhaps making use of the notes that the secretary has taken. The meeting notes need not be extremely detailed, but should serve to remind family members of what came up in the meetings, as well as what was decided to be done about it. The leader reminds members that agreements made must be honored until the next meeting, with no changes made midweek.

After the meeting is over, a family hug might be in order. Sounds a little silly, and, in fact, feels a little silly too, but in a good way; and the warmth of such a gesture goes a long way. It lasts much longer than it lasts, if you know what I mean. You might want to have a special dessert at the end of every family meeting. Honor the Japanese tradition of serving another rather than yourself: When your neighbor's milk glass gets low, refill it—don't pay attention to your own. Or you might want to break at a prescribed time to watch a TV show or a movie together.

The length of family meetings is up to you, but about half an hour is usually long enough; when children are very little, fifteen minutes may be better. It's important, though, that everyone leave the meeting feeling OK. Sometimes serious issues arise that make for tears and shouting. Perhaps you can't completely solve these issues in one meeting, but no one should leave feeling terribly upset. In a situation where the half hour is up and someone is feeling bad, it makes sense to go over the allotted time long enough for the person to feel better. Also, all should feel satisfied that the issue will be dealt with again at the next conference if necessary.

It is also important that family meetings be taken seriously. To that end, no phone calls or other interruptions should be tolerated. And no one who is speaking should be interrupted. This is a very hard thing to do, as it happens, but the skill is important for everyone to learn. There is a wonderful Native American custom of using a sacred stick

Finding Solutions

1. Listen carefully to all points of view.
2. Explore possible solutions through brainstorming, and have someone write these ideas down.
3. Choose a solution.
4. Discuss possible results of this solution: what you want or expect to happen, the desired outcome.
5. Obtain a firm commitment (verbal or written) and agree to evaluate the solution at the next meeting.

Call Home!

If a member is out of town, he or she may want to attend part of the meeting by speaker phone. Otherwise, have the leader report to the missing member directly after the meeting about what happened, and ask for input.

Weekly Minutes

Family conference notes might be kept in a special loose-leaf notebook used only for family meetings, and they might be written with a special pen, also used only for that purpose .

Decorate the front of your "minutes" book with photos of the family.

Post most-recent minutes on a bulletin board for members to refer to during the week.

during meetings. When you hold the stick, no one can interrupt you. You must speak from the heart, and when you are finished, you must pass the stick over your heart, to the left, on to the next person who wants to speak. Perhaps, in recognition of the fact that some members may filibuster, a time limit can be set on any one person speaking nonstop: no more than two minutes, say. But during those two minutes, it's important that everyone try hard to attend to what is being said.

A MODEL FOR A FIRST MEETING

Post a notice on the refrigerator saying where and when your first meeting will be held. At that time, the initiator can explain how the meetings will work, describing the roles of leader, secretary, and attendees; the form the agenda will follow; what the goals are. It is important, by the way, that the language used in family meetings makes you feel comfortable. If terms like "secretary" and "agenda" feel too much like business to you, use whatever terminology you'd like.

The item for discussion at this first meeting might be something for the whole family to do together next weekend. The leader could say, "Let's do something together next Sunday afternoon. We can afford to spend twenty-five dollars. Anyone have any ideas?"

AVOIDING "BLAMING"

When you are talking about something a family member does that is a problem for you, avoid using "you" language. This conveys blame and criticism. Instead, use "I," as in "I feel overwhelmed by all the housework I do. I need help." (As opposed to "You never offer to help me," which conveys criticism and lays blame.)

You may want to follow a certain pattern using an "I" message: (1) identify behavior that's a problem by saying, "When you..."; (2) state your reaction by saying, "I feel..."; (3) and explain why: "because..."

An example: "When you stay out past your curfew, I feel worried because I think something might have happened to you." When you speak in this way, the feeling is related to the consequence, not the behavior itself. It gets to the heart of the issue, speaks to what needs to be done to eliminate the problem for the speaker. It is therefore more likely to generate solutions.

BE A GOOD LISTENER

Good listening is not passive; it is active. When you are really listening to someone, you use not only your ears, but your mind and your heart. Your ears listen, your mind concentrates hard on what's being said, and you leave your heart open. Try, when someone else is speaking, to keep these things in mind:

LOOK AT THE SPEAKER Let him or her see that you are listening.

GIVE POSITIVE SIGNALS Use other body language to say that you are understanding; nod, say "uh-huh."

EXERCISE PATIENCE Never assume that you know what the speaker is going to say. Let him or her finish. Do not interrupt.

A Sample Agenda

One possible issue to resolve at your family conference is chore distribution. The meeting might go like this:

1. Brainstorm to make a list of all household chores.

2. Distribute chores to family members fairly, considering age and ability as well as time available. (A senior in high school in the middle of finals week has less time available that particular week.) Strong preferences may make division easier.

3. Establish chore deadlines. For example, the garbage must be taken out nightly. The bathroom must be cleaned every other day.

4. Decide on consequences if the job is not done. Example: If Johnny fails to take out the garbage, he will lose one dollar from his allowance for each time missed.

Family Conference Don'ts

- Wait till everyone in the family wants to meet.
- Start conferences late at night.
- Let meetings go too long.
- Let anyone dominate.
- Spend all the time on negative issues.

EXERCISE RESPECT   Do not patronize ("Well [snicker], that's a really good idea [benevolent smile], but...") or psychoanalyze ("You're just saying that because you want me to get in trouble").

EXERCISE TOLERANCE   Do not judge what is being said. Work to understand it and where it's coming from.

PAY ATTENTION   Do not formulate what you're going to say when it's your turn; concentrate on what's being said now.

CHECK YOUR UNDERSTANDING   When the speaker has finished, make sure you heard correctly, by rephrasing or summarizing ("So what you'd like is for me to..."or "So what you're feeling is...")

BE A GOOD TALKER

There are certain responsibilities in being a speaker, too. Be mindful that your task is clear and respectful communication. To that end,

MIND YOUR MANNERS   Be considerate. Do not shout or speak sarcastically.

BE AS BRIEF AS POSSIBLE   Do not say the same thing over and over. Try to make your point clearly and succinctly. Don't go on for more than two minutes, except in unusual circumstances.

TAKE RESPONSIBILITY   Try not to involve others, especially by blaming or criticizing. Speak for yourself.

WHAT YOU CAN EXPECT

If you're looking for immediate gratification from a family meeting, you can expect to have it, to some extent. It feels good to ventilate, regardless of what the issue is. Some results, however, may take a while. For example, we had an emergency family meeting one day because tempers were flaring like fireworks—everyone was in a terrible mood. It was difficult even to get everyone to agree to sit at the table together. Once there, we talked about what was wrong, and there were raised voices and tears. After the meeting was over, nothing changed for the rest of the day. People were quieter, perhaps, but everyone was still moody. But the next day, everyone seemed to make a special effort to get along. And I, who complained about not getting enough help around the house, received offers from every member to do a little something. That made me feel that the meeting, difficult as it was, was absolutely worth it.

Here is what can be guaranteed about family meetings: They will keep you in touch with each other; they will help you solve problems; and the benefits will spill over into other areas of family life. For example, sisters who work things out at a meeting are more likely to want to spend peaceful time together in other ways. And no matter who you are, when you're getting along with your family, you're more likely to get along with, and feel better about, everyone else.

Family Conference Do's

- Start with those willing to attend.
- Meet regularly.
- Start and finish on time.
- Put agreements into action as soon as possible.
- Hear all points of view.
- Record and post decisions made.
- Have some fun!

Keep it up!

First meetings are guaranteed to feel awkward for everyone. But you will get comfortable quickly, probably by the third or fourth meeting.

No-Reason Celebrations

It is all well and good to celebrate holidays and special events on their appointed days, but it is not well and good to let some wonderful idea die because it's unorthodox, or "doesn't make sense," or is something that we "shouldn't" do. The truth is, it's the spontaneous, different things we do in life that keep us from being dulled by routine, that keep us surprised, interested, awake.

As teenagers, we are in a big hurry to grow up, assuming that then we will at last be free to do anything—eat spaghetti for breakfast, drive to the next state for the weekend, sleep till noon. But then we become adults, and we don't do any of that stuff after all. Sometimes it's because we're being appropriately responsible. At other times our general reticence is proof that we've lost much of our imagination and our nerve, that we have forgotten how to play.

I believe it's a good idea to honor the small voice in us that sometimes suggests silly things, which can be anything from staying somewhere longer than planned to having a Christmas party for 40 in the middle of July. You can go outside for a family snowball fight when the first flakes fall, even though it's bedtime. You can keep your pajamas on all day. You can eat spaghetti for breakfast. And you know what? It's probably good for you.

Here are some ideas for "no reason" celebrations. There are a million more ideas inside you asking to come out. Why don't you let them? I'll bet you'll never regret it—or forget it—if you do.

THE WINTERTIME SUMMER PICNIC

It is good, when the freezing temperatures have lost their novelty, to recall the joys of summer. Some bleak day, when the sky is gray and the snow grayer, have a living room picnic.

THE SET-UP Spread a beach blanket on the floor. Set the "table" with colorful paper plates and reusable plastic flatware. Enlist the aid of the kids to make tissue "carna-

No Winter?

If you live in a climate that never really gets cold, have your picnic during the rainy season. Or throw a sun festival in thanks for the wonderful climate you enjoy. Or create an artificial winter: decorate your picnic area with paper snowflakes and make a gigantic papier-mâché snowman.

tions" and construction-paper daisies for the centerpiece. Hang a gigantic paper sun on the wall. Then, just for the duration of the picnic, turn up the heat high enough to let you be comfortable in shorts, or even a bathing suit.

THE FOOD This can be standard picnic fare: fried chicken, potato salad, sliced tomatoes. Or you can roast wieners over your fireplace "grill." Serve chips and fresh fruit, and fill your thermos with lemonade. Someone might even want to supply some fake ants.

THE GREAT OUTDOORS You can also have an outdoor winter picnic. On a pretty day, when the sun is out and the sky is blue and the snow sparkles beautifully, dress up warmly and have a picnic in the backyard. Haul out the picnic table, and serve warm and hearty foods: soups, stews, grilled sandwiches. Serve cocoa to drink and hot apple crisp for dessert. Warm bread is nice too.

SWEET ENDINGS Whether you are eating summer or winter food, it's always a nice ending to roast marshmallows and make S'mores.

THE NOT–THANKSGIVING THANKSGIVING DINNER

Have you ever sat around the day after Thanksgiving and thought, "Boy, that was good! I'd like to do it all over again!" Well, why not? There's no law that says you can have Thanksgiving dinner only once a year. I love the foods we eat on that day so much I make the same exact recipes at least three times a year.

NOT JUST FAMILY Sometimes it's hard to decide where to go for Thanksgiving. While our family spends Thanksgiving with relatives, we often thought we'd like to spend it with our friends, too. Thus was born "Thanksgiving, Part Two." We invite all our friends, and our children invite some of theirs, and we do it all over again.

NOT JUST NOVEMBER You can even have a Thanksgiving meal in the summer. Grill your turkey, or wait for an unusually cool day and cook indoors.

THE IT'S-NOT-CHRISTMAS CHRISTMAS GIFT

Much of the emphasis at Christmastime is on giving and getting gifts. Yet expectations are so high and obligations so many at that time of year that much of the joy is taken out of gift-giving. Some gray day in February, try an impromptu shopping trip with the whole family, with everyone getting one "Christmas present" they absolutely don't need. This is vastly different from grimly trudging forth to buy needed boots or school supplies. Rather, it may be closer to what gift-giving at Christmastime was meant to be in the first place—one small treasure to surprise and delight you, no strings attached.

NOBODY'S BIRTHDAY BIRTHDAY PARTIES

Occasionally, you have a longing to smell birthday candles being blown out and hear the rustle of paper coming off the presents. But nobody's birthday is coming for a long time. No problem!

THE UN-BIRTHDAY LOTTERY Have everyone in the family draw the name of another family member. Then have each person find a present for $1.00 or less at the local mall in half an hour or less. (A true challenge.) At home, everyone wraps and labels his or her gift and places it on the kitchen table. After dinner, have everyone make a party hat out of

Famous Birthday Celebrations

Choose a person whom somebody in your family admires. Then build a theme birthday dinner around that person. For instance, if you have a fan of impressionist painting among you, celebrate Claude Monet's birthday. Cook up a French dinner, decorate your cake with an Eiffel Tower done in icing, check out a book about Monet and his paintings, watch a French movie with subtitles, wear a beret, and hang a homemade French flag in the dining room.

newspaper and ribbon. Then place some candles on the cake, enthusiastically sing "Happy Un-Birthday to Everyone," and have everyone blow out the candles at once. Then take turns opening the presents.

BIRTHDAY OF THE UNKNOWN As an alternative, celebrate the birthday of someone you don't know. Perhaps it's a famous movie star; after eating "her" birthday cake, you could watch one of her movies that you've rented for the occasion. Or perhaps it's the birthday of a famous artist, and you'd like to visit the museum to see his paintings before you eat "his" cake. Or perhaps a relative would like to know that her or his birthday is being celebrated even though you are far apart. You can even sing "Happy Birthday" over the telephone!

ETHNIC NIGHT

It is always a valuable experience to learn about other cultures. Sometimes the simple act of having a different kind of food can lead toward appreciation of another people's ways.

MAKE IT YOURSELF It is common enough for us to eat Chinese food, or Mexican, or Greek, or Italian. But it is another thing altogether to make it at home. The whole family can be involved in shopping and preparing food you've never cooked yourself.

Most big cities have ethnic grocery stores. Visit one with the family and ask the proprietor for dinner suggestions. It can be fascinating to tour the aisles of these grocery stores, with all their exotic things. My favorite is when I can't read a thing on the labels because it's all written in another language. Talk about adventures in dining!

DECORATE It adds to the experience to use as many cultural trappings as you are able. For example, when eating a Chinese dinner, use chopsticks. You may also want to use a wok to prepare foods. On Mexican night, hang a piñata over the table.

GO AMERICAN! When considering other cultures, don't forget all the variety right here in the United States. How about a New England seafood supper complete with clam chowder and steamed lobster? (Don't forget to wear a bib!) The South is famous for fried chicken and barbecues and wonderful pies; New Orleans wakes up our palates with Cajun cooking. The Pacific Northwest, California, Puerto Rico, Hawaii—all have specialties to try. Also, if you've never tried vegetarian cooking, you're in for a treat.

It's a nice extra to have a member of the family do a little research on the history of the people whose food you are enjoying. Where do they live? What kind of jobs do they have? What is their government like? What kind of weather do they have? What are some of their customs? What have they contributed to our culture? Is there a reason they eat the kind of food they do? This job can rotate among family members.

DESSERT-FOR DINNER NIGHT

Do something you always wanted to do as a kid—have a dinner one night that is nothing but desserts. Cheese and fruit, by the way, are considered a dessert, and may go a long way toward making you feel less guilty. But the idea here, of course, is to be totally irresponsible, to do what

Food in the U.S.A.

Pacific Coast Salmon, king crab, razor clams and Pacific oysters. Fiddlehead ferns, wild berries, Tillamook cheese, and apple candy.

Southwest Barbecued beef, antelope, wild turkey, and bear. Enchiladas, tamales, chili, pickled okra, and garbanzo salad. Wild brush honey, agarita jelly, and mustang-grape pie.

South Grits, fried apples, hominy bread, collard greens, and black-eyed peas. Biscuits and gravy, shrimp Creole, country ham, dirty rice, and chicory coffee. Pecan pie.

Midwest Trout, bass, perch, poke greens, and wilted lettuce. Navy beans with ham hocks, cornbread, hot biscuits, and Chicago deep-dish pizza. Persimmon pudding.

Mid-Atlantic States Philly steaks, Maryland crab cakes, cherrystone clams. striped bass, and Chincoteague oysters. Beefsteak tomatoes, scrapple, and chicken pot pie. Shoofly pie, apple pie, and rich ice cream.

New England Lobsters, clams, scallops, and chowders. Baked beans, brown bread, maple syrup, cranberry sauce, red flannel hash, and corn on the cob. Wild blueberry glaze pie.

Skip Day

There comes a time when every working person needs a break, to call in sick and take a mental-health day. There may come a time in every child's life when he or she needs precisely the same sort of break: to be perfectly well, and skip school.

If your routine can accommodate it, let all family members have a skip day, to be used at their discretion. This is a day not to catch up on work, but to experience the joy of doing not much of anything, to be lazy and refuel.

If someone in the family takes great pride in perfect attendance, you might want to plan an alternative— a Skip-Chores Saturday, for example.

you used to imagine you'd do when you were finally a grown-up: eat chocolate cake and ice cream instead of the Basic Four.

A possible benefit of this dinner is that everyone will be so sick of desserts they won't want any for the next six weeks. But probably not.

THE REALITY OF MAKE-BELIEVE

One of the nicest afternoons I ever spent happened when my children wanted to know if I would like to attend their teddy bears' wedding. Yes, I said, I would. I would also, I added, like to help plan it. My children, aware of my abiding interest in love and romance, agreed. So we left the fiancés sitting on the sofa staring into each other's eyes, and went shopping at the discount party store. We bought a "lace" (plastic) tablecloth, and paper wedding bells to hang over the table. We bought wedding napkins and gift wrap. At home, I made a fancy three-layer white cake I'd been dying to try.

We dressed the bride and groom in random doll clothes, and put a paper doily and ribbons on the bride for a veil. We laid out pristine white paper towels in the hall for a runner and then performed the ceremony, with my older daughter as minister and me as photographer. (I must say that I excelled in capturing the post–"I do" kiss.) Then we had cake, and the newly wedded couple opened their gifts—things from around the house that we had wrapped up, everything from old dishes to rubber balls.

Children are great at coming up with ideas that we too often dismiss. Sometimes it's good to do exactly as they suggest, to play in earnest with them. If you get into a good game of hide-and-seek or tag, for example, you'll find out that it's still really fun.

It matters a lot to older children to have their parents' undivided attention too, of course—to share a good conversation, a movie, an awesome CD, an at-home shopping trip through a new catalog. Discover what playing means to your child, whatever her or his age. Then be ready and willing to participate!

THE AT–HOME CAMPOUT

Turn your living room into the great outdoors. Everyone sleeps on the floor in sleeping bags. Food is picnic style, no kitchen use allowed. (Bathrooms are OK, though!) Read stories to one another about the wonders of nature— anything from a children's encyclopedia explanation of how bees make honey to an E.B. White novel will do. After the lights are out, tell ghost stories around the "campfire" (imagined, created, or courtesy of your family fireplace). Stuffed animals arranged here and there can provide a certain ambience, especially if those animals are bears.

In the summer, of course, this campout can be moved into the backyard. Line up your sleeping bags and star-gaze together before you fall asleep. It's fun to pitch a tent in the backyard, too, and a tent does a lot for keeping out unwanted visitors such as mosquitoes and dogs and cats.

Go to Work with Mom/Dad Day

No matter what their ages, it is of enormous value for children to see where their parents work. That way, they have some sense of where you are when you're away, what it is that you do there. If your workplace allows it, bring your children in, one at a time, for at least half a day—to see your office, to meet the people you work with, to sit in your chair, to talk on your phone, to eat lunch with you.

Go to School with the Kids

It's a nice idea for a parent to spend a little time observing what his child does all day. Many children, as they get older, will object to having a parent in the classroom when school's in session, but you can usually watch what's going on when they're younger, provided the school allows it. If you can't watch on a regular school day, it's important to attend "open house" night.

ROLE-REVERSAL DAY

Offer your children a turn to take the reins. Have them be the parents one Saturday, and follow their lead all day long. Get dressed when they tell you to, wear what they put out for you. Go the places they want to go, for as long as they want. Eat dinner when they say it's time and, if they're old enough, let them cook it. Finally, go to bed when they say it's time.

This is a good way to understand some of the frustrations involved in being a kid, and a way for children to have a sense of the kind of responsibility parents feel. Plus, parents get to whine.

EVERYDAY THANKSGIVINGS

One very hot summer day, my children and I went to get sub sandwiches to eat in the park for an impromptu picnic. We ordered at a pizza shop where the air conditioning had gone out—it must have been well over 100° in there. Nonetheless, the woman who helped us (after she removed several pizzas from a gigantic oven that seemed, on this day, like Dante's inferno) was smiling, remaining relentlessly cheerful in the face of real adversity. We admired her spirit, my children and I, and we appreciated her kindness toward everyone she waited on. There was a florist next door to the pizza shop, so we went in and bought that woman a rose, handed it to her to say thank you, and enjoyed very much seeing the lift it gave her. She smiled and thanked us profusely, wiped her brow, and put the flower in some ice water.

We deal every day with people whom we can thank, in one way or another. Is there a helpful librarian who would appreciate a nice card? Would your mail carrier like a glass of lemonade on a hot day or some cocoa when it's cold? How about a pretty little plant for your secretary's desk, or a note to your child's teachers saying that you want them to know you appreciate the time they spent helping your child with math? Often it's the smallest gesture that means the most. Your children learn to notice the contributions of others through your example. And in giving to others, you will end up feeling pretty happy yourselves.

Family Award Night

Once a year, have your own award night. Give out trophies for award-worthy achievements such as these:

• helping with chores
• having such a terrific smile
• being a good friend
• getting swell grades
• working hard to earn the money that feeds, shelters, and clothes the family.

Inexpensive trophies are available, or you can have fun making some. Use milk cartons cut out to the desired shape and covered with foil, or get more fanciful. It might be fun for everyone to use "trash" and see what kind of trophy can be created. The point is to set aside some time to say that you appreciate certain qualities about each other, that in your family you are all winners to one another. There's room for humor here, along with some good old schmaltz.

Just Plain Fun

There are a lot of good reasons for families to play games together. For young families, it is a rare opportunity for your children to do something that you're doing, really. Playing games together is not about children imitating something adults do and receiving for their ever-so-cute efforts the usual condescending smiles. When children play a game with you, they seem to feel at last equal to you, and they thoroughly enjoy this elevated status, temporary though it is. Sometimes they manifest their pride with self—important postures: puffed-out chests, raised chins.

For families with not-so-young children, playing games is a way to help stay close, by doing things together. You can play games at home, thus avoiding being seen together in public places, something that embarrasses children of a certain age no end. Silly game-playing in the evening can often lead to a good, serious talk together later that night.

Perhaps best of all, though, playing games is just plain fun! Games are a good way to learn about cooperation and teamwork. They are also a way to learn to win and lose gracefully. Many games have no winners or losers. But let's admit that most of us are, at least a little, competitive beings who enjoy trying to win. Let's face it—it feels great to come out on top! And, although it may hurt a bit, it's instructive to lose. Games can teach us about being in both positions, and in that way help to prepare us for the realities of life. (Bear in mind that the younger the child, the less able he may be to tolerate the frustration involved in losing—choose games accordingly.)

When people hear the word "game," they may think of things like Monopoly or baseball. But there is much more to games than that. For example, I once witnessed my mother entertaining my two daughters for an incredibly long period of time with a simple box of toothpicks! (She also excels in card houses and games requiring only imagination. She also, regrettably, is not for hire.) As a child, I loved playing with nothing more than a waitress pad, taking orders from "customers" to turn in to my imaginary boss, the fry cook. (He was a deliciously unsavory character, who wore multiple tattoos, dirty T-shirts, and a white paper hat at a rakish angle; everybody loved his hash

What to Bring to a Family Game

1. Aligned priorities: Remember the object of any game you play is to have fun.
2. A sense of humor.
3. Positive feelings, with an emphasis on making everyone feel good while playing (no nastiness or criticism or put-downs).
4. Freedom for creation of new rules or changing the way the game is usually played, but not on-the-spot accommodations for the benefit of getting a player out of a jam.
5. If desired, a special game-playing outfit: a lucky hat, pin, scarf, shirt, tie. One family has matching visors for all to wear when they play table games.

Away From Home

Sometimes it's fun to play games with your family somewhere other than home. Try these:

Oh, Go Fly a Kite Even more fun when you make your own. (Remember to always stay clear of power lines.)

Playground Fun Swing, slide, ride the merry-go-round, climb the monkey bars. Other recreational areas provide swimming pools and exercise paths.

Standard Sports Games Try softball, basketball, soccer. And games like badminton, volleyball, and croquet can work with just four people. It's fun to go to a "professional" ball field for softball rather than staying in the backyard. If you can find an empty gym, play basketball there.

Contra Dancing Times and places are often listed in newspapers, and these dances (similar to square dancing) are fun for the whole family.

Miniature Golf Find the most elaborate course you can.

Swimming Try oceans or lakes, country ponds or city pools.

browns.) One family used their imaginations and spent an hour or two a week for months to create their own board game. The board started as a simple map from home to their vacation spot. It developed into a track-pursuit game full of adventures and pitfalls. (Some were based on real experiences, such as leaving a wallet at a roadside stand.)

The way I see it, a game is anything that has two or more of you engaged in the same thing for the purpose of fun—simply "playing." Games can be board games or sports games, yes; but they can also be dramatic or creative activities, peacefully quiet or exuberantly loud. They can take place at the kitchen table, on the living room floor, in an automobile, under a sheet "tent," or in the great outdoors. The only constant is enjoying yourselves together.

It may work for your family to have a weekly game night, where a couple of hours are routinely set aside for having fun. Imagine, for example, a winter Wednesday evening. Homework is done, bedtime is a couple hours away, and the family settles down for a card game. Popcorn is served; there is the comfortable sound of shuffling cards and the low chatter of you and your loved ones. The answering machine is taking telephone messages, for this is a special time for you and yours alone—you're having a good time together, and everything else can wait.

INDOOR GAMES

Sometimes you have an unexpected opportunity to play indoor games together. Maybe Old Man Winter got inspired overnight, and you wake up to a snow day. Maybe it's a national holiday important enough to cancel school and work but not demanding of certain traditional activities—Presidents' Day, for example. Or maybe you're on vacation, and you feel like just staying in for a while. These are all times to try some of these games.

INDOOR ACTION GAMES   Sometimes you actually get to have fun and do good things for yourself, too. These games are fun to play, and guess what? You're also getting a bit of a workout! You're doing aerobics, learning coordination and balance—and earning your next meal.

Obstacle Course Make your own with cardboard boxes, pillows, furniture placed different ways (a chair on its side for crawling over; a card table for winding around its legs, a soft ottoman for sliding over like a snake).

Aerobics Annie Someone is the instructor, and all must follow her directives. Play loud music and make up silly exercises: arm-fat jiggle, fanny buster, rapid heel tap, etc. Then let someone else be Annie.

Balance Beam Use a six-foot length of a two-by-four. Or lay a long piece of yarn, string, or ribbon along the floor, straight or zigzag. Players must walk this path without falling off. To make it more challenging, have players balance a book on their heads and sing while they walk.

Three-Legged Race Two members get bound together and are sent on silly missions that were written earlier and are now drawn out of a sack— "Go to the kitchen and bang on a pot for ten seconds."

Pillow Fight Use big, fat, soft pillows. Set the timer for two minutes, and go at it.

Balloon Basketball Make your own hoop with a coat hanger bent to shape. Hang it by the hook over the top of a door. Then take your shots!

Winners and Losers
The concept of "loser" is softened by people playing in teams.

Games for the Very Young

From the time babies are about a month old, they can be played with. The youngest enjoy looking at mobiles, stuffed animals, bright colors and patterns. They also like very gentle exercising such as lifting arms and legs to the count of one–two. Later, play ball by simply rolling one about. After children learn to walk, they can begin playing games such as Ring-Around-the-Rosy and London Bridge.

Board Games

- It's sometimes hard for a whole family to play together because of age differences among their children. It helps to play a younger child's game first, then move on to something more sophisticated in which the young child is "partners" with someone older.
- Creative rule-bending is often necessary, and is absolutely worthwhile. For example, in a game like Sorry, send a weaker player's piece back an agreed-upon number of spaces instead of all the way back home. In Monopoly, let the weaker player take two turns for everyone else's one.
- Make sure everyone understands what the rules are at the outset, to make sure there are no hard feelings later.
- Remember that older children are, after all, still children. Praise their efforts at helping their younger siblings. Encourage them to come up with their own ideas for rule modifications. Then they're more likely to tolerate them.

QUIET INDOOR GAMES   There are times when you really need games to be quiet. Perhaps someone in the house is sick, or napping. Perhaps bedtime is nigh, and you don't want to get everyone all hopped up. Or perhaps your body is tired, but your mind isn't.

Drawing in the Dark Each player gets a pencil and paper. The lights are turned out, and everyone draws a house. When the houses are finished, the leader says to add something, say, a tree in the yard, a sun shining down, flowers bordering a sidewalk, etc. When ten additions have been made, turn on the lights to reveal what happened—everyone will have lost their places and will probably have created a floating fantasy to rival Chagall.

Dictionary The leader finds a word in the dictionary that no one knows. She spells the word, then writes it down on a piece of paper, as do the other players. Then each person writes down, in secret, the definition. The leader writes the real definition; the others make something up, either a legitimate guess or something outrageous. All pass their folded-over answers to the leader, who numbers the responses, then reads them aloud. Players vote for the definition they think is right, and get a point if they are correct. Highest points at the end of an agreed-upon number of words wins.

I Spy A small object such as a thimble is hidden by "it" while all others are out of the room. The hiding place must be in plain view, but in an out-of-the-way place. When players return, they look for the object. When a player is close, "it" lets him know by saying he's "hot"; when he's far away, he's called "cold." When the object is found, the player calls out "I spy!" and picks the object up. Now it is his turn to hide it.

Indoor Golf Place several washed-out tin cans or plastic glasses on their sides around the living room. Then use a small rubber ball and a yardstick (or broomstick) to play golf. My father used this technique to practice putting. One day I came into the living room and found him attempting to get a golf ball into a glass at the far end of the room. I asked what he was doing and he told me. "That's easy!" I scoffed. "Oh yeah?" he asked. "Try it!" I tried it. I got it in. "Yeah, but do it again!" he said, and I did. He stared wide-eyed. I smiled. This is my single athletic accomplishment, and I remember it fondly, even if Dad doesn't.

OUTDOOR GAMES
OUTDOOR GAMES ON THE GO   How about taking a little trip and playing a game simultaneously?

Bicycle Follow-the-Leader Play as in the usual version, but on bicycles. The leader, as always, is obliged to make the journey as interesting as possible.

Wagon Walk Go for a long walk with the requisite red wagon or equivalent, and make sure everyone in the family gets a ride—even those who have difficulty fitting in!

The Wish Walk Take a walk in a new neighborhood, and have each person pretend he can have any house he sees in a given block. Thus, if you're walking past a house you admire, you can choose it. Perhaps there'll be one later that you like better, perhaps not; but you can't change your

Other Indoor Possibilities

Video Games Try playing some of your child's favorites with him. It may be an occasion for your child to share a certain passion with you; and he may be in the relished position of having to teach you, for a change.

Puzzles Buy one or make one. To make a puzzle, draw a picture or find one in a magazine, glue it to heavy-duty cardboard, and then cut it into as many pieces as will make for a challenge for the youngest player.

Card Games For the younger set, try "go fish." "Low card" is a game where cards are divided equally and each player puts his lowest card in the center of the table. The player with the lowest card claims all of them. The player who ends up with the most cards wins. As family members get older, move on to games such as "crazy eights," "hearts," or one of the many versions of poker.

All on One Side Volleyball

The ball is a balloon. All players start on one side. The object of the game is to get the players to the other side of the net and back as many times as possible. Each player volleys the ball to another player, then runs under the net. The last player to touch the balloon puts it over the net, then runs under himself. The process gets repeated.

mind. Make up a life to go with the house—an occupation, household help, cars of your dreams, etc. This is particularly fun in ritzy neighborhoods.

YARD GAMES   Imagine a warm summer night, the sun barely down, the grass newly mown, the stars on stage. Now imagine your family and you outside playing one of these games:

Tug of War This requires at least four family members with a little strength. Change combinations of partners.

Pillowcase Race Step into a pillowcase and hop off to your destination. Time each other.

Lawn Acrobatics The older members of the family may have to make do with slow-motion somersaults at best. But your children will probably be able to show you cartwheels, headstands, and much more!

Frisbee Make sure you include the family dog in this game of catch. In the interest of evening up skills, have the older or more able members of the team use their non-dominant hand.

Hug Tag The only time you're safe from being tagged is when you're hugging another player. Cuddle up!

Baby Baseball For playing when you don't have enough for teams. Players count off: 1 is the batter, 2 is the pitcher, 3 is the catcher, 4 is the fielder. Each time an out is made, players rotate positions, moving up the number scale.

CREATIVE GAMES

Sometimes less is more. Here are some games that don't involve fancy set-ups or lots of money. They encourage some pretty wonderful things, too: imagination, preservation, conservation. Try some and feel good.

MAKE IT TOGETHER   Ever wonder what to do with all the leftover stuff of living? There's no reason why you can't put it to new uses that pay off in great times with the people you love!

Recycle City Save cans, newspapers, milk cartons of various sizes, cardboard tubing from toilet paper and paper towels, Popsicle sticks, pieces of tin foil. Use these to create a city: buildings made of milk cartons (flatten the tops, cover with newspaper and paint with poster paint), ponds made of circles of foil, etc.

Sock Puppets You know all those lonely singles that you don't know what to do with? Make them into Muppet-like characters. Use buttons for eyes, yarn for hair, felt scraps for mouths. Old jewelry can be used on the ladies, old ties on the guys. After you've made some characters, use them to perform. Divide into teams and agree on what to do for each other. Perhaps each team must act out for the other a movie you've all seen recently. Or draw names of people you all know for the puppets to become.

Play Dough Projects First make the play dough, then decide on a project to make. How about a tea set for a teddy bear? Ashtrays? Coasters? Christmas ornaments? A garlic press, by the way, makes great play dough "hair."

Collages Decide on a theme: Our Vacation at Disney World, for example. Then provide a pile of magazines, and set your timer for about 20 minutes. At the end of this time, each person explains his artwork to the other members of the family. ("And over here is an elephant. I put him in here because he reminded me of Dumbo.")

No-fail Play Dough

1 c. flour
1/2 c. salt
2 tsp. cream of tartar

Mix above together in a medium pot. Then add:

1 c. water
2 tsp. food coloring (blue and green make my favorite, turquoise)

Cook over medium heat and stir. It takes about three to five minutes. Do not despair and think it's not coming out right—it will. Store in a plastic bag or in an airtight container.

Great Refreshments for Game Night

Popcorn
Chips or vegetables and dip
Rice Krispie bars
Slices of fruit and cheese
Finger sandwiches
Jell-O Jigglers
Homemade cookies
"Bridge Mix"
Wrapped assorted candies

Write a Story Book Each person writes a sentence, and the "book" gets passed around the table. Those who cannot write yet can dictate. Leave room on each page so that you can find pictures from magazines to illustrate the book, or draw your own.

LET'S PRETEND At the Children's Museum in Boston, one of the most popular attractions is the corner grocery store. This is a small model of the real thing, where a cashier sits on a stool to ring up purchases on his register, and customers fill their basket with fake oranges and bananas and pork chops.

However plain or fancy your props might be, "Let's pretend" is something that all ages can enjoy. Find me someone who has truly outgrown the joy of a pretend tea party. When I was five, I was the teacher at the foot of the stairs and my ten-year-old sister was the student, who advanced one step up each time it suited me. My mother often played Queen Victoria to my Princess Elizabeth; scarves and jewelry were very important. I now relish any role my daughters assign me.

Beauty Parlor This requires one customer and the rest of the family to be a shampooer, a hairstylist, a manicurist, a masseuse. The customer must submit to the real thing, barring a haircut (unless he's really brave).

Shoe Store Every pair of shoes in the house is brought out and arranged in the living room. Then one or two people are salespeople; the rest customers. When you buy a pair, you must invent the person who bought them!

Living Room Ballroom Everyone dresses up, complete with dramatic makeup for the gals, and great old band music such as that of Glenn Miller is played. Dance with different partners, different ways. You might want to get a book on dance instruction and give Fred and Ginger a run for their money.

Eagle on the Mountaintop Pretend that you're a bird family lodged high up on the side of a mountain. Fashion a nest out of pillows arranged in a circle, and send various members out "hunting." They can return with anything—a penny, a piece of Tupperware, a stuffed animal, a bag of potato chips. Practice waving arms and flying, with a good take-off leap from the side of the nest.

Block-Offs Use blocks, Tinkertoys, Legos, etc. Divide family members into teams with equal amounts of raw materials. Agree on an object or animal to make, such as an airplane or a bird. Set the timer for ten minutes or so. Go into separate rooms and create until the timer goes off, then compare your efforts.

There is a bit of the dramatist—and a lot of child—in all of us. Find it in you, and have a ball hamming it up with your kids! If you can get away with filming any of these games, by all means do. Your children will be at their most charming; and when you watch these movies later, they'll be the ones to put the biggest lump in your throat.

Taboo

This is an ongoing family game, wherein a word that has been particularly overused (e.g., "awesome" or "you know") is deemed by all family members to be taboo. Each time the word is used, a small fine, say 25 cents, must be paid to a kitty. When a fair amount is collected the money is used for a family treat: ice cream out, for example, or a game of miniature golf, or the rental of a video. Taboo is not for punishment! It is a game, so members should try to make each other say the word.

Seasonal Celebrations

One of our best parts is our appreciation for and ties to nature. We respond, sometimes despite ourselves, to nature's changes and to its messages to us. We rejoice in the new life that spring brings, hunker down with fat books and thick soups in the winter, understand the worth of water in the summer, become invigorated in the fall.

Every season is worth celebrating for its own sake, but also for what it may represent to us. Certain things suggest themselves at certain times. What better time for a block party than in the fall, when new friendships are being forged in schools all around us and can inspire us to make friends with our neighbors? Spring, the time of so much new life,

inspires our gratefulness to earth for all it provides us.
We take off from our day-to-day work lives in the long and
lazy days of summer, to rest, to have fun, to have long hours
with the people we might otherwise see too little of. Then in
winter we celebrate snow, appreciate the structure of the
leafless trees, do a little of our own kind of hibernating.

Whatever your individual approach may be toward
celebrating seasons, make sure you show your awareness of
the ever-changing drama that goes on all around you. Draw
the members of your family into your joy. Wonder about it
together! Reap the harvests that every season provides, and
be glad for the loveliness and variation that nature provides
to all of us, all the time, for free.

Spring:
Saluting Life

There has always been reason to celebrate the fact of the earth. It is beautiful, for one thing; and it is our home. But at this point it is clear that we have been careless with it— even abusive—and incredibly shortsighted. Now we are beginning to pay the price.

One might easily feel hopeless about the plight of the earth. Parents run the risk of frightening children in informing them about simple ecological facts that mean danger: You must wear heavy-duty suntan lotion because the ozone layer is depleted; you cannot drink that water or eat that snow "fresh" from the sky because of the pollution. But the fact is that everyone must learn what is happening to the environment, and make a serious commitment to making the world a better place. Perhaps the best motivation for doing so is to look around and really see what it is we have, to learn to love and respect the land, the water, the heavens, the animals, and each other. With love in place, caring becomes natural.

Spring is perhaps the best time to have a family Earth Appreciation Day. We are reminded then of the splendid optimism of birth and rebirth; the beauty of flowers and new leaves; the kindness of longer, warmer days; the solace of the inevitable cycles of life and nature. Set aside a day for you and your family to do some activities that will honor this planet we live on. But remember too that the respect we owe the earth must be ongoing, present in every one of us every day of the year.

APPRECIATING THE HEAVENS

There is something that happens to families that take in wonders of the earth together. You are awed, humbled, aware that there is much more to all this than just yourselves. It is a time to be satisfied saying nothing, to be thrilled at a thoughtful intervention that makes the world work better, to be heartened by the prospect that even

A Native American View

"This we know. The earth does not belong to man; man belongs to the earth. Man did not weave the web of life; he is merely a strand in it. Whatever he does to the web, he does to himself. All things are connected like the blood which unites one family. All things are connected."

Seathl(Chief Seattle)—1854

Make a Sundial

It used to be that the sun was everyone's shared timepiece. Make a sundial in your yard to illustrate how this was so.

Pick a spot that is never in shade. Drive a good, straight stick, broom, or mop handle into the ground at an angle equal to the latitude in which you live. (Check on a map to see between which parallels your city or town is located. If you live at the 42nd parallel, your stick must be at a 42° angle.) The upper end of the stick must point to the North Star, which is true north. You can find the North Star by first locating the Big Dipper. The two stars in the bowl of the Big Dipper point directly to the North Star, which is the end of the handle of the Little Dipper. The stick in the ground forms the gnomon (the vertical triangular plate) of the sundial. Its shadows will give you accurate time.

This project can lead to other discussions about using resources we ignore or forget about because of the seductive easy quality of modern-day alternatives.

small things you do can matter very much. You may even help shape someone's life work—a young man I know decided to become a marine biologist after his family took him on a whale watch. So consider, for example, the sun, the clouds, the stars, the weather, and the air around us. Learn about the life that lives here—in the air, in the water, in or on the ground. Here are some suggestions:

SUNRISE/SUNSET It's worth getting up early to see the sunrise together. Make it a special day by having a sunrise breakfast, perhaps accompanied by a reading from an ageless and inspiring tribute to nature. Check the writings of Walt Whitman.

CLOUD WATCHING Lie on your backs and look up at the clouds on a day when they're making interesting formations. Give everyone 30 seconds to decide what the cloud looks like. Then compare notes. This is not only fun to do, but it will provide insight into each other—how you "see," how you're different, how you're alike. Clouds change formations rapidly—about every five minutes—so when you're through with one picture, you can start imagining another.

GET WET For once, stay out in the rain. Pick a warm day when it's raining hard, but there's no thunder and lightning. Wear a bathing suit, if it's warm enough. Splash through puddles; take note of the busy little streams at the side of the street. Make leaf boats and sail them. Collect rainwater to use on your houseplants. This activity can be done by one, two, or all members of a family. How about making a rule that everyone have one play in the rain together before the first day of fall? (If it doesn't rain in your part of the country, do you like running through sprinklers?)

It's nice to see what's happening in other places in the world, too. Look in the newspaper to see what the temperature is in Paris. Where in the world is it hottest? Coldest? It can be fun to take a family survey, based on the weather, to see where each member would go "today."

STARGAZING Spend an evening under the stars. Before you go out, talk about the number, size, and brilliance of the stars, and the impossible fact that you see them after they're no longer there. Look at maps of constellations and have each family member "adopt" one, explaining to the rest of the family why he or she picked it. Then, when you go outside, find your constellation, and make a wish on it. (Be sure that you pick a constellation visible at the time of year you are looking for it.)

CEILING CONSTELLATIONS Use glow-in-the-dark sticker stars to create constellations on the ceiling. Perhaps you can make them for each other; then each person will get to see a surprise when going to bed. Imitate nature, or make up a design yourselves. Children may like to see their names spelled out in stars.

VISIT A PLANETARIUM When the lights go down and the stars come out, you will all be enthralled, no matter what your age or disposition.

MOON WATCH Each Monday for one month, take careful note of the moon. Draw it to see its changes. Have a family contest to see who can come closest to predicting when changes will occur the next month. Or how about the family writing a fantasy story about the moon? Each

Constellation Flash Game

Draw or cut out pictures of the most easily found constellations. Include approximate location as well as names of important stars in the constellation on the back of the card. When you learn these cards, it will be easier to find the constellation in the skies.

Meteorologists for a Month

Hang a thermometer outside, and keep a record of temperatures for a month. Draw a chart by making a horizontal column for each day of the month. Make a vertical column on the left side of the paper for the temperatures. You can graph the temperature and then color the square for what kind of day it was: yellow for sunny, black dots for rain, light gray for cloudy, etc. There is great value in paying attention to the nature around us: we learn to value it more, treat it better, understand the profound ways it can affect us. Watch people: how many ever look up at the sky? It's beautiful, free artwork—get in the habit of seeing what it offers you every day.

member contributes one sentence to make one paragraph on the observation/charting day. At the end of the month, jointly write the conclusion and read the whole—by the light of a full moon, if possible!

FOR THE AIR AROUND US   Once a week, don't drive. Take public transportation or walk. With a little planning, this is not so hard to do! Public transportation can be fun and interesting. Let everyone take part in deciding how to get somewhere, from the general mode of transportation to the specific bus or train or path to follow in walking.

APPRECIATING THE EARTH

Consider the earth below your feet: the soil, the rocks, the hidden gems, and the water that surrounds all of that. And consider what the earth supports: plants, flowers, vegetables, us.

A PLACE ALL YOUR OWN   Take the family to a woodland, field, or park. Have everyone find a nice spot close enough to hear one another, but far enough away to give a sense of privacy. Sit, doing nothing but listening, for five minutes. Regroup to share what you heard. You can revisit your place, bring it "gifts" (a pretty rock, a wildflower), and tell it your secrets.

ADOPT A TREE   This can be done in your own backyard. Name your tree. Make bark rubbings of it using crayons or charcoal. Create a leaf print by painting one side of a leaf and then pressing it down onto paper. Feed your tree by bringing leaves to the foot of it to enrich the soil. You can use an old tree for all of this, or plant a new one. If you do plant a new one, consider keeping a "baby book," with pictures and notes about the tree's growth. Also consider the tradition of planting a new tree to mark certain important events within the family—births, deaths, marriages.

MAY DAY ACTIVITY   Pick flowers (judiciously!), and wrap them up in a doily. Tie a ribbon around the bouquet, and use it to hang on friends' and neighbors' doorknobs. Part of the fun here is the anonymity—don't get caught making your deliveries! Here, at last, is an occasion where it's fine to ring a doorbell and then run away.

PLANT A FAMILY GARDEN   Give everyone a row that must be weeded, watered, fussed over, and, eventually, harvested.

THE NATURAL PICNIC   Use only foods direct from the earth. Have the food shopping/gathering/preparing be a family gig—just figuring out which foods are untampered with can be a real learning experience. Leave the place where you picnic cleaner than it was when you found it.

TAKE A HIKE   Put on a backpack and take off. You need not be in Yellowstone National Park to do this: There is always something interesting to look at outside. Bring a sketchbook to make a drawing of something you find—a horse chestnut, a flower, a rock. Observe your subject in great detail and draw everything you see. Everyone can contribute here toward keeping a family botany book.

THE JOY OF PLANTS   It is a fine thing to be responsible for the growth and flowering of a plant. Children, especially, are impressed with changes they can see daily. Create a family indoor garden. Plant a bean in a paper cup, sprinkle seeds on a sponge to sprout, or force narcissus bulbs inside. Potatoes and onions grow rapidly—use toothpicks to station them at the top of a water-filled container. Seeds

Making Mud Pies

Not only is this good, dirty fun, it teaches about the different kinds of soil. Loam, sand, and clay all make different kinds of pies. Make a point of finding and experimenting with different soils. Decorate your pies with berries, acorns, flowers, and leaves, and let them dry in the sunshine. And then, of course, serve.

Terrariums

City Garden Use potting soil instead of sandy soil. Plant slips of begonia, baby tears, grape ivy, etc. If a plant grows too high, replant it outside the terrarium, and replace it with a new baby plant.

Desert Garden After the layer of pebbles, put in about three inches of sand, then three inches of sandy potting mixture. Plant with potted succulents, cacti, sedums, and aloes. Keep in a sunny warm spot. Spray soil around plants, not plants themselves, about once a week.

from peas, oranges, lemons, grapefruit, pears, or apples will sprout readily. The tops of carrots or beets placed in a shallow dish with a little water will quickly send up shoots. Lima beans, if soaked in water for 12 to 16 hours, can be split open to view the tiny "baby plant" inside (a magnifying glass will show this very clearly).

MAKE A TERRARIUM A terrarium is a miniature garden under glass. A layer of moist soil covered with moss to prevent evaporation will support plant life as well as insects, frogs, snakes, and lizards. (If you use animals, make sure they are properly fed and cared for.) Use a fish aquarium and cover it with glass. You can vary the soil content and the plant life for different kinds of gardens.

Woodland Garden Start with a layer of clean gravel. Cover with two or three inches of sand for good drainage. Bits of charcoal mixed with the sand will keep the soil sweet. Next add a two-inch layer of slightly sandy soil that has been sifted and dampened enough to hold together when squeezed. Make your landscape interesting by molding little hills and valleys. Rocks can be miniature cliffs; a small, shallow dish can be used to make a pond— sink it into the soil and ring it with pebbles so the moss doesn't soak up all the water. Add a beautiful piece of bark or wood. Next, plant tree seedlings and other small plants that do not reach to the top glass. Cover the soil with mosses that grow on the ground, not those you find on rotting wood. Finally, wet down the terrarium with a fine spray of water, but not to the saturation point. Set the glass cover on loosely so that air can circulate. Keep in a cool place and out of direct sunlight. Keep the glass clean. Check hydration by watching for the formation of droplets of water. If there are many of them, remove the glass cover until most of the condensation evaporates. If the plants look dry, spray them. Once-a-month watering should be enough, but each garden is different. This is a good project for the whole family to create together. Assign responsibility for care on a rotating basis.

SAY THANKS TO WATER   At dinner some night, try to think of something on earth that does not require water. Good luck!

ALL IN A DROP   Collect pond water, and view it under a microscope. It is amazing how many forms of life exist in it.

VISIT THE OCEAN   Take a walk along the ocean. Consider how much of the earth is made up of water and what life forms live in the ocean. If you can, visit at high tide and low tide. Find something beautiful to bring home: a shell, a rock, even seaweed. Sit and listen to the sounds the surf makes.

APPRECIATING ANIMALS

While it is true that our culture does not consider animals to be as important as people, we do have great affection for them. What is missing is our respect. We have too many puppies and kittens put to sleep. We have too many zoos where animals blatantly suffer. We know too little about the conditions under which animals are raised for the meat industry. We do too little to educate our children about the worth and dignity of animals. Here are some ideas that might help.

LEARN ABOUT ANIMALS   Visit a natural history museum, a zoo, or a nature preserve. Watch films together, such as the ones made by the National Geographic Society. Try, in

Natural Forecasting

- Dew on the grass means fair weather.
- Mackerel sky (small, broken clouds that look like fish scales) and mare's tails (trails of soft, thin clouds) mean rain the next day.
- Red sky in the morning portends a storm; at night, it predicts that a nice day will follow.
- Birds fly high in fair weather, low if a storm's coming.
- Cows lie down in the fields when a storm is coming.
- The ground spider's web, if visible on the grass in early morning, means a fair day.
- Leaves on trees turn inside out (show their backs) before a storm.

Birdfoot's Grandpa

The old man
must have stopped our car
two dozen times to climb out
and gather into his hands
the small toads blinded
by our lights and leaping,
live drops of rain.

The rain was falling,
a mist about his white hair
and I kept saying
you can't save them all,
accept it, get back in,
we've got places to go.

But, leathery hands full
of wet brown life,
knee deep in the summer
roadside grass,
he just smiled and said
they have places to go to
too.

Joseph Bruchac
Entering Onondaga
(1978, Cold Mountain Press)

this way, to understand the contribution each animal makes, the inherent dignity in all animals, even if they're not cuddly models for stuffed animals.

VOLUNTEER TIME Helping at a vet's office or at an animal shelter will give you a new view of many animals and help keep the work of caring for them going.

FEED THE BIRDS There are many different kinds of bird feeders to make, from the simplest pinecone rolled in peanut butter and covered with seeds to the most complex of bird mansions. You can also buy a wide variety of feeders. Put your feeder somewhere where everyone can enjoy the sight of the birds coming. Find out the names of your most frequent visitors. Flash cards can help with this.

APPRECIATE INSECTS Reading E. B. White's *Charlotte's Web* together may help dispel some fears about spiders. Learn together about the genius of bees. Keep a grasshopper or a cricket for a day to observe it. Discuss the organized industry of ants, the reason for mosquitoes, the lovely metamorphosis of caterpillars, the number of hearts (actually, aortic arches) in a worm.

BRINGIN' IT ALL BACK HOME Remember to treat your own pets with respect. They are not playthings put here for our amusement. They need exercise and rest, proper diets, loving discipline, and the company of their caretakers. Make sure that the pet you pick is one you have time and resources for.

APPRECIATING ONE ANOTHER

It is a sad fact that our concern and involvement with the environment is not paralleled in improved relationships with one another. We continue to build up supplies of nuclear weapons capable of destroying populations, and the crime rate everywhere is soaring. The evening news and the daily newspapers should be X-rated. It may seem hard to believe that one small act of kindness can make a difference in the face of such violence and blatant disregard for human life, but the fact is that it can. We need those small acts of humanity now more than ever.

Think of things you can do to show your family and the people around you that you appreciate them. Turn off the television and talk to each other. Write letters to your friends. Give small gifts to the people you work with— bring in some chocolate chip cookies someone in your family made; be free with compliments; buy an inexpensive bouquet and give everyone a flower from it. Visit with lonely residents of a nursing home. Call your representatives in Congress to let them know your feelings about what the government is doing or not doing. Pick up trash on your street, or help to clean your favorite park.

SAVING THE EARTH

It has become "in" to be ecology-oriented, and information and suggestions abound. Books, magazines, and newspapers carry tips for recycling, for preserving resources, for conserving energy. Sometimes, though, the information is more overwhelming than helpful. How can you make them relevant to your family?

INFORM Make sure you understand what ecologists are talking about, why it's important to you. Be as matter- of-fact and as positive as possible when teaching about the environment; stress what we can do, not what it is too late to do anything about. It may be helpful to have a discus-

Make a Home Planetarium

1. Cut off the top and bottom lids of a large tin can.
2. Using the can opening as a pattern, draw a circle in the center of a piece of blank white paper.
3. Within the confines of this circle, draw the circumpolar constellations, using a good star map as a guide.
4. With a pin, prick the positions of the stars, making the holes big enough for light to shine through them.
5. Stretch this star map tightly over one end of the tin can and hold it in place with a rubber band.
6. Use a large flashlight to shine into the other end and, in a darkened room, project the star map on a blank wall.

Recycling Tips

- Coffee grounds, vegetable peelings, and used cooking oil can be put onto garden beds.
- Open-mesh onion and potato bags rolled up and secured with rubber bands make pot scrubbers.
- Recycle old greeting cards into postcards or recipe cards.
- Open your dishwasher before the drying cycle begins—the dishes will dry much faster.

It also is easy to start recycling newspapers, tin cans, bottles, even certain plastics. You might want to make your own "natural" cleaning products (vinegar works wonderfully well to clean windows, for example); to have a "light monitor" make sure only necessary lights are on at night. Make a policy of using junk mail for scratch paper.

sion about what all the terms we hear so often mean: What does recycling do? What is acid rain, exactly? What do the Brazilian rain forests have to do with us? What significance does it have if certain animals become extinct? Where are there droughts, and why?

ENFORCE Once you understand the necessity for recycling, for preserving our resources, for getting involved, do so! It may help to simply become aware of how much water you use by keeping track of how many times a day a toilet is flushed. (Put a notepad and pencil in the bathroom, and have everyone make a mark for every flush. At the end of the day, total the marks and figure out how much water you used. How could you have saved water? How about placing a brick in the toilet tank?) Or put a timer in the bathroom to remind the person showering when five minutes is up.

Tips that you find all over can be put on the refrigerator for a week, one at a time, to "sink in." Make them meaningful! For example, rather than saying it helps to carpool, put up a note saying, "Guess what? If each commuter car carried just one more person, we'd save 600,000 gallons of gas a day, and prevent 1.2 million pounds of carbon dioxide from polluting the atmosphere."

EVALUATE Once a week, take stock of what you've tried to do to help and how well it worked. Should you keep it up? Add something to it?

Whatever you choose to do, the point is to make it relevant and sensible. This makes for compliance and camaraderie. As temporary caretakers of the earth, we have an ongoing job. We must take responsibility for the way things are, and work always to make them better.

Although it is always fun to share good times, there is more to being a family than celebrating together. Banding together to act responsibly and to work together toward something you all believe in can make you close in a different kind of way. You learn and grow together. You feel the satisfaction of doing the right thing. You help each other deal with the inevitable fear and stress generated by stories about the terrible things happening to the environment. Try to make it a daily habit to honor your other mother, the earth, in every way you can.

Summer: Family Vacation

It's no secret that today's families are extremely busy. Adults must make a living and run a household, often simultaneously; and both jobs are demanding. Children, too, can be stressed out by their lives: they're faced with rigid schedules, homework, day care, problems with friends and teachers, to say nothing of uncooperative hairdos, pimples, and a wardrobe that is all wrong.

The pace of our lives seems to speed up more and more with no relief in sight. That is, unless we make for some relief, and schedule a vacation. Then, in addition to taking a break from our sometimes overwhelming routines, we get to really know the people we live with. We spend time waking up together, eating meals together, sight-seeing, enjoying different forms of recreation, and simply talking. In addition to these very important things, vacations are great for gaining perspective: for example, after a week or two away from a desk, we learn that the papers on it aren't the only thing to life after all.

Taking a vacation can cost a lot of money—really a lot of money, especially if you go to faraway places and stay in elegant digs. But vacations don't have to cost much at all— for instance, a stay-at-home vacation. The point is to be able, at last, to spend time with the people you love, doing something you enjoy that is different from what you usually do. The best time I had on my last vacation was sitting with my family and watching a dog named Candy on a beach. She liked trying to catch fish in her mouth, and we liked watching her bite the waves. This activity cost absolutely nothing, and if you ask me, it was more fun by far than the things we did pay for.

But: Often when people go away on vacation, they end up needing to come home in order to get a rest. What they had envisioned—a restful, enjoyable time—simply didn't happen. They return broke and irritable and disappointed. It seems to me that this kind of experience can be avoided by doing two things: lowering expectations and planning carefully. This does not mean that you head out on a

What About Grandparents?

Grandparents are often interested in traveling with their grandchildren. Travel agencies can help set up special trips that can accommodate their varying needs. Also, children may enjoy spending a week or so at their grandparents' house, doing not much of anything but enjoying one another's company.

Family Research Night

Go out for a quick dinner, then look for information together at the library. Check out some books on the places or subjects you're interested in. Ask the librarian for other sources you might consult, such as magazines and newspapers.

To Obtain Information

You can write to specific places such as dude ranches or resort hotels; you can write to chambers of commerce or official travel bureaus (address: State Travel Bureau at the capital city of states you might like to visit). You can call 800–numbers. You can also get information at travel agencies.

vacation sighing, expecting to have a terrible time—you should be full of enthusiasm, excited to be getting away, looking forward to all that might happen. It does mean, though, that you don't harbor illusions—about there being no fighting, for example. About everything being what it was "cracked up to be." About the world holding off on accidents or illness or other problems because you're on vacation. Problems will occur just as they do otherwise.

I have a friend who is a flight attendant. He tells me about the differences he notices in passengers returning home from vacations. "Some families are all smiles, so relaxed—you can see it did them a world of good to get away," he says. "They sort of lean into each other all the way home." And then there are the others. "You know it really didn't work for them," he says. "They're so tense, and you know they can't wait to get home and get this vacation over with!"

An annual family vacation is a good tradition to have. But like many good things in life, it needs care and feeding to make it work. With a little effort, you can be one of the families it does work for.

PLANNING

What you need to decide in a planning session is who's going on vacation, when, and where. This is a topic eminently suitable for a family conference. Initial planning should start far in advance, up to six months ahead.

A family vacation doesn't necessarily mean two adults and their children. You can bring along grandparents, aunts and uncles, friends of yours or the children's, your lumbering sheepdog. Single parents may want to join forces with a friend who is also a single parent. Sometimes families split up for vacations—a father takes one child to the ocean while a mother takes another child skiing. And sometimes kids go to camps and parents take a vacation alone together. There's nothing that says you can't combine things: Drop the kids off to visit with their grandparents for a week while the adults do something else; then pick them up and go somewhere together for a week.

There are times when families split up for vacations for other reasons. In a divorce situation, children may visit an ex-spouse rather than vacation with the people they live with. This may make for situations that need sensitive treatment. Leave yourselves open and ready for conflicts that may occur: difficulty adjusting to differing parental environments, ambivalent feelings about having a good time with one parent while leaving another behind, and so on. Regardless of how awkward or painful a situation may be, the thing to do is talk about it. Remember too, that oftentimes ex-spouses get along just fine, and pull-apart vacations go by without a hitch!

Most people vacation in the summer, but a winter vacation is also an option, especially during schools' Christmas vacation. It may be difficult to take off two whole weeks from work, but it seems to me people really need at least that much time. If we have only a week (or even less) for vacation, we might not ever unwind. Don't despair, though, if you can't take a long break, for whatever reason. Any break, taken together, is better than none!

Planning a vacation should be relaxed and a big part of the fun. Start early and give a wide berth to all. You may surprise yourselves by the creative things you can come up

Planning Ahead

Use the cold, bleak months of winter to plan your sunny summer vacation. It can be a treat to be surrounded by brochures about warm and beautiful places when it's freezing all around you.

- Once you know when you're going, start making reservations. In order to get the best deals on fares, you need to reserve at least three weeks in advance.

- Travel agents are very helpful, and don't cost anything to use. But keep in mind that if you let them do everything, you may miss out on some anticipatory fun!

- Everyone in the family deserves to offer input about where to go. Give consideration to the comfort and wishes of all, and try to come up with a plan to please everyone. Start with no limits—let everyone describe what his or her dream vacation would be.

- Get information about anything you think you might like to do, and anywhere you might like to go. Have some fun imagining yourselves at all the different places.

A Count-down Calendar

Include on it certain things that need to be done by a certain time. You might, for example, schedule first a family meeting to talk about vacations. Then write in a night to go to the library. As the time to leave comes closer, you'll need to do things like make reservations, arrange for pet sitters, have the car tuned up, discontinue newspapers. In addition to adding to the anticipation, this may also help to offset the stress that can dull your vacation fun.

with. The youngest members of the family may come up with the best ideas. (They may also be the most outlandish. But these are the things that keep you young, right?)

PLACES TO GO

My family went off to the mountains in New England to try skiing one winter, and we were dismal failures—at skiing itself. My husband slammed into the instructor, bending the instructor's brand-new (as he relentlessly pointed out) ski pole. I spent most of my time on my back contemplating cloud formations.

But we loved how beautiful the mountains and the falling snow were, loved drinking hot chocolate and playing board games before the fireplace in our rented condo at night, even loved a little bit making fools of ourselves as we tried to ski. For people who can actually stay upright, a skiing vacation will, of course, offer even more to appreciate.

TRADITIONAL VACATIONS AWAY

SKIING   Consider how difficult the terrain is, what other attractions besides skiing are offered, and whether family packages are offered. Also consider padding your derriere.

RESORTS   These offer sports such as golf, tennis, boating, fishing, hiking, swimming, biking, or horseback riding; meals; and entertainment. Many have free children's programs as well.

WHITE-WATER RAFTING   There are white-water rivers in nearly every part of America, and outfitters to provide you with a thrilling, but safe, adventure.

CANOEING AND KAYAKING These offer tamer ways for families to ride the rivers.

CITY VACATIONS Consider guided tours, museums, ethnic communities, sporting or theatrical events, zoos, parks, restaurants with regional specialties.

SAILING Consider a windjammer cruise. You'll spend time cruising for a few hours a day and also enjoy sight–seeing and swimming.

DUDE RANCHES Here you'll find fresh air and the openness of a ranch setting. You'll have a horse of your own. For a directory of Western ranches, send $1.00 to Dude Ranchers Association, P.O.Box 471F, LaPorte, CO 80535.

WORKING FARMS AND RANCHES Wake up to the sound of the roosters, have a huge old–fashioned breakfast together, milk cows, collect eggs, plant in the garden, bring in the hay, go on nature walks, play in the barn.

HIKING/BACKPACKING You can go with outfitters and learn the basics, or, if you have experience, take off on your own. Contact the Sierra Club (415–776–2211) or Appalachian Mountain Club (617–523–0636).

NATURALIST-LED WILDERNESS TRIPS Several nonprofit organizations provide family-oriented programs. Call 800–322–WILD to reach American Wilderness Adventure, which operates three- to five-day trips in Colorado, Minnesota, and Utah.

BICYCLING TOURS This is one of the most popular and least expensive family vacations. Some places provide a van that follows you and gives you a lift when you're tired. Be sure you find out how many miles are covered each day, especially if you're bringing young children.

Tips for Leaving Your House

- Leave a nursery monitor in your neighbor's house so they can hear any activity in yours.
- Leave an itinerary and a house key with the next-door neighbors.
- Consider using a pet-sitter service rather than keeping your animals at a kennel. The animals don't get sick; they get walked and petted and played with twice a day. Make sure you leave your vet's number and address.
- Cancel newspapers and mail delivery if someone's not bringing them in for you.
- Prepay bills that will come due when you're gone.
- Ask the police to drive by periodically.
- Get rid of all perishables in the refrigerator.
- Empty all garbage.
- Turn off the water supply to the washing machine.
- Unplug sensitive appliances like TVs, computers, stereos, VCRs, and microwaves.
- Set timers on lights.

Vacations at Home

You may want to tell others you're going away in order to have a better shot at a real family vacation. At any rate, figure out ways ahead of time to keep the time separate from non-vacation demands. Have every family member make a commitment to make every effort to honor the fact that you are all on vacation together. If you have a telephone answering machine, use it—make a rule that phone calls can be returned only at night when you've finished your activities for the day.

CAMPING Make sure the beauty of nature works its magic on you. Parks offer hiking, horseback riding, bird and animal watching, picture taking. Evening campfire programs are conducted by park rangers and volunteers. Junior-ranger programs are often available as well.

HOUSEBOATS These are available for rental all over the country. Call state tourist boards for information. Don't forget your straw hat and fishing pole.

CRUISES More and more, cruises cater to families. Here is a way to travel and stay put at the same time. Warning: You will gain weight from all the wonderful meals. And before-meal snacks. And after-meal snacks. And midnight buffets.

THE STAY-AT-HOME VACATION

This is my favorite. No packing, no unpacking, no traveling, no motel bills. Just an acknowledgment that you as a family are together, and time is your own. Have breakfast at home, and then take off, and don't come home except to sleep. Visit your own city as though you're a tourist. Go to three movies in a row. Tour potato chip factories, breweries, newspapers. Go swimming, hiking, biking. Ride the roller coaster at an amusement park. Visit a farm and pick your own strawberries. Spend some time at the airport just watching—see where all the planes are going, watch lovers kiss hello and goodbye, tour the control tower if it's allowed. Go to a play, a concert, a lecture, a playground. Take day trips to interesting places around you. Volunteer a day's time with an animal shelter or a soup kitchen.

Drive exactly 100 miles, with a rotating navigator telling you when and where to turn. (Each navigator dictates where to go for a given amount of time, say fifteen minutes.) See where you end up. Do something there, even if it's just having a picnic. Use a stay-at-home vacation to do whatever strikes your fancy; just make sure you don't hang around your house and work!

PACKING

This is much less painful if you get really organized and make lists in advance. Have everyone in the family who can, help.

THE PACKING GAME A parent puts all the children's suitcases in the hall. Armed with a list, she calls out, for example, "Bring me four pairs of socks!" The children race to find the socks. Add some nonspecific somethings, "Bring me something that will look great at the beach," or "Bring me something special for you to keep on your bed at the hotel." Or: Older children are given copies of the list—how many of what and a place to check each off.

KIDPACK In addition to packing clothes, let kids fill backpacks with things they'd like to do. The rule is, you can bring what you can carry. Have a practice run—let your kids carry packs around the house for an hour or so.

TRAVELING BY CAR

This can be a trial, but it can also be a wonderful way to really see where you're going. Remember that children (and most adults) cannot tolerate sitting hour after hour. Here are things to do to make the trip more enjoyable:

Wise Packing

Pack pajamas, toothbrush, hairbrush—everything you need for going to sleep—on top of suitcase or in a separate carrier. Include a swimming suit. You won't have to dig through suitcases to find what you need.

Things to Pack

- a board game for rainy days
- mail-in envelopes for sending in film (when you get home, your pictures will be waiting)
- electrical-outlet covers to protect babies and toddlers
- small bottle of detergent
- night light
- travel alarm clock
- sewing kit
- books for reading in motel rooms
- plastic bags for dirty laundry and wet swimming suits.
- a list of credit card numbers to report their loss—also health and auto insurance numbers
- your own pillowcases for a touch (and smell) of home
- rainwear
- first aid kit

To Prevent Car Sickness

- Don't let those sensitive to motion sickness read or draw in the car. Have them look out the window.
- Keep the car cool.
- Stop at least every two hours.
- Provide plenty of fluids.
- Avoid sweets; stick to fruit and salty food.
- Schedule driving to avoid rush hours.
- If you can, avoid winding, hilly roads in the morning—that tends to be the most sensitive time for many sufferers.

THE GREAT JUNK-FOOD SEND-OFF Before any road trip, we go to our local gas station for a fill-up, and into the little grocery store there to stock up on junk food. At the McDonald's down the road, we buy soft drinks for the kids, and coffee for the adults at Dunkin' Donuts. This must be done. Or the trip won't happen. And we'll have to go home.

I'LL TAKE THE SIDE ROAD Stay off turnpikes in favor of the more interesting side roads, at least a little. You will see so much more, find such interesting things! Forays may very well become the best parts of your trip.

MAPS AND TRAVEL JOURNAL Entries can be anything: what you see out of the window, funny signs you pass, what was best about the cafe where you just ate lunch, the way the driver drives, what was in the museum you visited.

STOP EVERY TWO HOURS Short, frequent breaks will help keep your spirits up and your stress level down.

TAKE TURNS Let each person have a turn deciding when to stop. For example, your eight-year-old daughter may dictate that at 4:07 you'll stop for french fries. When that time comes, go to the first place that offers same.

BRING IT BACK Stop the car, take a 15-minute walk, and bring something back. Then when you're off again, take turns every ten miles revealing what you got and how. These stories should be absolute nonsense. For example, "I saw this rock fall from a space ship. I picked it up and was temporarily frozen in place, but then they let me go."

AUTO SANTA Wrap up little gifts: a small box of crayons, costume jewelry, Mad-libs, little games like the kind where balls must go in holes, etc. Hand one out every hundred miles or every two hours, whichever comes first. Don't forget the teens and adults, who like presents, too!

LISTEN TO TAPES Enjoy books, comedians, all kinds of music. Learn about the genius of certain composers, the complex emotions in opera, the appeal of rap music.

SING Don't be shy! Sing rounds, old children's favorites, current rock songs. Put suggestions for songs into a container, draw one out. If you don't know the song, you have to pretend to.

IMPROVE YOUR MEMORIES Bring along photo albums and all those loose pictures you haven't gotten around to putting in them. When the scenery's dull, you can get around to it at last.

IGNORANCE IS BLISS Ignore fighting among children. Yes! Unless someone is in physical danger, just ignore it! Fighting is a form of recreation for children. Yes! And if you interfere, chances are it will only get worse.

QUIET TIME Require a five- to ten-minute period of silence each hour. This can be life-saving.

THE GRAND FINALE Each day should end with something special: a dip in the motel pool, a local movie, an outrageous dessert. At noon every day, start thinking of what that something might be. Take turns deciding.

In the Kid Pack

Consider coloring books, markers, blank paper, hand-held video games, tape player with headsets, blank tapes to make recordings, dolls, puppets, press-on games. Older children might bring personal stereos, address and phone books so they can send postcards to and/or call their friends, paperback books, certain items for grooming that must be in easy reach at all times.

Car Games

Before leaving home, put together a notebook with suggestions for things to do in the car. Some things to consider are:

ABC Think of sentences of five words, in which every word begins with the same letter: Edie eats everything, even eels. Increase or decrease the number of words in order to change the level of difficulty.

Psychic Make predictions about what you will see. Keep score. The winner picks the restaurant for dinner.

Groucho Each person picks a somewhat common word. The radio is turned on. The first person whose word is said, wins.

Traveling by Airplane

Book far in advance, up to a month ahead, for the best fares. You'll be told you can't get refunds, but if disaster strikes and you become ill and can't travel, you can get a note from your doctor in order to be compensated for a trip not used.

Kids in the Air

- **To help the discomfort of ear–popping, have infants suck on bottles or pacifiers on take-off and landing. Older kids can suck on hard candy or chew gum. Over-the-counter antihistamines or decongestants taken half an hour before the flight may help.**
- **Give kids the window seats, especially the younger ones. They will enjoy the sights they see, and it will separate them from passengers who may not enjoy sitting by children.**
- **Check with the airline to see if they have special kids' meals. If not, kids may like fruit plates, which are usually available, more than the usual fare.**

SCHEDULING YOUR DAYS—OR NOT

It's critical to remember that a vacation is meant to be a vacation, a reprieve from the stress of normal life. If you crowd in too much to do, you can end up needing a vacation from your vacation. Better to underplan, and prevent that frantic, frazzled feeling. Keep these points in mind:

SOMETHING FOR EVERYONE   Try to accommodate everyone to some extent every day—a splash in the motel pool, the Old Masters in a museum, shopping for CD's. When you know you'll get to do something you want, it's a lot easier doing something someone else wants. This is true whether you're four or forty-four.

DO-IT-ALL DAYS   This does not mean packing your schedule full. But pay attention to different types of activities, and try to include them all in one day. Do something physical (swimming), cultural (visiting a historical monument) and just plain fun (a park ride).

FAMILY PRIORITY CHART   When you arrive at your destination, have family members write down everything they want to do. One item gets four stars, one three, one two, and one one. The family should honor everyone's four-star requests, and then try to accommodate the other requests in order of their importance.

COMING HOME

Well, it's over. All you planned and dreamed about and saved for. Now you are back to face what you needed time away from in the first place. The good news is that the worse you feel, the better your vacation was. But here are some ways to make the homecoming sweeter:

END-OF-VACATION BLOW-OUT   Save some funds to spend at home. Eat out at a fancy restaurant, tour your own city, go horseback riding or sailing, or to the beach.

COME HOME EARLY   Return soon enough that you allow for "decompression" time. Veg out (and nothing more!) for a couple of days before you enter back into the fray. Take your time unpacking, doing laundry, opening the mail, shopping for groceries.

SOUVENIR GENERAL   Designate a part of your house for souvenirs from your trips—a corner, a shelf, a wall. Bring back hats from the different places you visit, rocks you keep in a beautiful basket, postcards, sand or shells from different beaches—anything that appeals to you.

SAVE THE MEMORIES   Some night after you've gotten all your pictures back, pop some corn and gather around the kitchen table to put them into photo albums, along with some brochures and maps in your albums. If you've brought back any food, have a little now, but be sure to save some for much later, too, when tasting something will bring back a flood of memories. "Remember the guy behind the counter, how funny he was?" Use this time to mail extra copies of photos to friends and relatives, to edit VCR footage. It's a way to enjoy your vacation again.

Traveling by Train

There are a number of advantages to going by train. It's inexpensive, you can really see where you're going, and you can get up and move around. There's food and a bathroom available, other adults and children to make friends with. You can build a vacation around taking Amtrak's Seattle/Los Angeles Coast Starlight. On long-distance western trains, you can get a route guide with a map and a description of what you're going to pass. There are also movies and games in lounge cars. *Call 1–800–USA–RAIL for information and to get the Amtrak Travel Planner, "with over 500 great places to take kids."*

Remember!

What kids need most on their vacation is unstructured time with their parents.

Fall:
A Block Party

Fall is seen by many as the real New Year, because it's the time when we begin things again. School starts. The pace of our work lives picks up to normal now that everyone's back from vacation. It's time for all of us to put on our new shoes, literally or figuratively, and enter back into the fray.

A block party at this time of year, when almost everyone's home, can be a good thing. Why? Well, for one thing, a block party may be the only opportunity you ever have to meet the people who are your neighbors. And it's a good thing to know them. You feel less alienated in an alienating culture—you feel as though you belong somewhere.

A block party can also teach you about the history of the place where you live. Those who have been on the block for 30 and 40 years have a lot to say about what's happened there over time. A block party gives you an excuse to ask some things you've been wondering about for months or longer (Is it true your job is playing violin for the symphony? Who built your deck for you? How did you find your au pair? How do you like your new car?). It reinforces the understanding that the world is made up of all kinds of people, and that it behooves us to get to know each other and learn to get along. It's also a wonderful family activity, because there's a job to do and a benefit to be gained for just about everyone.

WHEN?

Personally, there's nothing I like better than a late after-noon party on a Sunday. That's a likely time for people to be home, for one thing. Also, a Sunday afternoon party chases away Sunday night blues, that vague sense of malaise a lot of people feel when the weekend is over. You can plan for a block party to start a half hour or so before eating, then allow at least an hour and a half for dinner and another half hour or hour for post-dinner socializing. So

Rain Dates

A note on rain dates: Supply one if you want. I don't believe in them, because there's no guarantee it won't rain on the rain day and because I feel it's anticlimactic. When I plan block parties, I figure if it rains, we'll all squeeze into my house. It never has, though.

you might set the hours for 4:30 to 7:30. This makes it easy for people to take care of things they need to do during the day, and to get little children home and in bed on time. It also leaves enough of a night for people to do something else, if so inclined. You might want to pick Labor Day for your party.

Another option to consider is a Sunday brunch—a block party breakfast extraordinaire. It's a nice way to get the day going. It's also a great excuse to buy a whole bunch of those gooey caramel rolls you ogle every time you go to the bakery.

WHERE?

I like block parties that are held outdoors. There's room for everyone; spills are no problem (in fact, any dogs attending the party will look upon accidents as a bonus); and groups of adults can sit and talk while groups of children run around at breakneck speed. So I've used my backyard, as well as my neighbor's when we've needed it. I've also used the driveway for food and adult conversation, and the adjacent front yard for the gymnastics and general enthusiasm of the younger set. Other people I know block off their street via police order, and then give the participants the run of the place. Children, especially, seem to adore the freedom of standing (or, more commonly, lying spread-eagle) right in the middle of the road with no horrified adult holding onto the sides of her head and yelling, "Get up from there before you get killed!" If you opt for using your yard, make your bathroom, telephone, and kitchen sink available to anyone who needs them.

Another option is to invite the entire block to meet at a park for a picnic. This works well for a condo party, or for city dwellers who want a country atmosphere.

HOW?

When I first gave a block party, all the people I invited expressed admiration and sympathy for "all that work." The truth is, there isn't much work, because it's a potluck, so the work is very much shared. All I do is invite people, and then provide the space as well as the food I make.

INVITATIONS It's a good idea to send them out about two weeks early, giving people time to plan. You can buy all manner of invitations, or make your own. Children are almost always willing and eager to help design such things. (The last invitations I sent out featured this scene at the top of the page: Smoke rising from houses nestled cozily along a tree-lined street. Flowers standing up proudly in neatly tended beds. Cats out on their rounds staring disdainfully out at the invitees, and a sun shining brightly in a sky full of puffy clouds.) Let the invitation read something like this:

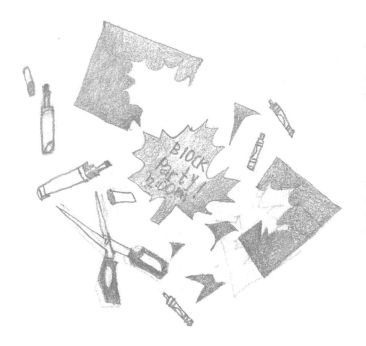

PLEASE COME TO A POTLUCK BLOCK PARTY
SUNDAY, SEPTEMBER 2
4:30–7:30
CALL 339–9932 TO R.S.V.P.
MEET YOUR NEIGHBORS! OVEREAT!
ALL WELCOME!

RSVP

Keep a list handy, in a central location, such as on your refrigerator door. Then anyone who takes a call can make an entry. Here is a sample RSVP list:

Name	How many	House #	Bringing	Phone
Brown	4	77	mexican dip	330-8723
Sullivan	2	12	green salad	883-9263
O'Brian	5	89	plates & cups	838-7457

Whatever your design, indicate on the invitation the nature of the party, the date, the time, and the number to call to RSVP. Then have your children deliver the invitations to each house on the block. You can make them mailpersons, with a backpack to be the mailpouch. They might even like a "uniform" complete with a hat. Older children, who might eschew such costumes, are usually still willing to deliver invitations. I have also enjoyed this role—it's fun to see what everyone's mailbox looks like! The last time I made the deliveries, I had a delightful chat with a woman a few doors down from me who was out on her lawn with her new puppy.

As hostess, you handle the RSVP calls and get the following information: name, number coming, house number, food bringing, and phone number. You can assign foods (usually four to six servings is plenty) such as salads, appetizers, desserts, entrees, or beverages; or you can request that the people bring paper towels, cups, plastic flatware, or napkins. There are those who believe that a good way to have a potluck is to have the hostess supply the dishes, then let the participants bring whatever they feel like bringing, no disclosure necessary. If you end up with 30 desserts, what the heck? Enjoy yourself! While there is something appealing about this notion, I like better, as participant and hostess, to deal with specifics: "We have three desserts coming, so would you like to bring a salad or an entree?"

If you have an answering machine, you can make your greeting say, "This is 555-9932. Please leave a message after the tone. If you're calling about the block party, please leave your name, your house number, the number coming, the food you'd like to bring, and your phone number." That way, you'll need to call back only if there's a problem.

One good thing about a block party is that no one has to go far if something is forgotten. Another is that guests can bring along their own chairs—no worries about how you will seat everyone.

DECORATION Anything goes! Hang things from your trees: feathers, bells, cut–out decorations such as fall leaves or little houses designed to look like those on the block, wind chimes, a pinata. Tie a big balloon bouquet to your front yard lamppost—one for every "house" attending, marked with the name and the house number. Set up a picnic table (or, better, join two end to end) for the food, and decorate with many little bottles scattered randomly here and there, all holding one flower. Children are wonderful sources for decorations, of course: Just tell them you want some, give them raw materials (paper, glue, scissors, fabric scraps, buttons, ribbon, foil, glitter, macaroni, etc.) and let them go. You may want to provide a children's table at the party with a paper tablecloth. They can decorate it with crayons or markers you've provided on a tray in the center of the table. You can scatter colorful blankets or sheets around the yard for people to sit on.

FOOD A potluck provides you with a wonderful variety of foods. People who hate cooking night after night for their family are often inspired by a block party to show off a little and bring a favorite, terrific dish. As the host, you may want to provide hamburgers and hot dogs fresh off the grill. Just be sure if you do that the grill is kept far away from the children's area.

The No-blow Tablecloth

To keep a tablecloth from blowing up over the food, sew up the corners into triangles, creating a pocket to hold golf balls or stones.

Closed Block

To block off your street, you may need to submit a petition to the traffic department, signed by residents of the block. Call to find out the procedure in your town.

Pet Corner

If pets come to your party, leave out bowls of water for them. Put up a sign calling it the "Filling Station."

Popular Party Foods

- deviled eggs, carried in an egg carton lined with plastic wrap
- spinach lasagna
- fried chicken
- pasta salads
- meatballs (provide toothpicks)
- fruit salad
- brownies
- homemade pies
- homemade breads
- chips and dip
- chocolate chip cookies
- crispy rice cereal bars

(Note: Be careful about foods sitting out too long. Some people may want to bring freezer chests to store their contributions in after the first pass.)

You may want to put "like" foods together—have an appetizer area, a salad area, a dessert table, for example. Or you may want to mix and match—put down your apple pie next to your neighbor's Greek–style chicken wings. (I love this idea, because then no one sees me going up to the dessert table six times.) Finger foods work very well at block parties—people like to walk around and mix with other guests while they eat. Bear in mind, too, that people tend to eat twice—once when they arrive, and later after they've warmed up.

ACTIVITIES

MEET YOUR NEIGHBOR The best part of a block party is simply getting to know the guy who lives two doors down from you. To this end, it's fun to play this game. When your guests arrive, have them write their name and house number down on a press-on label. Put that label in a jar. When it appears most of the people have come, have each person draw out a name. Then have guests find each other: For example, you've drawn Sandra Brown at 54 Green Street—now you must find her and give her her name tag.

OLD AND NEW Have the person who's lived longest on the block talk about when they moved here, and why. Then do the same with the newest on the block.

WHAT'S MY LINE Each person stands and gives two general hints about what they do ("It's indoors; I wear a uniform"). Then the others guess at the occupation.

BALL GAMES In my neighborhood, a playground and a ball field are close by. If you have the same convenience, you might want to organize an after-dinner softball game or other sport. People who don't want to play can be spectators or cheerleaders: provide pom-poms made of newspaper strips. (Tie long strips at the center with yarn. Leave enough yarn to hold onto.)

THE GREAT JUNK EXCHANGE Tell everyone who RSVPs to bring something still good that they don't want anymore. We've all had the experience of receiving a nice gift that we really don't use, or of buying something that ends up sitting on the shelf. (I've had a wok for about 15 years that I've used exactly once.) Provide a table or an area of the yard for people to dump their junk. The only rule is: If you bring something, you must take something home. If you're so inclined, you can have an auction, with proceeds going toward the next block party or to a charitable organization.

NEIGHBORHOOD TRIVIA Gather interesting facts about the neighborhood and give a ten-question exam: How many houses are on this block? (No fair counting.) How many people live here? How many children under the age of one? How many oak trees line this street? Ask the kids for help on this one.

CHILDREN'S GAMES Set out riding toys, dolls, board games. Also remember old favorites like drop the handkerchief, tag, hide-and-seek, drop the clothespin in the bottle. There's no reason adults can't join in, if the kids are willing.

THE GREAT GIFT GIVEAWAY Decide on a theme: the beach, a picnic, romantic bathing, gourmet cooking, etc. Then, as host, provide a large, attractive, but inexpensive basket. Have each guest bring one thing to put in it: For the beach, someone might bring suntan lotion; someone else, a sand toy or deflated beach ball. For gourmet cooking, try exotic spices or vinegars or a miniature whisk. For bathing, special soaps or lotions or an extra-thick washcloth. Have a

Things for the
Great Junk Exchange

Cookware
Books
Movies
Toys
Small pieces of furniture
Lamps
Curtains
Vases, other knickknacks

drawing to choose a winner. If you've used balloons to decorate, you can put pieces of paper inside each balloon before you blow it up. One of them will have an "X" on it. At the appointed time, have each house pop their balloon; if they got the X, they are the winner. (Of course, when you make the pieces of paper, you must mix them up, folded tightly, before you put them in the balloons, so you don't know who gets the X!)

GRAB BAG FUND If you like, ask everyone coming to contribute a couple of dollars to a "grab bag " fund. Then let everyone choose a little wrapped gift: a kitchen towel, pretty rocks or crystals, a great big candy bar—take a walk through the dime store and see what might work as a gift.

Although it can be fun for you to provide some activities, remember that you don't have to provide any. People at block parties are very much interested in simply getting to know one another, and children will always make up something to do. Your goal in having such a party is not to win host awards but simply to provide a way for people who live on the same street to know one another.

THANKS FOR THE MEMORIES

Provide large resealable plastic bags and encourage guests to take home doggie bags. Also, take photos and, if you're feeling generous, send copies to your neighbors with a "thanks for coming" note. You can videotape the activities, and begin next year's party by showing a little movie of last year's party.

A block party is a wonderful way to get the whole family involved in an event. From invitations to food to activities, there are ways that everyone can contribute. In addition to the warm feelings fostered by working together, you may find an extra bonus: meeting a whole family that "fits" with yours!

Winter: Warming It Up

There aren't many people who say that their favorite season is winter. But my 11-year-old daughter does. When I once asked her why, she said, "Because it snows! And because I have more energy."

Cold weather is energizing, it's true. For one thing, you have to keep moving or you'll freeze! And almost everyone will admit that there's something thrilling about snow. No matter what your age or level of cynicism, there's something magical in the way the flakes fall down and transform the out-of-doors into a kind of fairyland. For people who ski, snow is reason for celebration; and even the most unathletic people (like me) can get a charge out of going down a good hill on a sled. I once watched my then 65-year-old father whoop and holler when he rode a red plastic sled down a hill on a golf course near his house. Accompanying him on the sled was his toy poodle, Molly. When he came back up the hill, pulling the sled behind him, he said, "Boy! That thing really goes!" Molly, barking excitedly behind him, seemed to agree.

I also love seeing the snowmen (and women!) that people build, those quiet and friendly sentinels who are suffused with enough high spirits and goodwill as to seem nearly alive.

When the winter weather grows fierce and being out-of-doors is too uncomfortable, a certain kind of coziness can move in, and you can enjoy doing a great number of indoor activities that you would never do otherwise. This can be a time when families who rarely spend much time together, do. When no one has to get anywhere, I actually enjoy being weatherbound. We re-learn, at those times, the real pleasure in simply being with each other.

If you live in a climate that has no snow—or even cold weather—you can still create winter traditions. The notion of "hunkering down" and enjoying a day inside together

Dressing for Warmth

Think layers—long underwear, flannel shirts, wool sweaters! Wear gloves, warm socks, good boots, scarves. And don't forget your hat! We spend a lot of money on bathing suits that we usually wear only one season. Why not invest in good winter wear (check ski shops for snowsuits for all ages, for example) that can be worn many seasons over? If we're warm outside, it's much easier to enjoy ourselves.

The Do-it-yourself Rink

Choose a level area on the north side of the house. Try to find an area shaded by trees from the afternoon sun.

Make the perimeter of packed snow or bales of straw. Using the fine spray nozzle, spray water slowly. Don't flood, or the water will seep through into the ground and cause a thaw. A thorough base spraying will take about 45 minutes, and for best results should be done in freezing weather. Spray again several times. What you want is a good foundation of ice. Four to five inches is best.

Maintain the rink. Fill holes and cracks with ice shavings, then level it off. Scrape ridges with the edge of a shovel. Then spray over a new coating a couple of times.

Take care of your hose. After you use your hose for this activity, it will ice up inside and out. Lay it out in the basement to let it thaw before coiling it.

depends more on the warmth in your heart than the cold temperatures outdoors. Make time, in the winter months, to have a few close, warm days together. Take advantage of a rainy day to act as though you're snowbound. Or "visit" snow—take a vacation to a cooler climate. Whereas most people try to get away from the winter, those of you who live in a warm climate can seek it out.

SOME FREEZE-SEASON ACTIVITIES

FEATHERED FRIENDS Visits to frozen lakes to feed the birds are always gratifying. Make sure you bring lots and lots of bread; even then, you'll wish you had more.

MAKE YOUR OWN SKATING RINK If you have a big and level lawn, try making a skating rink. (The effect on the lawn is that it will take an extra two to four weeks for the grass to look normal when the warm weather comes. But you can hasten the process by dressing the area with black soil and reseeding it in early spring.) You need only a snow shovel and a garden hose with a fine-spray nozzle. The ground should be frozen a good two or three inches deep before you begin.

WINTER WALKS It's always worth it to take a walk in the cold—even if you start out chilly and complaining, you end up warmed and invigorated. Make a family outing of a walk: Have a certain time limit or destination, and when you come back, have some cocoa—with no limit on marshmallows! If you have a fireplace, now's the time to really enjoy it. In fact, what marshmallows don't get used in the cocoa can be roasted over the fire. If you're feeling indulgent, have S'mores.

SOME SNOW ACTIVITIES

SLEDDING Sledding is fun for everyone—even dogs. Our dogs are too big to fit on sleds, but they love running beside them when we go down hills. They seem to feel that they have a job, too, which is stealing the hat and/or mittens off the driver. There are sleds made of plastic or wood that you can buy—oblong or disk shaped. You can also use an inner tube, the lid of a garbage can (with the handle flattened or removed), or even a large piece of cardboard. You get great exercise walking back up the hill, a walk well worth it for the thrill in going down again.

SKIING Try cross-country and downhill. Many places offer lessons for the whole family. Children tend to do well even at very young ages. You can make a whole day out of trying out a slope—have a hearty breakfast, hit the snow, and then have a warm and nourishing dinner together.

SNOW WALKS Taking a walk in the snow is a beautiful and peaceful experience, especially when it is falling or fresh. There is a unique kind of quiet to be enjoyed, and it is fun to see everyday objects like mailboxes transformed into something beautiful. The sun glistens diamondlike on the snow in the day; a beautiful bluish glow seems to emanate from it at night.

BLAZING TRAILS Paths through the snow can be made by one person who starts out ten minutes earlier than the others, who then follow in his footprints exactly. If you're the trailblazer, make it interesting: go under and over things, make circles and zigzag patterns.

SNOWBALL FIGHTS Remember to keep the balls large and soft. If you have a big enough freezer, save a few of these for a surprise activity on a July day.

A Recipe for S'mores

Take a graham cracker square, place half a plain chocolate bar over it, top with a perfectly toasted marshmallow, and cover with another graham cracker. If you can eat just one, you are superhuman.

Build a Snow Family

Make a mother, father, baby, even a snow dog. Be creative—use things you find outside like rocks, red berries, pinecones and boughs. And then use some things from inside:

- scarves, hats, jewelry, sunglasses, shoes, shawls
- "wigs" made from mops or beards made from shredded newspaper
- food coloring or water paint "makeup"
- shopping bags, purses, golf-ball pop-out eyes

Make sure you put the snowmen where you can see them when you're inside. And remember, there's no reason they have to be standing—you can build your snow people lying down or lounging in lawn chairs. In addition to snow people, make snow animals, or houses, or cars.

SHOVELING Yes, even this can be fun! Make a game out of it by letting the whole family join in. You can outfit everyone with a shovel of appropriate size. Wax the blades and the snow will slide off easily. Even small children can accomplish a good deal of work when they're "playing" shoveling—and if you hide pennies in the snow for them to find, they're especially motivated. Give everyone a strip of snow and have a race to see who finishes first.

SQUIRT GUN ART Fill your pistols with colored water and go out to make some art. "Draw" a garden full of snow flowers, a portrait of the family, some abstract piece of genius.

SNOW ANGELS We find these nearly irresistible to make when the snow is new. Lie down, move your arms up and down, and your legs in and out. Then carefully stand up—voilà!

TREASURE HUNTS The snow makes for great hiding places. Have someone hide the goods, then draw maps for the rest to find clues, and, ultimately, the treasure. This can be a cigar box full of treats, or tickets for a movie.

SOME INDOOR ACTIVITIES

Even if you very much enjoy being outside, you can still spend a lot of time indoors in the winter. Try to use at least some of this time as an opportunity to enjoy your family. Many activities can be "saved" for bad weather days only, thus making a potentially boring and restless day into a special treat.

READING ALOUD This is nice to do in front of a roaring fire. Have the family sit in a circle and share a book. You can take turns reading each time, or have one person read.

When you have very young members of the family, try nursery rhymes and some of the many wonderful children's books available. You don't have to be a child to enjoy James Marshall's books about George and Martha, two lovable—and really funny—hippos; or Lillian and Russell Hoban's Frances books.

BAKING   Food, warm and fresh from the oven, is satisfying for all ages, and everyone can help. Make some good old chocolate chip cookies, or look in your cookbooks for something entirely new that you've always wanted to try. Making bread is easy—it just takes time; when you're weathered in, you've got that.

CARD HOUSES   Test your family's skill with a pack of playing cards. They can go from simple two- or four-walled structures all the way to multi-tiered extravaganzas. Work individually or in teams.

MAKE A MOVIE   Use a video camera—one you own, rent, or borrow from a friend—for this one. Write a script, pick your actors, rehearse, and shoot. Then make some popcorn and watch.

TENT CITY   Get out your sheets from the linen closet and see what you can come up with. Take over the living room, and have dinner inside your new quarters.

WATCH A CLASSIC   There are many wonderful old movies that we rarely have time for. Use an indoor day to share the joy of watching Fred Astaire, Bette Davis, Humphrey Bogart.

REVIEW FAMILY MEMORIES   Take out the scrapbooks, and savor all the memories. If you're like most families, your books need work too—this is the time to sort pictures and

A Good Read for All Ages

Poetry Try Robert Frost, Shel Silverstein.

Plays Shakespeare can appeal even to the very young. Otherwise, consider such classics as *Our Town* or scripts for favorite stories such as *The Wizard of Oz*. Let everyone read a role, and ham it up!

Animal stories Try James Thurber; James Herriot for short stories; the Black Stallion or Lassie series for longer works. You can have a novel such as *Black Beauty* set aside just for bad weather days.

Drama Truman Capote's "A Christmas Story" and *The Diary of Anne Frank* are well–written and worthy of follow–up discussion.

Make Something from Nothing

Go around the house looking for things you don't need that might be used to make ... well, something. Then fill a box full of the things you've found: feathers, sequins, fabric scraps, buttons, and ribbons; Tupperware, plastic baskets that come from the grocery store, old children's clothes, stuffing, and nylons; cardboard boxes, cardboard scraps, tissue paper, and magazine cut-outs.

Warm Treats for Cold Days

- cinnamon toast
- herbal tea
- hot honey lemonade
- soup
- hot spiced cider
- cocoa and marshmallows
- hot buttered popcorn

put them into the books where they belong. This is also a good time to enjoy watching the family movies you rarely have time for.

A POTLUCK DINNER   This is a nice way to pass the bad-weather time with your neighbors as well as to get to know them better. Send the kids out with impromptu invitations, and see who wants to come.

LETTER WRITING   Being "stuck" indoors is a good time to catch up on letters you owe friends and relatives. Perhaps there's something you'd like to tell the President. Or the current rock idol. Or a secret flame. The whole family can write a letter to Grandma—pass the paper around and have everyone write a paragraph or two.

INTERIOR DECORATE   Put the names of all the family members into a hat. Draw a name, and have the whole family brainstorm about what can be done to make that person's bedroom better. Reorganize it; redecorate it; add to it. Or put all the rooms of your house into the hat, and draw one out, and then go to town on that. Have a planning/brainstorming session. Be as creative as you can—when it comes to suggestions, anything goes.

MAKE A QUILT   Save scraps for just this purpose. Quilts come in amazing varieties, from the most basic sewing together of six-inch squares to stunning and amazingly complex pieces of art. The whole family can work on making one block apiece, and when you have enough, you can put them together for a summer picnic blanket or a wall hanging or even a bedspread for some lucky recipient.

LISTEN TO MUSIC   Now is the time to sit together quietly and hear a symphony. It is nice to know something about the composer you're hearing—use your encyclopedia, or library books, or even the back of the album to learn something about the person behind the sounds you'll hear. "Peter and the Wolf "is excellent for young children and adults, too. But there's nothing preventing the youngest members of a family from thrilling to Chopin and Beethoven, too.

WRITE TOGETHER Consider putting together a family newspaper, which can be mailed to all your friends and relatives.

While it's true that most people prefer warmer weather to winter, we miss out on a lot of the year if we only endure winter. We owe it to nature and to ourselves to try to enjoy it. And no matter where you live, or what winter means there, it's at least one more good excuse to create and maintain family traditions, even if it's a "First Day of Winter Beach Party"!

Everybody Playtime

Coloring Get out the crayons and the coloring books and the blank paper. If you think you've outgrown this, just take a whiff of a crayon.

Paper Dolls Use ready–made or, even better, make your own. You can cut "people" out of magazines, and cut out things to go in their "houses." Or you can draw people, and the clothes to fit them.

Play Store Set up a "store" in a corner of the living room. Let one member of the family be the store-keeper, the others shoppers. You can use paper money from your Mo-nopoly game, or make some. Or if you have a stash of coins, use that. A TV tray makes a fine "counter." Use canned goods for your inventory.

Hide-and-Seek Everyone can play. We have on occasion made our poor dog be "it." Actually, he seems to like it. For one thing, when he's all done with his job, he gets a treat. Anything's worth a "pupperoni."

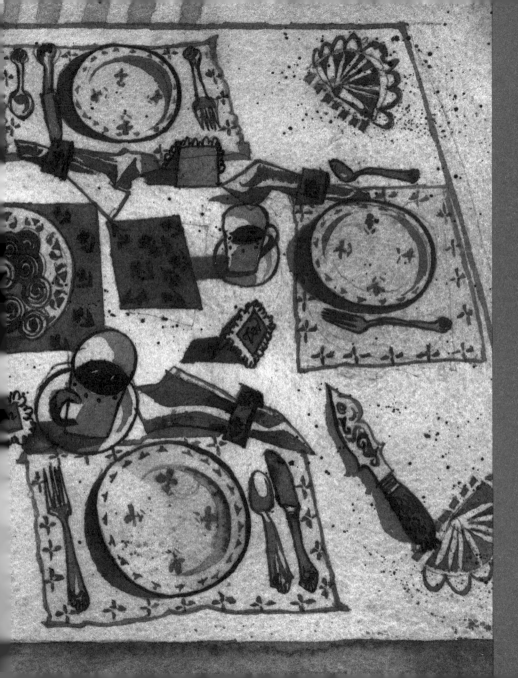

Family Holidays

Despite our age, past experience, or level of general cynicism, something about these holidays can make us all open-hearted children again.

If only we let ourselves, we can look forward to and enjoy so much in them!

It may be the candy and sentimental messages we get on Valentine's Day, the soft colors of Easter, the dramatic reminder of our country's independence on the Fourth of July. Perhaps it's the charming transformation of our children—or ourselves—on Halloween, the agony of overeating on Thanksgiving, the joy of giving at Christmas. All of these we can anticipate with mounting excitement, year after year.

Holidays have their serious sides, too: Memorial Day, with its bittersweet tribute to those who have gone before us;

Passover, with its hard-earned message of the importance of freedom. These, too, offer us the chance to celebrate.

There is the prospect of a new beginning that the New Year suggests; the honor of being appreciated as parents on Mother's Day and Father's Day; the quiet surrender to contemplation before the candles of Hanukkah.

It's worth the effort to not let these opportunities for joy and recognition pass us by. We need to mark our family calendars, plan things to do, create and carry on wonderful traditions around holidays. If we let them, they can make us and those of our culture more aware of who we are.

Valentine's Day

When we think about Valentine's Day, perhaps what we remember most are the shoe boxes or paper bags full of valentines we received as a child. Some were beautiful; some were ingenious; some were downright insulting. There probably isn't a parent around who doesn't review in depth all the valentines a son or daughter brings home, and remember the stomach-gripping thrill of seeing who "loved" you and who did not. For although the selection of valentines may be quite arbitrary, we like to pretend it is not.

Valentine's Day is not just for children. It's just as much fun for adults to make, send, and receive valentines as it is for children to do so. And on what other day of the year can we buy and receive such wildly decadent boxes of candy? The best thing about Valentine's Day is that it's an excuse to say "I love you." We tend, for the most part, to be shy beings who have difficulty saying the things we ought to. Though it never hurts to say "I love you" to other family members, there are times when it's more important than usual. Perhaps there's been a lot of fighting lately between certain members of the family—or all of them? Perhaps a family has undergone changes due to remarriage or adoption or other reasons, and the new members of the family feel very much on shaky emotional ground. Valentine's Day helps us remember the need to express our affection, in good times and troubled, and gives us a skirt to hide behind while doing so. That alone makes it a holiday worth celebrating.

THE STORY OF VALENTINE'S DAY

Valentine's Day was first observed in the Middle Ages. The day honors St. Valentine, but which St. Valentine is open to interpretation. As many as eight St. Valentines have been identified. In perhaps the most popular story, one of the Valentines was imprisoned, fell in love with the jailer's daughter, and sent her letters signed, "From your Valentine." St. Valentine is to this day the patron saint of engaged couples.

The Unknown Rule

Valentines are always supposed to be anonymous.

Who Loves Valentines?

England, France, and the United States are the greatest Valentine's Day celebrators.

Who Is It?

An old custom says the first person you see on Valentine's Day will be your valentine.

A Japanese Custom

In Japan, girls give chocolates to the boys.

Who Needs Valentines?

Your family members
Your friends
Your co-workers
Your children's teachers
Your mail carrier
Your grocer
Your favorite movie star
Your neighbors
The dog down the street that your dog
adores ("sign" with a pawprint)
You! (Buy yourself a rose)

The custom of putting valentines in boxes comes from Roman days. During the feast of Lupercalia (in honor of the pastoral god Lupercus, whose job it was to keep wolves away), the names of young women were drawn from a box and matched to those of young men. Those couples would be game partners for the year. Later on, in France, it became customary for both sexes to draw from boxes—the men drew from the women's names, and vice versa. In England from 1660 to 1685, ladies drew men's names in Valentine's Day lotteries. Then the men gave gifts to "their" ladies.

In 1723, there appeared valentine "writers" who made booklets with an assortment of verses and messages to copy. Commercial valentines appeared about 1800. Today, some estimate that the number of Valentine cards sent each year is second only to that of Christmas greetings.

MAKING YOUR OWN VALENTINES

While an enormous variety of valentines can be purchased, there is much to be said for making at least a few of your own. Homemade valentines are more interesting and more heartfelt, and, best of all, bear the individual mark of the maker. Pick a day (or two, if you're making a lot) to do this as a family, and after dinner sit around the table and see what you can come up with. It's great to see others' designs emerge—and to have a ready audience for all of your creations. Often, siblings who don't ordinarily get along very well will work harmoniously on a crafts project. While you're cutting and pasting, share stories of romance:

how you met your first boy/girl friend; what you love about your current flame. Older children, especially, will enjoy this.

A word of advice, here. Don't make valentines too far in advance, as you may misplace them. On the other hand, don't wait until 9:30 the evening before they're needed, when the rush to complete things will take the joy out of doing it. Be advised that young children are often unwilling to part with something they've made and are proud of. It helps to make one extra valentine, and let a child pick his favorite to keep. Older children may not want to share everything about the valentines they make. My older daughter will show me her outside design, but not her inside verse.

Valentines can be as simple or elaborate as you like (though remember that valentines to be mailed must be kept relatively flat, and excessive decorations will probably fall off). Every member of the family can help. The goal is not perfection of product, but enjoyment of the process: to witness the charm of little hands cutting out hearts, sprinkling glitter, printing "I love you"; to realize how creative your older children have become. Try including some of their friends when you do this activity. Sometimes something a teen views as goofy—in the bad way—becomes a lot of fun when friends take part. Take some photos of the process, or videotape it. An instant photograph could, in fact, become the cover of a card: Here's a picture of your valentine making your valentine!

Recycled Valentines
Save homemade valentines and use them to decorate the front door each year.

Object Valentines

Use your imagination here, and let an everyday object glued or taped on a heart help say your message. Some examples:

pine needles: I pine for you

a penny: I'm not worth one cent without you

a Band–Aid: Don't wound me; be mine

safety pin: I'm stuck on you

pebble: Don't have a heart of stone; be mine

a piece of wrapped candy: I'm sweet on you

"googly" eyes: I've only got eyes for you

button: I'd bust my buttons if you'd be mine

TRADITIONAL VALENTINES These are the red paper–white doily variety. You can cut out red hearts and put them on white doilies; you can cut out white hearts and put them on red doilies. You can make a large red heart as background, and use a round white doily in the center with a smaller red heart on that. There are, in addition to white doilies, silver and gold ones.

In addition to the usual heart-on-doily motif, you can use the doilies as wrappers for a hearts "bouquet." You can make heart ladies with doily dresses and/or parasols. You can make a red heart and white doily garden. You can make a white doily "plate" with red valentine "cookies." You can go modern and make abstract valentines.

FABRIC VALENTINES Get out the sewing machine, and appliqué hearts made from fabric onto construction paper cards. You can use plain red or white fabric or red and white prints, or get fancy and use velvet or lace. An alternative is to use tulle (netting) for the heart, and put "gifts" behind it: potpourri, pieces of ribbon, candy hearts, pressed flowers. For a more extravagant offering, put in two tickets to a play or concert, or a valentine bracelet or necklace. The respective ages and relationship of sender and receiver will help you make these choices.

3-D VALENTINES Cut out a 6-inch (or larger) heart from lightweight cardboard. Then cut out a fabric heart an inch bigger. Silky red or pink lining is nice for a woman; consider denim or burlap for a man. Glue the fabric onto the cardboard three-quarters of the way around, and let it dry for a good 20 minutes. Then cut tissue or paper towels into half-inch strips and stuff the heart loosely and evenly. Glue the open side shut. After it's dry, this heart can be decorated with jewelry such as pearls or pieces of costume jewelry, glued or sewn on. Use fabric paint to write a message, or pin a note on fancy paper to it. You can also sew around the edges, or use yarn with a large-gauge needle for a more masculine effect.

HIDDEN-MESSAGE VALENTINE Use words and/or pictures from magazines to put a message on a blank sheet of paper—standard-sized or cut into a heart shape. Put the words or pictures in random places, in equal-sized boxes. Then use tracing paper to mark the location of the boxes, and transfer the markings to the piece of paper that will be the cover. Carefully cut around three sides to make doors that will be closed over the message. Glue or tape the cover sheet to the bottom sheet. Number the doors in the order of the message, by putting a number below and/or the appropriate number of hearts on the door. The receiver will open them one by one for his valentine message. Try using red construction paper for the message and a doily for the cover, or vice versa. For children who don't yet read, valentine stickers can be put under the doors. This could be a wonderful month-long valentine with twenty-eight messages (one for each day in February) to send to your college student child or distant parent.

GLAMOUR-GRAMS Make two equal-sized hearts from white poster board. Put one upside down below the other so that you have what looks like a heart–shaped face and a shapely figure. Glue together and decorate with poster paint, crayons, or markers. You can attach real earrings—the hoop or pierced variety (without stem)—or use red foil

Savory Valentine Food

Veggie Platter Use red and white vegetables, such as radishes, red peppers, cherry tomatoes, beets, peeled cucumbers, cauliflower.

Bread Hearts Use a cookie cutter to cut heart shapes from bread slices, top with cheese, and broil.

Ribbon Sandwiches Use five slices of very thin bread. Cut off crusts. Fill each layer with either deviled ham, peanut butter and strawberry jelly, cream cheese dyed pink with beet juice, or tomato and cucumber slices with mayonnaise or cream cheese. Wrap and refrigerate for one hour. Then slice sandwiches into four even strips, and lay the strips on their sides.

Pizza Make the dough into a heart shape. Use a white cheese.

Barbecued Chicken Breasts Use the whole breast, spread open into a heart shape.

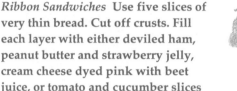

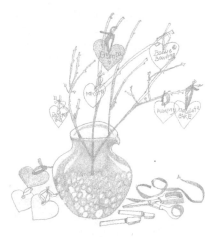

Tree of Love

Find a branch outside and put it in a jar, with an inch or so of marbles to stabilize it. Hang hearts from the branch with the names of people and things you love. Mix and match—go right ahead and hang a heart with "Grandpa" right next to "pasta with pesto sauce." You might want to start this a week early, and leave paper, pens, scissors, and ribbon out. Your tree can come into full love–ly bloom as family members slowly but surely fill the branches.

hearts as earrings. One of the most fun things to do with these valentines is to use real makeup: blush, lipstick, even false eyelashes.

COOKIE PORTRAIT VALENTINES Bake oversized sugar cookies. Place them in resealable plastic bags on which you have painted heart faces resembling the person you'll give the cookies to. Or paint the portrait on the cookie itself, using food coloring.

PRINTED VALENTINES Before you start, put newspaper over the kitchen table, and aprons over yourselves. Pour red poster paint into disposable pie tins.

Method 1: Cut a potato or sponge into a heart shape. Dip the potato or sponge into the paint, and press it onto the front of your card—a piece of paper folded into halves or fourths. (If the paint seems too thick, add a couple of drops of water.) Let dry completely and then write in your message.

Method 2: Draw your heart onto a piece of Styrofoam that is no larger than the card you want to print. Sponge paint onto the Styrofoam. Put the paper over the Styrofoam, and roll over it with a rolling pin. Practice with scrap paper first.

SOME LOVE–LY THINGS TO DO

Cards and gifts aren't the only way to express love on Valentine's Day. Look through these ideas and see what else might appeal to you.

FILL A VALENTINE'S JAR WITH LOVE NOTES   Make a valentine's jar from an empty mayonnaise, pickle, or other large-sized jar. Decorate the jar elaborately. Each year, a week before Valentine's Day, set out the jar in a common room such as the kitchen. Encourage each member of the family to write anonymously something he or she loves about every other member of the family. Don't forget pets! Examples might be: Julie is good at helping with homework. Or: Jenny has a terrific smile and a great sense of humor. Or: Mommy makes the best chocolate cake around. Or: Daddy has kind and beautiful eyes. On Valentine's Eve, pass the jar around, taking turns reading the notes aloud.

A VALENTINE MAILBAG Use a large grocery bag. Make a valentine animal such as the mouse shown. Cut a "mail slot" in the middle, and then tape or staple the bag closed. Use it to hold the valentines you're given.

SHOEBOX MAILBOX Here is a more traditional kind of valentine holder. To make one, cut a slot in the top of a shoebox. Tape the top down. Then decorate the whole thing outrageously. Too much is not too much here.

TELEPHONE LOVE CHAIN Decide as a family whom you'd like to call just to say "We love you." Then tell that person to call someone he or she cares for, have that person call another, and so on.

VALENTINE SCAVENGER HUNT Before dinner on Valentine's Day, have everyone look around the house or the yard for three heart-shaped objects. That will "earn" them their dinner. Interpretation of "heart-shaped" is loose here, or dinner will get cold. You may want to provide centerpiece space and arrange the valentine finds on the table.

A GESTURE OF LOVE Make Valentine's Day the day you show love to someone else. Visit a nursing home with valentines or valentine goodies, and talk with a lonely resident. Go to a park and pick up litter for half an hour.

Sweet Valentine Food

Filled Cake: Angel cake with strawberry or raspberry and whipped cream filling: Make an angel cake. When cooled, carefully slice off the top inch and a half. Dig out some cake to form a circular tunnel (don't go through the bottom!), and fill with whipped cream/fruit filling. Replace the top.

Heart–shaped Cake: Bake one layer in an 8-inch round pan and one in an 8-inch square pan. Cut the circle in half; place the halves against two adjoining sides of the square to form a heart. Use white frosting and decorate with red candy hearts. Stand valentines up in frosting.

Sugar Cookies: Cut out in heart shapes.

Frozen Yogurt: Top pink frozen yogurt with red berries and serve in elegant, long-stemmed glasses.

123

14 Reasons Why
I Love You

Think of one reason for every day of February leading up to The Day. These can range from the silly to the sublime, for example:

- *"The way you pour syrup on your pancakes."*
- *"The way you make me feel better when I feel blue."*
- *"You watch The Three Stooges with me, and laugh when I do."*

Bring some canned goods to a food shelter, or some dog biscuits or toys to an animal shelter. Offer to sit for a friend's children for free one night.

DENTAL DAY OFF Consider letting Valentine's Day be the one day a year when you eat sweets with every meal: gooey caramel rolls for breakfast, a candy bar with lunch, a cake with dinner. You may have plenty of friends who would like to be invited to such meals! Decorate the table with a white sheet and scattered valentines. Use red carnations in a white vase for a centerpiece, or your "heart tree." Doilies can be placemats. If you use paper plates, you can decorate around the edge with lace. (Use glue on the underside of the plate!)

HOW TO WRITE A LOVE LETTER

Okay, pull out all the stops. Get sloppy and sentimental. Everybody likes to get a love letter, and everybody can write one. In addition to what occurs to you spontaneously, try something unexpected! Dads, write to your sons; mothers, to your daughters. How about a sibling admitting she cares a great deal for another sibling? Appoint a secretary to take a letter from the family pet.

Do you think this is a good idea, but feel stuck? Here are some ideas for love letter themes that might get you started:

FANTASY LETTER Pretend you can go anywhere, do anything. Write a letter to your valentine explaining exactly what will happen. For example:

"My dearest valentine,

At exactly 7:00 tomorrow evening, a solid gold limousine will arrive to take you to the airport, where we will board my private jet. I have a little dinner planned in Paris, after which we will..." You get the idea.

NOSTALGIA Write a letter talking about the first time you met, what you liked immediately, what has grown to be your favorite thing about the person. If writing to your child, you can tell her about the day she was born, or something endearing she did "when she was little." I heard about a family with an adopted child for whom they wrote and illustrated a book about the day they decided to adopt. It was done with great love and sensitivity; the child shows it proudly to everyone.

THE TRUTH When all else fails, try the truth. Tell your valentines why you love them, honestly—for their own qualities, as well as for the way they make you feel. Mail your letter so that it will arrive on Valentine's Day, or hide it somewhere where you know the recipient will find it. These letters need not be elaborate examples of the beauty of the English language. The truth is, any declaration of love—real and from the heart—is a lovely thing, and will be cherished by the receiver forever.

Valentine Drinks

Hot and Spicy Mix equal amounts of cranberry and apple juice with a few whole cloves, 2 cinnamon sticks, and a few raisins; then heat and serve.

Cool and Fruity: Make ice cubes out of cran/raspberry juice. Use the cubes in pink grapefruit juice. Or mix plain seltzer with a red juice. If you feel like splurging, make yourself a strawberry milk shake.

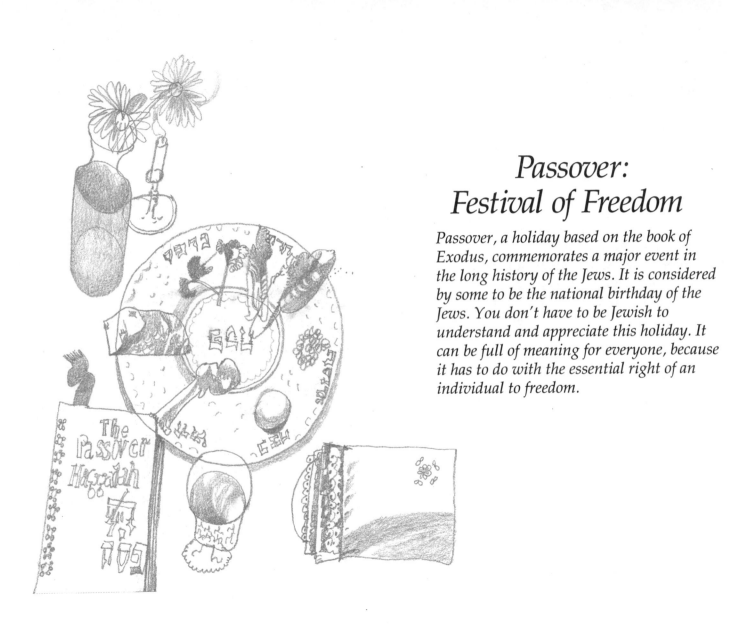

Passover: Festival of Freedom

Passover, a holiday based on the book of Exodus, commemorates a major event in the long history of the Jews. It is considered by some to be the national birthday of the Jews. You don't have to be Jewish to understand and appreciate this holiday. It can be full of meaning for everyone, because it has to do with the essential right of an individual to freedom.

Passover starts at sundown on a day in early spring, and lasts for eight days. It is ushered in by a Seder, a religious service celebrated in the home rather than in the temple. A Seder is a carefully orchestrated meal, full of stories and rituals and symbols. Participants eat special foods in a certain order, drink wine, share parables and legends, ask traditional questions and receive traditional answers. There are benedictions, songs, and chants.

The idea behind a Seder is to endow the events and miracles of the historical exodus with a certain immediacy, to make participants feel the relieved joy of sudden freedom after so many years of slavery. Christians are often invited to Jewish tables for a Seder during Passover. If you have the opportunity to attend a Seder, by all means do. It will teach, entertain, and inspire you—to say nothing of filling you up.

THE STORY OF PASSOVER

Two thousand years before the birth of Christ, the Israelites were slaves to the Egyptians. Moses, a Jew who had been raised in Pharaoh's household and who was determined to free his people from a bondage that had lasted 430 years, asked Pharaoh to let them go. Pharaoh refused. As punishment, God sent ten plagues upon the Egyptians.

During this time, the Pesach festival was held in the spring, at the time of the vernal equinox. The night just after Pesach, when the moon was full, was designated by Moses to be the night that the Israelites would escape. He told his people to sacrifice a lamb and to sprinkle its blood

Understanding Matzoh

Here is a little experiment to show children why matzoh is flat bread: Fill two glasses half full with warm water. Stir some flour into one glass. In the other, dissolve a little yeast in the water before adding flour. Set them both in a warm place for an hour, then check on the results.

on their door. This would do two things: show defiance to the Egyptians, who worshipped the lamb as a sacred animal, and show the Israelites' faith in God.

On this same night, for the tenth plague, the angel of death came and took the oldest son in each Egyptian family, but "passed over" the Jewish sons. When Pharaoh learned of this, he ordered the Israelites to leave immediately. They complied in great haste. But the next morning, Pharaoh changed his mind and sent his army to bring back the Israelites. Trapped with the Red Sea in front and the army behind, Moses miraculously parted the sea and the Israelites passed through safely. However, when the pursuing Egyptians tried to pass through, the sea surged over them and they drowned. The Israelites then followed Moses to the promised land.

For almost 4,000 years since, Passover has celebrated this event. Its purpose is to remember the saving of the firstborns and to celebrate the redemption from slavery. But it is also to teach children that freedom is a great privilege that must be won and kept, and that doing so is not always easy.

The first and the last days of Passover are observed by Jews as holy days. Matzoh, or unleavened bread, is eaten during this time as a reminder of the long flight from Egypt. The Jews had no time to let dough rise, so they had to bake their bread without the advantage of this process. They rolled it into thin wafers and put it on flat boards, then baked it in the desert sun.

THE SEDER

THE PREPARATION To strictly observe Passover, the house must be prepared. It is searched for and cleansed of chometz (leaven), as no leavening agents except eggs can be used in the preparation of Passover food. This search can be done by the whole family, going from room to room, with everyone helping.

As this is also a springtime holiday having to do with renewal and optimism, the house must be refreshed—"spring cleaned." Some people use this time to paint, wallpaper, slipcover, or recarpet. Stoves and refrigerators are cleaned; new pots and pans are bought or the old ones boiled.

Setting the table is important. Many times the number of people attending is large—Passover is a time for extended family and friends. The host family sets the table with linen tablecloths, special china and silverware. Some people have china they use only at Seders. A candelabrum, fresh spring flowers such as tulips, daffodils, and anemones, a bowl full of beautiful fruit and nuts—any can serve as both centerpiece and reminder of today's plenty.

THE SERVICE

Seder means "celebration order" and this traditional family dinner does indeed follow a very particular order. The Haggadah, a book that tells the story of the Exodus, is read aloud, and it determines what happens in the Seder service. Most people follow a traditional Hagaddah, but there are alternative services, such as the Women's Hagaddah.

Christian Seders

Christian Seders are increasing in popularity. It is a not an offense for non-Jews to understand and appreciate Jewish customs and beliefs, as well as pay tribute to an important concept. Use the time during a Seder to talk about what freedom means specifically to you and your family members, as well as to others in the world.

Haroseth

This is good by itself, or spread onto matzoh.

Mix 1 c. finely chopped apple

1/4 c. chopped nuts

1 tsp. cinnamon,

2 T. grape juice or wine

Its preparation varies the world over. In this country, it is usually finely chopped apples and nuts spiced with cinnamon and sweetened with wine. In Venice, it is made with pureed chestnuts and apricots; in Yemen from chopped dates and figs, coriander and chilies.

At a certain point in the Seder, the youngest child asks the question, "Why is this night different from all other nights?" The answers explain the contents of the Seder plate as well as other items on the Seder table. The Seder plate, which is put in front of the leader of the Seder, is a special plate, often with indentations to hold the representational foods. On it are the following items:

Roasted Shankbone of lamb recalls the animal sacrificed on the night of the Passover. It is prepared by being held over a flame until it is charred. A chicken or turkey leg sometimes is used as well. Vegetarians or others who object to this practice may substitute a broiled beet.

A Hard–boiled Egg, a sign of spring and of life, symbolizes the survival of the children of Israel, and the perpetuation of existence.

Bitter Herbs (usually horseradish) represent the bitterness of slavery.

Haroseth symbolizes a morsel of sweetness, to lighten the burden and allay the bitterness of the bricks and mortar used by the Hebrews to build monuments and cities for Pharaoh.

Parsley, a sign of new life, is dipped into a bowl of salt water, representing the tears of slavery. The greens (which can also be watercress, celery, or chicory) represent the poor diet of the Hebrews as well as spring, hope, and redemption.

In addition to the Seder platter, the host places matzoh on the table to remind participants of the haste and hardships of the long flight from Egypt when there was no time for the bread to rise. Three perfect matzoh, for three tribes of Israel, are placed one on top of each other in matzoh covers, or folded separately in one or two large napkins. The middle matzoh is broken into two uneven pieces. The smaller one is returned to the cloth. The large one is shown to the children and then hidden by the leader. The children then search for it. Whoever finds it will receive a special gift for returning it to the leader. Although this gift is usually money, it might also be a book that has to do with freedom in some way—a biography of Martin Luther King, Jr., say, or *The Diary of Anne Frank*. The Seder can't end until everyone has tasted a piece of the hidden matzoh, called the Afikomen—the last item of food eaten at the Seder. The Afikomen goes a long way toward keeping the children alert.

A wine glass or goblet is at each place setting, and a filled wine decanter at the center of the table. The ceremony requires that the wine glass be filled four times, symbolizing the fourfold promise of redemption: "I will bring you out...I will deliver you...I will redeem you...I will take you to Me." Children take only a sip, or are given very small cups. (A nonalcoholic beverage may be substituted for abstaining adults as well as children.) An extra glass of wine is placed on the table near the leader's place for the prophet Elijah. After the fourth cup of wine is poured and a prayer is said, the door is opened so the spirit of Elijah can enter. This honors the belief that he will someday return to lead the Jewish people back to Palestine and to bring new peace and happiness to the whole world.

A pillow or cushion is put at the left arm of the leader's chair, or on another chair close to it. This symbolizes the freedom from bondage, during which slaves had no time for leisurely meals.

A Suggestion for a Passover Menu

Start with hard–boiled eggs, dipped in a dish of salted water. Then serve gefilte fish or chopped liver. Follow with chicken soup with matzoh balls. Roast chicken with matzoh dressing can be the main entree. For the vegetable, serve steamed asparagus or artichokes, or try tzimmes, a candied carrot concoction. Dessert can be macaroons, sponge cake, honey cake, or nut cake with fresh fruit.

During Passover, try a special breakfast treat of matzoh brei: matzoh soaked in water, coated with egg, and crisply fried. My husband loved this as a child, and now regularly makes it for his own children during Passover. They also love it.

For lunch try matzoh meal pancakes, potato or noodle kugel, potato pancakes, and blintzes.

Some Passover Recipes

MATZOH

Mix and knead 3 1/2 c. flour and 1 c. water. Roll out the dough on a floured surface and transfer to a greased cookie sheet. Prick all over with a fork and score into squares with a knife. Bake in a preheated oven at 475° F 10 to 15 minutes or until lightly browned.

MACAROONS

4 egg whites
3/4 c. sugar
1 1/2 tsp. matzoh meal
1 c. coconut
1 1/2 tsp. lemon juice
1 1/4 tsp. potato starch

Beat egg whites and sugar and add remaining ingredients. Spoon onto a greased cookie sheet and bake until brown, about 20 minutes, at 325° F.

The Seder ends with hope for the future: "Next year in Jerusalem, next year may all men be free."

The Seder normally takes a very long time, and follows the order set in the Haggadah. But since part of the purpose of a Seder is to inspire children to hand down the tradition to the next generation, it can be shortened to accommodate the natural restless nature of children (and some adults as well). The important thing is that the message of this holiday be understood. It has been said that to say we must leave Egypt is to say that we are able and willing to break out of our own narrow-mindedness and to let ourselves be free to achieve our full potential.

The four questions, asked by the youngest child and answered by the leader, can be impetus to ask other questions about our religion or our way of life. Discussing the freedom of the slaves so long ago in Egypt can make us wonder about our own country: Are all people here free? Why or why not? How has the legacy of slavery in the United States affected present-day attitudes and practices? Consider those who are discriminated against because of their color or religion or because they have certain diseases or handicaps. At the last Seder I attended, much time was spent discussing the plight of Ryan White, the teenager with AIDS who was not allowed to attend his school after being diagnosed. What can be done about this, on a personal or political level? What might the consequences be if nothing is done, individually and as a country?

It is rewarding to celebrate Passover, for many reasons. But perhaps the most important is that it makes us look very deliberately and directly at what freedom—or the lack of it—really means to individuals. This is also a good time to discuss the fact that freedom on any level carries with it certain responsibilities: what we do will create consequences. Are we aware of them? Are we prepared to deal with them?

Though Passover is based on important historic and far-reaching events, it can also precipitate a much-needed discussion in your family about freedom of the individual members. For example, how do you decide how late children can stay out, and why? When is the right age to go places alone? If you've recently gotten a license, what are your responsibilities as a driver? What rights do all members have for personal time and space? Are we free to be ourselves all the time? Should we be?

The questions you can come up with are endless. Settle down at the table for a good meal and a great discussion!

Easter

"We didn't have much money when I was growing up," a friend of mine says. "But one thing we could always count on was a new outfit for Easter. We got everything, even new embroidered hankies for our new patent leather purses." A spring outfit, complete with Easter bonnet of course, is one of the distinct pleasures of this season, but there are lots more.

I remember waking up early one Easter morning and descending the stairs to silently search for my basket of goodies. I could smell chocolate in the air. I found my brother's basket first; then I discovered my sister's; I left them undisturbed (after eyeballing the contents, of course). But I couldn't find mine.

I was reviewing ways I might have inadvertently offended the Easter Bunny when suddenly I spied my basket. It was nestled in the bookcase, green "grass" spilling out from it, marshmallow chicks and chocolate bunnies and cream eggs and jelly beans packed into it. There were fuzzy yellow "chicks" to play with, adorable as they listed to one side or the other on their skinny orange feet. And there were beautifully colored hard-boiled eggs that I'd helped make and then left out for the Easter Bunny to use. I loved eating those eggs, provided I had a salt shaker close at hand. I would crack open the shells on my head, making sure anyone in the room with me noticed what I believed was a unique talent requiring bravery as well as good aim.

I liked wearing a new dress to church, scratchy new petticoat notwithstanding, and I liked especially the warmth from the rays of the sun coming through the stained-glass windows. Easter signals the end of a long winter and the time of birth and rebirth, and gives an excuse to fawn over baby chicks and ducks and lambs. It feels like relief and hope combined together, colored in lovely pastels.

Everybody's In!
Remember: Easter baskets are not just for the young!

Natural Dyes

Use coffee, saffron (5-6 pieces), blueberries, raspberries, grass, spinach, leaves, shredded raw beets, cherries, turmeric, red cabbage (for blue eggs). These make soft and lovely shades.

Technique Put eggs in pan, then 2 cups natural dye materials. Cover with water, and add one tablespoon of vinegar. Simmer eggs for 15 minutes, then leave for one hour. When dry, brush with cooking oil.

The Egg

- The egg is the symbol of the universe. It is also a symbol of the rebirth of the earth out of the bleakness of winter.
- Colored eggs have been a part of Easter since the 15th century.
- Hard–boiled eggs are good 3-4 days at room temperature; up to ten days refrigerated.
- Before dyeing, wash eggs in a mild detergent to remove oil coating. The dye will adhere better.
- Freeze raw eggs out of the shell. Add 1/8 tsp. salt for every two eggs.

THE STORY OF EASTER

Long before Christianity, the Anglo-Saxons in northern Europe held a festival in honor of Eostre, the goddess of springtime. After the time of Christ and the beginning of Christianity, the name Easter, meaning "new beginning," was kept for recognizing the day of the Resurrection, the day Jesus Christ arose from the dead.

In A.D. 525 the Easter date was decreed to be the Sunday following the first full moon after March 21, which is the spring equinox. Easter was not celebrated widely as a holiday in the United States until after the Civil War.

For many, the religious significance of the Christian Easter has given rise to distinctively religious rituals and celebrations. But some of the traditional symbols of the holiday cross religious and cultural lines.

The egg has always been a symbol of new life, and a feast of eggs was used to honor Eostre. Colored eggs were rolled over fields to help make the earth fertile.

The tradition of the Easter rabbit is also very old. According to legend, Eostre's favorite animal was a large bird. But one day when the bird angered her, she changed it into a rabbit. Thus we have the combination of rabbits and nests with colored eggs. Chocolate Easter eggs were introduced around 1880.

THE FUN OF COLORING EGGS

Egg-dyeing is fast and easy to do, and the whole family can participate. There is nothing wrong with purchasing a commercial set-up for dyeing eggs. Kits usually produce the standard, single-color egg, lovely as far as it goes. But there are many, many other styles you might want to try.

Then you may want to save some of your better efforts in egg cartons, to be used each year at Easter (only if they're "blown out" eggs, of course). Also, you can save beautifully decorated eggs as unique Christmas tree ornaments. Consider setting aside a day before Easter for the family to try a few of the following:

GLITTER Make some really fancy eggs: Glue glitter onto eggs, one side at a time so the glue can dry. Make an even application of single or multiple colors of glitter, or create a fancy design.

"ENGRAVING" Scratch a design in the shell with a needle, then dye it. The design will show through.

FAMILY CARICATURES Write everyone's name down, each on a separate slip of paper. You can make it your immediate family, or include grandparents, aunts, even your pets. Put all the names into a bag. Each family member draws an equal number of names, then proceeds to try to make a caricature of each person (or animal). Use cotton or yarn for hair, pipe cleaners for glasses, construction paper and/or paint and pens for features. Mostly, use your imagination! Keep the finished eggheads upright by making a construction paper holder—a five-inch-long strip glued together into a circle. When all the caricatures are finished, put the name slips back in the bag. Take turns drawing them out and trying to match the name to the egg.

GLAMOUR-GIRL EGGS Make up your eggs using false eyelashes (bought from the dime store or made from curled, black construction paper), eye shadow, blush, lipstick, and hair made from yarn or curly ribbon or

Decorations Galore!

A Fine Shine Gloss up your dyed eggs by wiping a lightly waxed or greased cloth over them.

Plaid Put rubber bands or thin strips of tape on the egg before dying.

Tie-Dyed Wrap the egg in fabric, and secure it at the ends. (The egg will look like wrapped candy.) Soak it well in dye, then let it dry overnight. Remove the cloth.

Bejeweled Use rhinestones or other colored stones available in craft and dime stores—simply glue them in place. Also consider sequins and beads, even fancy buttons, or a mixture of all.

Beribboned Glue into place delicate satin strips in pastel shades, then tie them into a pretty bow at the top. Also consider decorated ribbon. You can also use rickrack, lacy seam binding, or satin cording.

Stickers Buy some or make your own by cutting out pictures from magazines or catalogues. (Seed catalogues are wonderful for supplying pictures of beautiful flowers.) Wet them slightly so that they adhere to the egg, then shellac into place.

The Perfect Boiled Egg

Have eggs at room temperature to keep shells from cracking. Put in a clean, grease-free pan without overcrowding. Don't use aluminum or the dye won't hold on the eggs. Add cold water to reach one inch over the top of the eggs. Heat until water boils, then immediately remove pan from stove. Cover and let stand 25 minutes. Rinse with cold water.

How to Blow Out an Egg

Have eggs at room temperature. Using a large-sized sewing needle, make a small hole at one end, a large one at the other. Try to puncture the yolk with the needle as well. Hold a straw against the smaller hole and blow contents into a bowl. Rinse the eggs out with water thoroughly! Then, as the shells air dry, have yourself some scrambled eggs. When the shells are dry, put clear glue around the holes to keep them from cracking further.

embroidery floss. Add a lace (or some other fabric) collar and earrings made from pearls, rhinestones, or other stones or metal.

ANIMALS Make a bunny by turning the egg on its side, then adding a cotton tail, a tiny pink pom-pom for a nose, construction paper ears and whiskers, and black beads for eyes. Whiskers can also be pieces of white thread, stiffened with hair spray. A bird can be made using tiny fan-folded pieces of paper for wings and a tail—glue them on or make a tiny hole in a blown-out shell. Add a construction paper beak and feet. Make bugs by adding construction paper or pipe cleaner legs and antennas. This is just the beginning! Use your imagination to make everything from pigs to porcupines to puppies.

JELL-O EGGS Use blown-out eggs that have been thoroughly rinsed with water and left to dry. Then cover one hole with masking tape. Into the other hole, pour liquid Jell-O. Let harden in refrigerator overnight. Peel carefully and put into a dyed-green coconut "grass" nest. Use around one-third cup less water to guard against melting.

CLAY Transform eggs into sculpture. For example, let the egg be the face or the belly of a cat, and use the clay for the ears, arms, and legs. You can also put clay through a garlic press to make "twigs" for a little nest. Use jelly beans as eggs for the nest.

MONSTERS Create Easter beasts by adding googly eyes, wild hairdos, and huge construction paper feet as bases.

SCENES Use blown-out eggs that have been chipped away enough to make a kind of "frame." If you can get goose or duck eggs, you will have a larger egg, and therefore more room to work. With the egg on its side, paint the inside sky blue, then add white cotton clouds and a tiny nest with a jelly bean egg. Or stand a toy chick amid tiny flowers. A tiny rabbit figure can be holding a very tiny Easter basket. Check out dollhouse accessories to help you on this. After the figures are glued in, cover the opening with plastic wrap and glue it to the sides. Then cover the edges of the wrap with trim or lace.

If you want an even bigger area to work with, consider making papier-mâché eggs. Blow up a balloon, and cover it with overlapping strips of newspaper soaked in a mixture of flour and water. Let it dry thoroughly. Then use a pin to pop the balloon, and cut out an area to put your scene into. Paint the outside of the egg a pastel color or cover it with foil.

You can also make a string egg. Blow up a balloon as above, then wrap crochet thread around it. Leave plenty of space between the threads for an "open weave" effect. Then, using your hands or a sponge, cover the threads with fabric stiffener. Let dry, pop the balloon, and cut out an opening. This creates a lovely, fragile shell.

CHICK-IN-A-SHELL Use half an egg shell, width-wise. Glue one cotton ball to another. Glue that into the shell. Glue on a tiny orange construction paper beak, and two black bead eyes (or draw them on or use sequins). You can also make a cotton-ball rabbit—use the same two cotton balls, but make construction paper bunny ears, and a pink nose.

EGG-SHELL VASES Take off just the very top of a blown-out shell, much as you would if you were eating an egg in an egg cup. Use construction paper to make a base, and curled paper strips to make curlicue handles. Then fill with tiny dried flowers.

Ukrainian Pysanky

There are fancy kits available that older family members skilled at detailed work may want to try using. Check out craft stores and get Ukrainian Pysanky kits for the artist in your family. These kits include the tools and supplies for multiple layers of wax and different colors of dye. The finished eggs represent a centuries-old Ukrainian tradition.

Step 1

Step 2

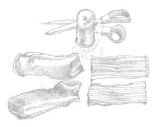

Step 3

(Continued on page 141.)

SOME OTHER THINGS TO MAKE

Today's frantic pace of living makes us quick to dismiss things we have to make from scratch, whether it's cakes or clothes. But it is well worth the effort to make something with your own two hands. One reason is the feeling of accomplishment it gives you. Another is the way that something homemade, however clumsy and imperfect, is cherished by the people you give it to. Children genuinely appreciate even small efforts in this direction, and often hold on to something you've made for a very long time, if not forever!

Often, these homemade offerings do not take more than half an hour to make; many of them take only a couple of minutes. A friend of mine tells me that she used to make everything, including gifts, by hand, because she couldn't afford to buy anything. Later, when she "graduated" to store-bought gifts, she found that her friends and family—both children and adults—were terribly disappointed. "And in a way so was I," she adds. "There's something about putting your time and creative energy into a gift that makes you feel really good. It feels more sincere, because it's really coming from you."

I made my first sock lop while my husband and I sat at the kitchen table and my children slept upstairs. It was fun, honest! We talked about the headlines while I glued on whiskers. I try to provide at least one homemade thing in each Easter basket every year. Of such things are memories—and traditions—made.

SOCK LOP You'll need one pair of socks—color and size up to you. Step one: Fill the foot of one sock up to the top of the heel with soft material. Tie it tightly with string that

(continued)

matches the color of the sock. Step two: Split the upper half of the sock down the middle in front and in back as far as the tie, and trim the bottoms of the resulting pieces in a rounded fashion for "ears." Tie a ribbon under the head area to separate it from the body—the heel of the sock becomes the rabbit's nose.

Step three: Cut away the heel portion of the other sock. Cut in half the ribbed area and the foot area that you have left. Use these four pieces for arms and legs—sew the bottom and sides into "tubes," turn them inside out and stuff them, then sew them onto the body. Step four: Decorate the face using paint or embroidery floss. A pink pom-pom can be a nose. Whiskers can be thread stiffened with hair spray or sewn-on pipe cleaners. You can use googly eyes if you like them, under embroidered or drawn-on eyebrows. You can also buy eyes used for stuffed animals at button, fabric, or dime stores. Put on miniature hats, if you like, perhaps with veils and flowers for the ladies. These bunnies can be put in your Easter baskets, or in a larger sock and hung by the fireplace for a new variation on an old theme from another season.

MARSHMALLOW BUNNIES   Stack up three marshmallows for the body, then split two in half for the arms and legs. Use construction paper for ears, gum balls for eyes and nose. Don't forget a bow tie, made from ribbon or paper. This guy can sit with a bunch of Easter friends in the center of your Easter dinner table.

Step 4

Step 5

141

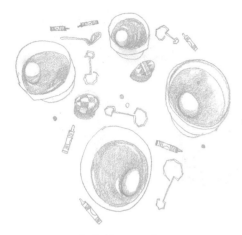

Adults-only Egg-coloring Party

Parents can dye eggs for their children in secret. Of course, you needn't have children of your own to have fun doing this. Make colored eggs for other friends, for your office, for yourself.

AN EASTER TREE Find a nice-looking branch. Keep it natural or paint it white or any other color you like. Then anchor it in a can filled with florist's clay or sand or stones. Hang decorated, blown-out eggs with glued-on ribbon loops along the branches.

EASTER BASKETS Use halves of milk cartons, oatmeal boxes, or containers from strawberries, covered with crepe paper or foil. Even egg cartons can be used, with each indentation holding a different treat. Or try a straw hat turned upside down. When the goodies are emptied out, decorate the hat for wearing or hanging.

"Grass" can be strips of green construction paper, or newspaper painted green and cut into strips, or dyed coconut. How you handle Easter baskets depends upon your belief systems: If the bunny comes to your house, baskets must be made in secret and hidden. Or you can make baskets together and leave them under the Easter tree for the bunny to fill. (Don't forget to leave out carrots for him!) If nobody believes in the Easter bunny, make the baskets together, but fill them apart from each other. (You never lose your love of surprises and presents, right?) You can draw names, and provide equal amounts of money to shop for presents.

You needn't use only candy—consider books, a small doll or stuffed animal, bubble bath for Mom, golf ball "eggs" for Dad, crayons, paint boxes, a package of flower seeds. Perhaps you want to have a tradition of using only things in pastel colors—nail polish, soaps, stationery, socks. Give each family member time alone in the wrapping room, and then an opportunity to hide the basket.

If the family is making baskets for relatives and friends, create a factory-like assembly line, and let everyone have a job to do.

SOME THINGS TO DO ON EASTER

There are many people who make it a point to attend a church service on Easter, even if they don't attend regularly throughout the rest of the year. Whatever your religious beliefs, there is something pretty wonderful about the idea of a resurrection. I like to sit in an Easter service of almost any denomination and think about the notion of being able to start things again. I also find the sight of little children in their Easter outfits with jelly bean stains around their mouths irresistible.

In addition to such a service, Easter is for enjoying the birth of spring and being with each other. You might want also to consider some other time-honored activities.

EASTER EGG HUNT Hide the eggs in the backyard, and then turn the kids loose. The winner gets a chocolate bunny, or to pick the restaurant the next time the family eats out. If there's an age difference among the kids searching for eggs and you want to keep things fair, suggest that all find the same number. Whoever finishes first helps those still short of their goal.

HARD-BOILED EGG FIGHTS Holding a hard-boiled egg in your hand, tap it against your opponent's egg. If his egg cracks or breaks, you win it; if yours does, he takes it. At the end of the game, the person with the most eggs wins— and the loser makes egg salad.

Easter Outfits

If your budget allows, buy your family all new outfits— from underwear up. On the day you all shop for them, treat yourselves to a fancy lunch or tea, perhaps at a downtown hotel or a museum cafe. You might want to include the "Where should we eat?" question in your family conference the week before.

Easter bonnets can be decorated yourself. Start with a basic hat and add flowers, feathers, netting. It's fun to be as creative as possible—use tiny stuffed animals or eggs, even little nests. Hats need not be beautiful— they can be just plain silly. The important thing is to have fun making and wearing them. Videotape or photograph yourselves every year in your Easter outfits. Keep the photos in a special Easter Album if you like.

Hot Cross Buns

Make a tradition of serving these
every Easter morning:

1/4 c. milk	3 eggs
1/3 c. sugar	4 c. sifted flour
3/4 tsp. salt	3/4 c. currants
1/2 c. shortening	1 egg white
2 pkgs. active dry yeast	1 tsp. cold water
1/2 c. warm water	White frosting

1. Scald milk, add sugar, salt, and
shortening; cool to lukewarm.

2. Sprinkle yeast on warm water; stir
to dissolve.

3. Add eggs, yeast, and 1 c. flour to
milk mixture; beat with electric mixer
at medium speed for two minutes,
scraping bowl occasionally. Stir in
currants and enough remaining flour
to make dough easy to handle. Beat
well. Place in lightly greased bowl;
turn dough over to grease top. Cover
and let rise until double, about 90
minutes. Punch down, turn out onto
lightly floured surface.

(Continued on page 145.)

EGG ROLLING   If you don't get invited to the White
House, don't despair. Any yard will do. Each person has
an egg and a wooden mixing spoon. The egg is put on the
starting line, and when someone shouts "Go!" each person
pushes his egg toward the finish line. The egg must not be
hit or batted.

EASTER PARADE   Dress up everyone in Easter finest,
including homemade Easter bonnets from paper plates, if
you wish. Then take a walk through the loveliest place you
know. Or take a stroll through your neighborhood, asking
people to join you. You might want to organize a neighborhood Easter parade a few days in advance—drop in
everyone's mailbox invitations to meet at the corner
mailbox at high noon on Easter.

FEED THE BIRDS   What better day to honor the ducks you
know? Visit a local pond with a big sack of bread crumbs
for them, perhaps a picnic for yourselves. Be prepared for
the ducks to invite themselves to your picnic if you sit too
close to them.

RABBIT MAKE-OVERS   Almost every house with children
also has a few stuffed bunnies. Gather every one you can
find and dress them up for Easter. Include hats, ties, and
jewelry. Put them in a wagon and pull them in your own
Easter Parade. Let them sit outside your house when
you're done. If your family has no bunnies, dress up some
other stuffed friends. Who says there's no such thing as an
Easter bear!

EGG THE TREES   Hang some of your beautiful blown
eggs from the tree branches outside.

EASTER DINNER

Perhaps your children are at the age when they no longer appreciate an Easter basket or a parade. Well, there's still Easter dinner to look forward to. After all, people never outgrow (or grow to be embarrassed by) special meals!

It's a nice tradition to have the same thing every year. For many of us, that means baked ham or roast lamb and plenty of wonderful side dishes. Cover your table with a pastel cloth, and hang pink, green, and yellow streamers and balloons around the room. Ask your children to find pictures in magazines that suggest spring, and use those, too—either spread on the table or taped to the wall. Center-pieces can be some of the things described above, or use a stuffed animal (lamb, bunny, or chick) or a lavishly deco-rated basket. Give each person an egg cup with a "person-ality" egg in it, one decorated to look like a person, real or imagined. Personally, I am drawn to eggs with mustaches. And bald heads. Except for a little fringe on the side.

Easter may be the holiest day of your year. Or it may simply mark the turning of the seasons. Whatever it means to you and your family, it provides another opportunity to build a tradition of good times among you and those you call your family!

Hot Cross Buns (continued)

4. Roll or pat to 1/2 inch thick. Cut in 2 1/2–inch rounds with biscuit cutter; shape cutouts in buns. Place 1 1/2 inches apart on greased baking sheet. Let rise about one hour, or until doubled.

5. With a very sharp knife, cut a shallow cross on top of each bun. Brush tops with unbeaten egg white mixed with cold water.

6. Bake at 375° F for 15 minutes, or until golden brown. Cool on wire racks for 5 minutes. Then fill in crosses with white frosting. Best served warm. Makes 1 1/2 dozen.

White frosting: Mix 1 c. sifted confectioner's sugar, 1/2 tsp. vanilla, and 2 T. hot water until smooth.

145

Mother's Day and Father's Day

It's a good thing there's an annual reminder for us to pay our respects to the people who raised us. Otherwise, most of us would put off forever what really should be done regularly. We would hold latent in our hearts all the love we would like to offer, but don't quite know how or when to do it.

The problem with Mother's Day and Father's Day comes when we try to find a gift that will express our feelings. Is a box of candy or a tie really going to do it? Beyond that, how do we honor for a few hours, on one day, someone who for years changed our diapers, ministered to our illnesses, endured our adolescence, helped shape us into the people we are today?

Well, we do the best we can. If we've time, we spend hours at the card racks looking for the proper sentiment: not too sweet, not too funny, something that feels real. We agonize over gift ideas, pick up and put down a million things in the stores, and eventually come up with something we guess they'll like—often, if the truth be told, a box of candy or a tie. We call on the phone when we live far away from them, and haltingly wish them a happy day. When we don't have time for shopping, we send a bouquet at the last minute, or ask someone else who lives nearby to take care of buying and delivering a gift. But no matter how we handle looking for cards or gifts, we almost always feel we've come up short. The truth is that there isn't anything that will fairly represent the important message we hold within, the gigantic thanks.

This could be discouraging. But when we have our own children, we learn an important lesson: our children thank us daily, simply by being themselves. We are rewarded by the fact of their unfolding lives, which we brought about. BUT: We also learn that it's pretty swell to get breakfast in bed, just for being a parent; to be given some acknowledgment of the job we've tried to do, whether it's a handprint in clay or a cruise to the Bahamas.

Working at Loving

Not all of us, of course, had idyllic relationships with our parents. There may have been very painful parts of our past with them that we have had to learn to forgive (or are still trying to). But as we are not perfect, neither are our parents— after all, they came from parents with their own problems. One of the tasks of adulthood is coming to terms with the pain we endured in childhood, whether it was a little or a lot. To that end, we work toward loving our parents as best we can, regardless of our circumstances. It is never too late for that, and it is always worth doing.

Make a Date With Your Parent

Find something for just the two of you to do, and present the coupon for it on the special day. Places to go:
• a play
• a movie
• a ball game
• shopping
• your place for a lunch or a dinner you make
• a nice restaurant

Take them someplace they used to take you when you were younger:
• the zoo
• a playground, just to watch the children

Whatever you do, make sure you leave time for talking.

The moral of the story? Realize that perhaps nothing you do for Mother's Day or Father's Day is going to "pay them back" for all they've done. And then make every attempt to do so anyway.

THE STORY OF THE DAYS

Father's Day formally preceded Mother's Day by four years. Its beginning is credited to Mrs. John Bruce Dodd of Spokane, Washington. She, along with her brothers and sisters, was raised by her father after her mother's death. At her suggestion, the Spokane Ministerial Association approved the proposal that the third Sunday in June be set aside for honoring fathers. It was first celebrated on June 19, 1910.

The rose is the official flower for Father's Day—red roses as a tribute to a living father, white ones for remembrance.

In the late Middle Ages, to "go a-mothering" meant for young people who had to live away from home—apprenticed or in domestic service—to go home to visit their mother church. On that "Laetare" Sunday, in mid-Lent, they had a chance to visit their biological mothers too. They brought presents to them as well as to the church.

The suggestion for Mother's Day came from Miss Anna Jarvis of Philadelphia. She was one of eleven children, and, as such, surely had keen appreciation for what mothers do. In 1907, on the anniversary of her mother's death, she arranged for a church service to honor all mothers. The following year the whole city of Philadelphia observed the day. Then, on May 9, 1914, President Woodrow Wilson made the second Sunday in May the official national day.

Americans were asked to display the flag "as a public expression of our love and reverence for the mothers of our country."

The tradition of pink and white carnations as Mother's Day flowers—pink to be worn for a living mother, white if the mother is dead—was established in memory of President William McKinley, who always wore a white carnation, his mother's favorite flower.

THE GREAT CARD SEARCH

If you think what a card says doesn't matter, think of the last one you received. Didn't you read the message, and, especially if it was "serious," take it to heart at least a little? Finding the right card for your mother and your father can be a lengthy—and frustrating—experience. Cards tend often to be overly sentimental and romantic when they are serious ("You were a perfect mother! I want to be exactly like you!"), and make the sender feel somehow dishonest. Funny cards seem to keep the sender from saying something meaningful. Many women, in looking for cards for their mothers, find that the images and messages make them, the daughters, feel like children again, when what they want is to convey a message of love from one adult to another. Also, cards tend to stereotype mothers and fathers in antiquated ways—most mothers do not spend all of their time cleaning and cooking, and most fathers do not spend all of theirs fishing or lying back in their recliners with their newspapers. Consider, too, that there are plenty of times when the person who mothers you isn't your biological mother at all. Generally, cards seem to be slow in keeping up with changes in today's families.

Buying for Men

I once heard that men like only gifts that can be eaten, drunk, or spent. While this is probably not entirely true, it is true that men are generally harder to buy for than women. Therefore, here are some things that might appeal specifically to a man:

- Shine all his shoes, and get new shoelaces for his sneakers.
- Buy him a record he liked when he was a teenager.
- Clean his car thoroughly. In the glove compartment, put in coupons for another wash as well as some new maps.
- Do all his least favorite chores for him, such as cleaning up the yard of all the doggie "calling cards," or washing out the trash bins, or mowing the lawn.
- Get him a great tool—a torque wrench, a nest of screwdrivers.
- Provide him with a comfy hammock and a great novel.

Love By the Yard

Make a gigantic ruler out of cardboard. Measure everyone in the family and put messages of love beside your height. You can get as creative as you like: Draw a bouquet of flowers beside your number, and make up a little poem: Four feet two, and I'm crazy about you.

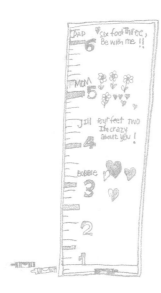

That having been said, you can sometimes find cards that say exactly what you want. You just have to spend the time looking for them. But why not consider another option? Why not make one?

One man I know buys his father a card with a beautiful picture on the outside and a blank inside. He writes his own message to his dad on the inside, one he describes as "pretty passionate." "I really think a lot of my father," he says, "and once a year, I make sure he knows it."

You can make your own design for the front of a card, if you'd like—use natural materials such as flowers and leaves, or draw or paint something, or use a photograph. You can also simply write a letter remembering, in detail, some experience you enjoyed sharing with your parent. This can be something from long ago or from just last week. The important thing is that your parent understand his or her own worth. You can also list the things you are grateful to your parent for doing for you: braiding your hair every morning; teaching you how to burp your baby; reading you stories at bedtime; helping you understand the necessity for honesty and the value of a buck. My precocious 16-year-old daughter wrote on the inside of her father's card: Thank you for helping me through these difficult years.

SOME GIFT SUGGESTIONS

Make it personal. Do something for your parent that suggests you are recognizing an individual. What are his hobbies, his passions? What would she call a good time?

TICKETS TO A PLAY OR CONCERT Depending on how elaborate you want to get, you can include dinner out (simply call the restaurant of your choice and give them your credit card number—they will bill you).

MAIL A MEAL I have a friend who, every Mother's Day, sends a lobster dinner via the mail. And every year, his mother sends back a photograph of herself wearing her lobster bib, holding up the empty shell, and grinning for all she's worth. "It was DEEEEELICIOUS!" she always writes on the bottom of the photograph.

AN ENLARGED PHOTOGRAPH Find an old photo of your parent, one he or she has forgotten all about, and have it enlarged and framed. Or, perhaps even better, find one of the two of you together. You might also consider a photograph of one of your parent's favorite places. (Remember, though, that enlargements take time—plan for this a couple of weeks in advance.)

VCR SPECIAL Transfer old home movies onto VCR tape. Assuming your parent has both a VCR and some old movies, this makes a great gift.

IMMORTAL WORDS Have a favorite saying, or prayer, or even recipe framed. Or have it made into a plaque, or embroidered onto fabric. There are many free-lance artists who do this kind of work. Contact local art centers or check out the newspaper or Yellow Pages.

PERSONAL WRAP-UP A "bath sheet" of high quality, monogrammed, can make a person feel special. Add other bath products if you like.

PREDICTIONS Arrange for a reading by a psychic.

Home Services

Get that malfunctioning TV or radio or blender fixed. Have someone mow the lawn, clean the house, wash the windows. Hire someone for the day to do small repairs—fix the leaky faucet, get rid of the creak in the front hall closet door, repair the broken window shade, paint the bathroom ceiling. A caterer can come to your parents' house to make a meal and clean up afterward.

To Wrap It Up

When you wrap a gift for a woman, consider placing a gift within a gift: a sewing basket may hold sewing treasures; a purse may hold a new wallet; a beach bag, a new bathing suit, and/or towel; a picnic basket, a variety of gourmet foods, and a pretty tablecloth. If you use gift wrap, consider adding real flowers—simply cover them with tape, and they will retain their color for several hours. For men, you can make a "shirt" box. Use striped or white or plaid paper (or fabric, for that matter), glue on buttons, and make a paper collar and bow tie. Spray with men's cologne.

BASKET OF GOODIES Make up a gift basket, filled with something your parent loves. My father is big on gourmet foods. My mother loves stationery. Gifts baskets can be built around themes such as these.

TOYS Don't forget the child in your parent. Does your mother love dolls? Your father, model airplanes? Think of something that will let them play. (Kites? Toy boats? How about renting a fancy car for the day? Put a picnic lunch and a nice blanket in the back seat.)

TECHNOLOGY If they don't have them, would your parents like some of the modern appliances? Consider a microwave, a coffee maker with a built–in timer or grinder, a cordless phone, an answering machine, a food processor.

BEAUTY How about a day at the beauty parlor for Mom? Get her a manicure, a facial, a pedicure, a leg waxing, and a hair cut and style. Dad might appreciate some of the same or a great massage.

NATURE Plant a garden for your parent, and add to it every year.

THE OLD RELIABLES If all else fails, you can rely on bouquets or jewelry or candy. But make it as special as you can— a small arrangement of very special candy in a pretty box makes more of an impression than a big box of the mediocre stuff.

Whatever you choose as a gift, remember the incalculable value of simple time and attention. Whatever your age, your parents never want to stop feeling needed and enjoyed as well as loved by you.

Also, don't forget that Mother's Day and Father's Day provide prime opportunities for multi-generational activity. For example, a little girl sitting at a table with her mother, her mother's mother, and her mother's mother's mother ... well, you get the idea. That little girl will be enriched by the experience of just being with so many generations all at the same time. It will add texture to her life, inform her in essential ways as to who she is. And all the stories and gestures (spoken and unspoken) she is witness to will not be lost on her—or on any of her tablemates, either.

HELPING YOUR CHILDREN GIVE GIFTS

When Mother's Day comes around, you, the father (or father figure), can help your children plan something for their mother. Similarly, a mother (or mother figure) can help children with Father's Day.

THE GREAT WHITE TORNADO   Send the parent to be honored away. When she returns, the house is immaculate, a good dinner is cooking, and presents are on the table.

WRITE A "BOOK"   Put several pieces of paper together and fold them in half, creating a book. Or cut the papers in half, punch holes in the left margin, and tie the book together with yarn or ribbon. Title the book, "This is My Father/Mother," or the equivalent, and then fill the book with anecdotes, pictures, photographs. You might want to include things the parent excels at, by drawing or making a blue ribbon reward, the caption saying something like, "This award given for outstanding Caesar salad" or "For wonderful storytelling."

Junior Chefs
Let the children decide on a dinner menu. Their idea of "fancy" is often wonderfully creative, tenderly amusing. When my daughter Jenny was younger, her idea of gourmet fare was buttered egg noodles, cucumber slices, crumb-topped cherry pie, and orange juice (served in a wine glass, of course).

A Memory Collage

Have the children collect items that remind them of Mom or Dad. Consider photographs; pictures from magazines of things they like (people as well as material objects—from Kevin Costner to a Porsche); a shopping list; ticket stubs from somewhere they went with them; an envelope from a letter sent to them. Add words cut out from magazines or newspapers: TERRIFIC, SUPER, BEST, GREAT, etc. Put this all together in a collage in an overlapping design. Then "frame" it with construction paper, or a real picture frame.

A TREASURE WALK The child takes the adult on a trip to find a hidden present.

THE HOME THEATER Present a play for the honored parent. Help the children write, produce, and perform it. Make construction paper programs and tickets. Set up the living room as the theater. Make the play about anything you like, or make it tie in with the day: how to be a good parent, a re-enactment of a family event (perhaps the birth of the actor?), imagining parents of the future, etc. Remember, humor adds a lot to home productions. Provide refreshments at intermission, of course.

THE DAY OFF Give the parents an entire day off from parenting. Banish them from the house after a wonderful breakfast they neither prepared nor cleaned up after. Tell them to go do something they love—all alone, if they'd enjoy that, at the pace they want to, as though they had no family obligations at all. You may want to provide tickets to something for them, or even call a friend of theirs to spend the day with them. Parents of very young children may appreciate this more than anything else. When they come home, have their pajamas laid out, and a piece of wonderful chocolate candy on their pillowcase.

SPECIAL SITUATIONS

Sometimes children's parents are alive, but not living with them. It seems wise, in these cases, to follow the child's instincts about whether to honor that parent's day. Perhaps the separation is due to divorce, and the child has a good relationship with the absent parent. In this case, expect that the child may want to spend at least part of the parent's day with him or her—and should. If the parent is far away, the child should be helped to send a card or gift.

Other times, the relationship is not as good—and can be as bad as when children have been removed from a home. While it is never a good idea to encourage hate or bitterness, it is equally wrong to try to force love and respect. If a child wishes to ignore a biological parent's day for complicated emotional reasons, he should be allowed to. He may want to recognize a substitute parent in his biological parent's place, feeling that he or she is his "real" Mom or Dad anyway. If, on the other hand, a child wishes to pay respects to a frankly abusive parent, he should be allowed to, in a way that is safe for him.

When a parent has died, there are bound to be sad feelings that come up on that parent's day. Don't deny them. Healing is hard work, and requires getting through some pain in order to reach acceptance. You can also use the opportunity of the dead parent's day to talk about all the good times you had together.

Whatever you decide to do to recognize Mother's Day or Father's Day, remember that the aim is to make as clear as you can how much you appreciate them. Everybody deserves to hear that at least once a year.

Memorial Day

When we think of Memorial Day, we usually think of warming weather. And why not? After the rigors of winter, it's great to think about going outside without a coat, enjoying longer days, and seeing all the new life that spring and summer bring. But birth is not the part of life that Memorial Day is about. Instead, it is about remembering those who have died.

In our culture, we spend a lot of time and money and effort denying death. It's hard to think there's much sense in that, given death's inevitability. When we deny death, we find it that much harder to accept. Why not, rather, acknowledge it as a perfectly natural part of life? It's not that we won't feel sad or angry or at a loss when someone close to us dies. But at least we're not surprised.

Memorial Day can be a good time to remember, in the most positive and loving way, those who have gone before us. It can help us to understand death, to be not so frightened of it, to begin, in that way, a lifelong process of preparing for it. A deliberate attempt at keeping memories alive can also help us to be very much aware of the character and worth of certain members of the family we might not otherwise remember. It can reinforce the fact that almost everyone who lives has something of value to leave behind: something as simple as Grandpa's recipe for gravy, for example, or Aunt Estelle's way of telling stories. This carrying on of small parts of people's lives creates a certain continuity that never dies. It brings us warmth and comfort, as well as profound appreciation for the fact that we are still here.

THE STORY OF MEMORIAL DAY

Memorial Day is also called Decoration Day. It began two years after the Civil War, when some women of Columbus, Mississippi, decorated the graves of both Confederate and Union men. This was a well-received gesture in those sensitive times. The custom spread, and in May 1868 General John A. Logan, commander-in-chief of the Grand

Army of the Republic, made the practice official. He named May 30 as the day "for the purpose of strewing with flowers or otherwise decorating the graves of comrades who died in defense of their country." Today we use Memorial Day to remember not only soldiers but also other people who were important to us and have died.

TALKING TO CHILDREN ABOUT DEATH

Every child will experience death through the loss of a pet, a neighbor, a friend or a relative. Children's attitudes toward death are, like other attitudes they have, learned from their parents. The parents' job is to support them and explain reality. Otherwise, children make up their own answers to the questions that arise in their minds about death. Sometimes those answers are much more frightening than the truth.

After a death, it is natural to grieve. Mourning is hard emotional work. Both children and adults must go through the stages of grief: denial, anger, bargaining, depression, and acceptance. However, children have special concerns that must be addressed. For one thing, young children believe that death is temporary, and that the one who died will return. It must be gently reinforced that they will not. They also have fears that the dead still feel—are in pain, scared of the dark, lonely and cold. Again, the truth will need to be told to them several times over. Finally, it must be made clear to children that a death is not their fault. They are very likely to feel that their bird died because they forgot to feed it once, or that Grandpa died because, in a moment of anger, the child wished him dead. Simple

About Death

Books written for children that deal with the death of a fictional character— a pet, fantasy figure, family member or friend— may provide a safe-feeling context for discussions about death.

explanations are appropriate here. Let the child know he is in no way responsible: Grandpa died because he was very old and his heart stopped working.

Sometimes children make a natural association from the dead person to their parent, and ask if the parent is going to die, too. It is important for the parent not to deny death, but to suggest that it is unlikely for now. An answer such as, "Well, I could, but I take very good care of myself, and I plan to be alive for a long, long time" will do.

It is important that we continue to talk about death as children grow (and age) through life's many phases. The answers given to a 5-year-old will change as the child reaches 10, 15, and so on. We adults experience changing views too, having to do with reaching mid-life, ourselves or our friends suffering serious illnesses, and the death of our parents.

It is my belief that there is much wisdom in the hearts and minds of parents, if only we allow ourselves to access it. But sometimes it is helpful to have other sources to get us going, or to support us. There are many, many books on death and dying available in both adult and children's sections in libraries. These are, for the most part, sensitively written; and there is a great variety in approach—whether in poetry or prose. There are also pieces of art and music meant to help accept and express feelings about death, to learn to grieve, to prepare for death, and so on.

Make a Rubbing

You can do this yourself:
Find a gravestone that you find
meaningful for its message or design.
Hold or tape in place a piece of paper,
and rub a pencil or crayon against the
gravestone. The design will transfer
through.

We give her body
to the earth.
She has in Heaven
a second birth.

A TRIP TO THE CEMETERY

There are some people, children especially, who are spooked by cemeteries. For a long time, my own children had a practice of holding their breath every time we even drove past one. When I asked them why, they informed me that it was to keep a dead soul from replacing theirs. I suggested that maybe they'd end up with an even better soul, but they'd have none of it.

Cemeteries don't have to be regarded as creepy places. They are, in fact, usually quite beautiful—quiet, peaceful, full of birds and flowers and wonderful bits of human history spelled out on grave markers. In New England, where I live, many of the gravestones are very old, and tell interesting, if brief, stories of the people who lived so long ago and now lie below them. It can be an enriching experience to walk among the graves, read the little biographies, and think about times and people gone by. Many times there is beautiful artwork on gravestones, which is what inspires gravestone rubbings.

Cemeteries tell us there is value in every life ("Here lies Anna Huble, beloved wife of Charles, mother to Elisabeth, Sarah and William. Died at 30 years of age of pneumonia. She tended us with loving hands.") They also remind us that every life ends, whether at 3 days or at 100 years. There are glorious markers and modest ones, but the fate of those they identify is all the same. There can be immense comfort in this.

There is comfort, too, in going to "visit" someone you've loved and lost, in having a consistent place to be while you once again talk to them. I have a friend who used to visit gravesites with her mother every Memorial Day.

She remembers being quite young, around 5, and sitting in the back seat of the car surrounded by pink geraniums and gardening tools, on her way to spiff up the final resting spots of some of her favorite people.

"It was wonderful," she tells me. "I remember the smell of the earth and how black it was. The flowers were planted quite efficiently by my mother, and my job was to pat down the soil. When we were done, we would have a little chat with every person in every grave. Oh, I knew full well they were dead, but I still believed they could hear us. In a way, I still do."

So the practice of visiting the dead can in fact be quite pleasant. It can be educational, emotionally satisfying, and an opportunity to be with those we no longer see. If those you loved are buried near you, consider visiting them on Memorial Day.

THANKS FOR THE MEMORIES

Even if you don't visit a gravesite, you can make a practice of remembering people on Memorial Day. Pick a quiet time—after dinner, perhaps, and let the family share memories of relatives and friends who have died. Talk about how they looked, things they said, things they did. Remember times they made you laugh and times they made you mad. Retell funny stories, recall presents you got from them or gave them. What holidays did you spend together? What did you do then? Where were some places you went together? Get out photos or videotapes and review those. Rather than mourning the fact that they died, celebrate the contributions they made to your life. How did

The Custom of Flowers
The custom of placing flowers on graves is an old one, and can be found in many countries. The Greeks put flowers over each new grave and believed that if they took root and blossomed, the souls were sending back the message that they had found happiness.

they affect you and your family? Are there ways that you can see their influence in your daily life? If so, can you feel that, in that way, they keep living?

PET CEMETERIES

Pets are usually very important to families, and their deaths can be nearly as painful as the death of a human. You may want to consider burying small pets such as fish and birds in a special place in your backyard.

Some aspect of ceremony can ease the pain and pay a small tribute to the pet you've lost. Bury it in a nice handkerchief and/or box. My mother once gave me a beautiful jewelry box to bury my dime store turtle in—velvet on the outside, satin on the inside. Her gesture made me believe that she understood the depth of my feeling for my little friend. Mark your pet's grave with a pretty rock, painted or plain. If you'd like, you can have the family take turns saying goodbye out loud.

Each year when Memorial Day comes, pay a formal visit to the graves again, bringing along some small thing to decorate each site, and taking time to remember once again the positive things each pet brought to your lives.

OTHER THINGS TO DO ON MEMORIAL DAY

MAKE A MEMORIAL ALBUM Sit down as a family and have each member who is able draw a picture of or write a story about something or someone he or she loved very much but lost. This can be a person or a pet now dead, a toy long gone, or a friend who has moved away—whatever represents loss. Now have everyone do the same thing for someone or something he loves that has come into his life since that loss happened.

Peace Talks

While Memorial Day is traditionally for honoring soldiers who have lost their lives in service to the country, it may also be a good day to talk about the avoidance of war. Discuss how certain wars got started. Were there other things that might have been tried instead? Talk about the role of leaders and the role of citizens. What do antiwar activists do? Does it make sense? What can we do as individuals to promote peace not only in the world but around our supper tables?

CELEBRATE LIFE GOING ON Plant a tree. Plan a vegetable garden. Treat your front yard to flowers. Wear a favorite relative's clothes, or make her favorite meal and eat it in her honor.

SEND A MEMORIAL If your parent is dead, find a resident in a nursing home with the same birthday, and send him or her a present in your parent's honor.

DECORATE A SPECIAL PLACE Sow wildflowers in a place you used to walk with a person you've lost.

Use Memorial Day not only to honor the dead but to acknowledge and celebrate the fact that you and many of those you love are still here. Taking a more self-conscious look at death can encourage us all to take a deeper swig of the joy of being alive.

Memorial Day provides a special challenge: to reach new levels of appreciation for all aspects of life, including the end of it. No matter what our age or circumstances, I believe, we can meet that challenge.

Sharing Legacies
When you don't know how to divide things up from a loved one's estate, establish a kind of lending library where those things rotate every year from one house to another.

Fourth of July

When I think of the Fourth of July, I think of
my grandfather. He initiated the annual
Independence Day picnic that all our
relatives attended. We held our picnics in a
huge park and it was a good thing, because
there were lots and lots of us—mothers with
their hair tied back, setting out pastel bowls
full of potato salad and baked beans and
Aunt Tish's marinated cucumbers; fathers
in their T-shirts throwing softballs around
and manning the barbecue; and children
everywhere you turned.

Babies sat stunned-looking on blankets, toddlers ambled aimlessly about and occasionally removed the thumbs from their mouths in order to taste whatever looked good (which of course was not always food). There were school-age kids chasing each other in zigzag patterns or organizing on-the-spot games, and there were teenagers sulking magnificently while they huddled around someone's transistor radio.

We ate hot dogs and cold meatloaf sandwiches, fried chicken and hamburgers, casseroles and salads, watermelon and chocolate cake, and we drank soda kept cold in huge containers loaded with ice. Grandma and Grandpa sat regally smack in the middle of the action, in lawn chairs the color of summer. The rest of us sat in the few other chairs available, or on the benches from the picnic tables, or on one of the blankets spread on the ground, or on a good piece of ground where the grass was thick and the ants were not. After we ate too much and said we couldn't fit in another thing, we ate more. And then we had roasted marshmallows.

Sometimes the day was insufferably hot and humid, and we spent most of our time in the park's swimming pool. One year it was so cold we built a bonfire. Sometimes we played vigorous team sports; sometimes we were lazy and exercised only our jaw muscles, swapping stories with each other. But always at the end of the day, when the dark came, we watched the wonderful display of fireworks, oohed and aahed with the rest of the massive crowd at the park over every colorful burst we saw light up the sky.

Digging Into the Past

Consult one of the kids' history books, or take a trip to the library to gather information about Independence Day. Then have a family discussion about the colonists' grievances. Talk about how they arrived at the decision to write the Declaration; what their justifications were for doing so. Then have each member of the family who is capable of doing so write a first paragraph for such a document. Be serious, or funny. Read these paragraphs aloud to each other. Then read aloud the real first paragraph. The eloquence will take your breath away!

My grandfather died on the Fourth of July after a long illness that had kept him hospitalized and away from our annual picnics. There was some discussion about whether to have the picnic that year, but in the end we went ahead. I think everyone felt that to do so would be fitting tribute to Grandpa's memory. He was on all of our minds that day, all day long. I decided he died on the Fourth so that he could come to the picnic after all. Certainly he was with us in spirit—that year, and in all the years since.

I now live far away from Minnesota, where those picnics are held, and so I don't get to go to them very often. But picnics like that are what the Fourth of July was made for. That, and fireworks, and ice cream, and parades, and acknowledgment of the fact that our country has an exhilarating history beginning with a declaration of independence. Think of all that act of rebellion has brought us!

THE STORY OF INDEPENDENCE DAY

The Fourth of July is a legal holiday in every state in the United States. It is surely the biggest birthday party imaginable. (Aren't you glad you don't have to make the cake?) What we celebrate, of course, is the birth of this nation.

It was in Philadelphia that the Continental Congress passed the Declaration of Independence. With that act, the American colonies made their first break with Great Britain, declaring us free and independent states. It was a long-awaited move. Oppressions by the mother country had not ceased despite numerous petitions and pleas. On June 7, Richard Henry Lee of Virginia proposed dissolving the political link between Great Britain and the colonies. John Adams seconded the motion. A four-day debate then followed; in the end a committee was appointed to prepare a declaration to this effect. That committee consisted of Thomas Jefferson, Benjamin Franklin, John Adams, Roger Sherman, and Robert B. Livingston. The actual writing, however, is Thomas Jefferson's.

The Declaration of Independence was presented to Congress on June 28th, and after another week of earnest debate, it was presented to the president of Congress, who signed with that most familiar of signatures, John Hancock. Crowds had been gathered around the courthouse since dawn that July 4th; at two in the afternoon, the Liberty Bell finally rang to announce that the declaration had at last been signed. This was a serious thing: If their new nation failed, every one of the delegates whose signature was on the document could be convicted of high treason and put to death. But these were brave men, our forefathers, and party animals to boot: John Adams wrote a letter to his wife saying that the day should be celebrated with "pomp and parade ... guns, bells, bonfires, and illuminations, from one end of this continent to the other." The country took him up on his suggestion then (some of the boys getting really fired up and beheading a statue of George III—too much grog, probably) and continues to do so now.

PARADES

What would the Fourth be without a parade? We can all thrill to the sound of a big brass band and seeking out that kind of fanfare is a great thing to do. Check your newspaper for listings of such events. But don't forget that there's more than one kind of parade. A serpentine passing by of

John Hancock's Pen Made at Home

1. Get a ballpoint pen with a straight, round barrel—the kind that looks like a pencil.
2. Cut out a piece of construction paper to wrap around the barrel (do not include the tip).
3. Tape the paper down securely.
4. Now cut a triangular piece of paper the length of the pen. Make it half as wide as the pen is long.
5. Make several cuts into the slanted side in order to make a feathery fringe.
6. Wrap your fingers around the barrel of the pen as though you were going to write. Tape the fringe above this point.
7. Now, pretend you are John Hancock. Take a deep breath, and sign!

Wear Red, White, and Blue

Add stars if you like, and hats with confetti hanging from them.

The Family Parade

There's nothing to say you can't keep a parade small. March around your backyard or your block. Let crepe paper banners fly from Popsicle sticks.

The Bike Parade

Cover your route on your bicycle, first decorating the bike with red, white, and blue crepe paper.

The Toy Parade

All the kids who participate march with their favorite toy. If they have many, they may need to pull the adored ones in a wagon.

exuberant folks in your neighborhood may thrill you more than any straight lines of uniformed strangers, no matter how impressive their band!

ALL-THE KIDS-IN-THE-NEIGHBORHOOD PARADE   Round 'em up and head 'em out. Deliver notices to all the houses in your immediate vicinity asking that all children who would like to participate in a Fourth of July parade dress up and meet at your house at noon. Ask that they bring an instrument of any type—a kazoo, a whistle, a harmonica, a guitar, cymbals (finger or bigger), rattles, pots and pans with a wooden spoon "drumstick," bells, even combs to play with their fingernails. The more outlandish the instrument, the better. Then, on a signal given by the leader, march around the neighborhood—on the sidewalks, please!

ALL-THE-PETS-IN-THE-NEIGHBORHOOD PARADE   Same idea as above, but this time the pets march. Dress them up a little if they'll let you (red, white, and blue hats, or at least ribbons around their necks), then take them out and about. Make sure they're on leashes or in cages, as altercations can break out.

NEIGHBORHOOD PARADE   Get the adults and teens in there with the kids. March to the sound of great band music on someone's boom box. If a playground is close by, march down there for a Fourth of July baseball game. (One street versus another. Women versus men. Ranches versus two-stories. Decks versus no-decks. Dog-owners versus cat-owners. Or pet-owners versus no-pets. If you really get organized, you can have people wear team shirts. Fabric-paint the name on a T-shirt.)

SOME ACTIVITIES FOR THE FOURTH

FLAGS Display them, big and small. Put a gigantic white sheet on your front lawn, and have everyone help paint the flag. Use quick-drying latex, and 3- or 4-inch brushes for stripes, smaller brushes for the stars. Put small flags, painted with water colors or poster paint, in the windows.

HAVE A JOHN HANCOCK CONTEST At the beginning of the day, have a look at the famous signature on the Declaration of Independence. Then, several hours later, have everyone try to imitate it without looking at the original. When all are finished, compare their efforts to the original. The winner gets a new fountain pen.

THE GREAT FOURTH OF JULY COIN RACE Guess who's on the nickel? Thomas Jefferson, of course! Have a nickel race in his honor. Line up three nickels on the kitchen table, head at the beginning, two tails following. Indicate the finish line with a string (make the distance shorter for younger players).   Then, on the count of three, and using only one finger, push on the third (last) nickel to make all three move. Keep them in line, be the first to reach the string, and you win.

HAPPY BIRTHDAY AMERICA BUTTONS Using a small can, such as a soup can, as a guide, draw a circle onto cardboard. Cut out the circle, and decorate it with paint or markers. You can say, "HAPPY BIRTHDAY, USA!" or draw a flag-like motif, or make a wearable firecracker: create a glittery design, and hang tinsel from the edges. (If you don't have tinsel on hand, cut tin foil into long, thin strips.) Make a tape loop and affix your button to your (red, white, or blue) shirt. You can also purchase pins for backings at craft stores.

Eat Red, White, and Blue

Berries do well here, of course: blueberries, strawberries, raspberries. So does ice cream! But there are also mashed potatoes, beets, radishes, rice, etc. Make a white cake decorated with raspberries and blueberries. Place a tiny flag, stuck in a red or white gumdrop, at each place setting.

Play it Safe

The sale of fireworks to individuals is illegal throughout most of the country, and for good reason: they often injure and occasionally kill their users. Even the most innocuous-seeming of things, sparklers, can cause injury if you touch the burning end, which can reach 2,000 degrees. Better to forgo putting on your own show, and go instead to a municipal fireworks display. These displays are so spectacular that even the most reserved of people are oohing and aahing along with the crowd. You just can't help it.

FIREWORKS

Our family follows the same protocol every Fourth of July. We pack up a huge picnic dinner: deli cold cuts, rye bread, white rolls, cole slaw and potato salad, sliced tomatoes, fresh fruit and cookies. Then we head out early for an Army base an hour and a half away from our home. We spread out on a blanket near the parade ground, read, play games, take walks and eat dinner until the sun goes down. Then we listen to the Army band play selected tunes, the finale being the "War of 1812 Overture," complete with cannons being fired. You can feel those cannon shots reverberate in your chest, feel the ground shake. It's scary, but it's all part of the fun. Then comes a fabulous display of fireworks that lasts 45 glorious minutes. I don't know of many places that have such a long display, but if you can find one, by all means go to it.

CELEBRATING SUMMER

If you live in the North, as I do, it takes the Fourth of July to let you know it's really summertime. What that season means to me is lazy days, later (and later) bedtimes, dinner made from the gifts of the garden, bare feet on sidewalks still warm from the sun even after the stars appear. It means the smell of fresh-cut grass and the sound of children yelling exuberantly at one another as they play outside. We slice through the waves at beaches, and we slice through tomatoes we take from our kitchen window-sills. Oftentimes we salt those tomato slices and eat them right from our hands.

Though our obligations at work may remain the same, there is something inherently relaxing about summer. Some of that is undoubtedly due to the fact that school is out, but this sense of ease has also to do, I think, with things more instinctive and magical in us: we respond to certain rhythms of a season almost in spite of ourselves. The less frantic pace of summer living lets family members see a little more of one another, be together in ways they cannot be at other times of the year. Here are some activities to honor that notion:

ICE CREAM HOGS This is for the grossly indelicate. Go to your favorite ice cream store, and get a flavor of ice cream you have never tried before. Then come home, dish it out on paper plates, and have an ice cream eating contest. No utensils or hands allowed; and whoever finishes first, wins. If this is a little too much for you, consider mere ice cream decadence instead. Go to an ice cream parlor that makes those HUUUUUGGE ice cream sundaes, usually designed for several people. Order one for the family. Eat it all. (Be prepared to endure staring from everyone else in the store. Don't feel bad. They're only envious.) Then go home and begin a fast.

PAPER CUP WATERFIGHT Everyone gets a paper cup. Everyone gets access to a water supply. Everyone tries to soak everyone else. Or, if you don't object to having toy guns around, take a trip to the toy store, equip yourselves with squirt guns, and then go home for all-out warfare. I must tell you here about something terrible I did, so you won't do it. I bought one of those big, black squirt guns that look like a submachine gun. The stream of water from those things travels incredible distances. I couldn't wait to

Make a Paper Firecracker

Use a sheet of construction paper and a piece of lightweight typing paper to make a hand-held popper:

1. Fold the construction paper in half horizontally, and glue the two halves together. Let dry.

2. Firmly fold one corner up diagonally, so that left side edges meet.

3. Cut off the section that sticks up behind the triangle you've made.

4. Trace this folded construction paper triangle onto typing paper.

5. Cut out the typing paper triangle and fold it in half.

6. Unfold the construction paper triangle. Press it flat, so that it now is a square. Unfold the typing paper triangle, and line up its center fold with the center fold of the construction paper square. Then tape the two together, at the outside edges only.

7. Fold the square together again, with the smaller piece of paper inside, into a triangle. Now, holding the triangle at the end that is opposite the taped end, snap your wrist. The paper will make a loud pop.

Summer To-do List

Sit down with the family and brain-storm about everything you'd like to do this summer. Let this run the gamut from the fanciful (take your dog to visit his "mother," the kennel who sold him to you; take up skydiving) to the practical (take a day trip to somewhere near your house; learn to type); from the doable (try the new Mexican restaurant; make an entire dinner of Vietnamese dishes) to the impossible (eat dinner in Paris). Hang the list up somewhere, and the next time you're looking for something to do, consult it.

get home to play with it, so I filled it up with water for the ride home. I shot it out the window, having a real bang-up time, until someone pulled even with our car, saw me pointing the gun out the window, thought I was aiming at them, and nearly had a heart attack on the spot. So, if you buy a squirt gun, don't be like me. Control yourself. Until you get home. Then don't control yourself anymore.

FORM A BASEBALL TEAM   Look for willing players from your neighborhood and/or among your friends. Anyone want to start a just-for-fun summer league? All should be welcome, kids and adults, for Friday night or Sunday afternoon games.

MAKE A FREEDOM GARDEN   Prepare a small area of ground and plant some beautiful flowers. Find a rock, paint a message of freedom on it (or just the word "Freedom") and put it in the middle.

VISIT A HISTORIC SIGHT   If you live in Philadelphia, you're all set. But no matter where you live, there's something there that speaks of the history of this country—if not on July 4th, 1776, then on another day. Consider visiting the oldest street in town, a monument of some kind, an old cemetery, etc.

The Fourth of July is a good opportunity to discuss with your family what freedom means. Is it the same thing to all people? Are there certain inalienable rights with which we are endowed? If you were to guarantee certain freedoms to all people on earth, what would they be? Where do one person's rights begin and another's end? Is any country in the world rebelling against its government right now? Where? Why? Should our government be involved?

Finally, consider what the reasons are for laws. First look at the government of our nation. Do you know of any laws that you feel are outdated? Are there no laws about something for which there should be? Now move onto the family: What are the laws here? Why do they exist? Do any need changing? Why?

Halloween

My younger daughter starts a countdown on the first of October, X-ing off calendar days in restless anticipation of Halloween. In part this is to give me ample warning to get going with her on costume ideas—she and I both remember the time I was at the sewing machine madly finishing her "Dorothy" skirt 15 minutes before she and Toto were ready to leave. But in part it is just because Halloween is so much fun.

One reason for the anticipation, of course, is the candy. I am afraid I understand this love of the sweet all too well. I used to spend hours trick-or-treating—staying out until people wouldn't answer their doors anymore, and even then standing hopefully on darkened doorsteps a long while after I'd knocked, just in case they were coming after all. Finally I would go home and dump my loot all over the living room floor. I'd give away the few things I didn't like to my parents or my brother and sister. The rest of the candy would live under my mattress, where I'd steal from it every night after I went to bed. I'd lie staring at my ceiling in the dark, blissfully sucking on Milk Duds or Butterfingers or Tootsie Roll Pops. No wonder I amaze my children when I show them my fillings! "EEEEWWWWWW!" they say. "Mom!!"

Another fun thing about Halloween is the theater of it all—being able to become someone else for a night. There are many costumes you can make at home that are inexpensive and easy. Please consider trying some of these, and get the whole family involved in the process. Finally, remember: Just because you're the adult who answers the door doesn't mean that you can't get dressed up, too! How about a whole family of werewolves or pirates or mummies or...?

THE STORY OF HALLOWEEN
Hundreds of years before the birth of Christ, the Celts (pronounced Kelts), who lived in the British Isles and France, began the new year on November 1. On the night before, they held a festival called Samhain, which means

An Original Good Scare
Mary Wollstonecraft Shelley, the wife of poet Percy Shelley, wrote the book Frankenstein *when she was 18 years old. It was considered so shocking it was published anonymously. It became an instant best-seller.*

Halloween Words

"Ghost" comes from the Old English word gast, which meant the life force, the thing you lose when you "give up the ghost." Later it meant soul or spirit.

"Skeleton" comes from the Greek skeletons, meaning "the dried up thing."

"Trick" comes from the Old French trique, meaning a stratagem for cheating. "Treat" comes from the Latin word tractare, which meant "to drag," and later took on the meaning of negotiating.

"Witch" comes from the Old English word wicce, meaning "one who practices magic."

"the end of summer." Priests, called druids, offered sacrifices to the sun god and the god of the dead. It was believed that during the Samhain the ghosts of the dead came back to earth, and so the Celts lit bonfires and waved burning wisps of braided straw held aloft on pitchforks to frighten those ghosts away. As a little extra insurance, they also wore grotesque costumes and masks. They hoped that if the goblins weren't frightened by the fire, they would assume that the dressed-up Celts were one of their own, and not harm them. Thus was born the tradition of dressing up for Halloween.

Many years later, the Romans came to Britain. They added customs of their own to the festival, including that of bringing gifts of apples and nuts to Pomona, goddess of the orchards. This is why we bob for apples on Halloween.

When Christianity took the place of druid and Roman religions in the ninth century, November 1 was set aside to honor all saints. It was called All Hallows' or All Saints' Day, and the evening before it was All Hallow E'en, which means "holy evening." Later, this became shortened to Halloween.

"Trick or treat" came about this way: Long ago, poor Irish farmers decided to ask rich people for food on Halloween. If they didn't comply, the farmers played tricks on them and blamed the ghosts who, as everyone knew, were out and about that night.

MAKING COSTUMES

Halloween is a great time to rediscover your and your children's rich imaginations. Give yourselves a night of brainstorming a couple of weeks before Halloween and see what you can come up with. Don't forget the first rule of brainstorming, which is that anything goes! Sometimes what sounds at first like a ridiculous idea turns out to be the best one. For materials, check out dime stores, second-hand stores, fabric stores, and your own places for storage at home. Set aside an evening to make the costumes together, for your kids, for yourself, for any and all in the family. Don't wait until the last minute, as I once did; in your desperation to hurry and finish, you rob yourself of the fun of it all.

Witch Some year, someone will probably want to be a witch, particularly if he or she has been impressed with the crème de la crème of meanies, the bad witch in *The Wizard of Oz*. Start with a black pointed hat, and add a mop wig or do a sensational job of messing up your child's long hair. Cut a cloak from crepe paper. Tape on long black paper fingernails, and glue a clay wart on nose or chin. Tie a black cat (stuffed, please!) onto a broomstick. This is a dark costume, so consider a reflective lightning bolt taped to the back, and a flashlight to carry in front.

Cat Take an old white pillowcase and cut a hole in it for your face. Use rubber bands to pull up fabric for ears. Then decorate the pillowcase with stripes or spots, using felt–tip markers or fabric paint. Use pipe cleaners for whiskers, or draw some on. You can put stripes or spots on your face, too, if you like. Tape on claws made from construction paper. Wear a collar if you'd like. For a

Coats and Costumes
If you live in a cold climate, think in terms of costumes that can be worn over a coat, not vice versa. Also, remember to make sure that your children can see and be seen.

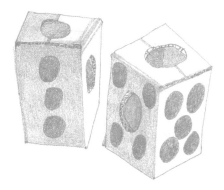

Start-with-a-box Costumes

Birthday Present Use a large upside–down cardboard box with holes cut for arms and the head. "Wrap" it beautifully, attach a gigantic birthday card, and put it on. Wear ribbons on shoes and in hair.

Pair of Dice: This is a great idea for two pals trick-or-treating together. For each friend, paint a box white or cover it with paper, and add big black dots (construction paper or drawn on).

trick-or-treat bag, use an empty box of cat food with a string on it. If you want to be gross, carry around a toy mouse in your mouth—swinging by the tail, of course.

GYPSY Another very popular costume is that of a fortune teller. Wrap a scarf around your head, and tie it in back. Wear a white blouse cut very full, a long multi-patterned skirt, and a shawl. For jewelry, try multiple rings and bracelets and gigantic hoop earrings. Your trick-or-treat bag can be decorated with playing cards. Blue eye shadow is essential, as is the reddest red lipstick. Tell a quick fortune to everyone who answers (or comes to) the door: "Your future will be dandy if you give me lots of candy!"

LADYBUG Cut two large circles of cardboard from a large box. Paint them red, and then glue on black construction paper dots. Cut two holes at the top of each circle, and tie the circles together to make a sandwich board. Make a headband out of black construction paper, and staple pipe cleaner antennae to it. You can add wings made of netting over a coat-hanger frame, if you like. A nice accessory is red sneakers with black dots drawn on—you can still use them after Halloween.

WEREWOLF Start with a deceivingly "regular" outfit, such as jeans and a sweatshirt. If your hair is short, slick it back from your face, or make it stand startlingly on end with some gel. If your hair is long, put it in a ponytail. Put a thin layer of cold cream on your face. Outline each eye with black eye pencil. Then color the area from the side of your nose to halfway under each eye. Also color half of the upper eyelid, letting the color merge downward into your lashes. Make a horrible face as you look in the mirror, and use the lines you see to guide your pencil in drawing lines up from the corner of your eyes. Draw short lines for eyebrows and have them meet in the middle of your forehead. Draw lines along the edge of your nose to meet the corners of your mouth. Draw another from under your eyes obliquely across your cheek. Smudge black under your nose and in the indentation above the middle of your mouth. Then make your lips black. There is actually black lipstick available, or use eyebrow pencil. For fur: Use about two yards of spun yarn, or "roving wool," which fluffs up when you unravel it. Cut ten or twelve 6"x 8" pieces and set aside. Rub a sticky syrup along the sides of your face, down the middle of your forehead, and in a triangle from your eyebrows to your hairline. Rinse and dry your hands and then apply wisps over the syrup. It's a nice, creepy touch to add some to the back of your hands—imagine how swell they'll look reaching for a Kit Kat. For a new twist, try a baby werewolf, wearing a diaper and a bonnet, and carrying a rattle and a pacifier.

DOROTHY (from *The Wizard of Oz*) Cut a rectangle of blue and white checked fabric. Sew up the side, put in an elastic waist, and you have a skirt. Next, cut wide strips for straps. Sew white buttons to the waistband, and wear the jumper over a white blouse. Put hair in braids, and a black stuffed dog in a basket, which you will use to collect treats. Spray red glitter paint on an old pair of heels, and wear innocent white socks with them.

SNOWMAN Use two white pillowcases. One is the hood, from which you will cut out a small rectangle to allow for clear vision. Draw "coal" eyes with black magic marker on either side of this rectangle. Also draw on a "coal" smile.

Fast Disguises

- Use a large brown paper bag for a wig: Cut away enough of the front section to show the face. Cut the top into strips and scissor-curl them for bangs. Fringe and curl along the bottom.

- Use an egg carton to make a pop-eyed mask. Use two adjoining cup sections, cut holes in the bottom to see out of, and poke holes on the side to tie strings through.

- Make a curly beard out of construction paper. Fold a 9" x 12" piece in half. Cut up in thin strips almost to the fold. Scissor curl it. Poke holes in the sides for string so that you can tie it on. Cut a mustache out of paper and tape on.

- Paper noses or beaks can be made by cutting out a triangle, folding it in half, then attaching it to the wearer's nose with masking tape.

Treats for the Needy
An alternative to the usual practice
of trick-or-treating is to send kids out
in costumes to collect canned goods
for various shelters. This is a nice
activity for older kids who may
eschew begging for treats but relish
getting dressed up.

The other pillowcase will be the body, in which you will cut arm and leg holes, and then stuff with newspaper for a rounded effect. Tie a scarf around the neck to hide the pins you have holding the sacks together. Wear black leotards and winter boots and carry a broom. Use construction paper in appropriate colors for buttons and a carrot nose. Don't forget the hat! The trick-or-treat bag can be decorated with snowflakes.

THE TREATS

If you really hate candy, consider giving out fruit roll-ups or small bags of chips or popcorn. You can also give out handfuls of pennies, or colorful pencils, or Halloween stickers. Some people buy children's books in perfect condition at garage sales all year long, and then hand those out at Halloween. If you want to make cookies or other homemade treats, give them only to children you know, and then with your name, address, and phone number on the bag they're in.

At our house, we wrap our goodies in Halloween fabric and tie with black and orange ribbon. The kids seem to like the fabric as well as the treats, and there are great selections to choose from: silver spider webs against a black background, green-faced witches, creepy skeletons. The last time I did this, the kids saved the fabric.

We also frequently hand out Tootsie Roll Pop ghosts: center a white tissue over a pop, then tie a length of very thin black or orange ribbon around the stick, under the pop.

WHAT TO DO WITH LEFTOVER CANDY

I let my children have all the candy they want for a couple of days, provided they brush their teeth after they eat it. Then the rest goes to my husband's workplace.

If your children are little, "The Sugar Witch" can show up at your house much as Santa Claus does. Her job is to take away extra candy, and to leave behind coupons for other gifts—a day at the roller rink, perhaps, or a new book. She may "leave behind" a few straws from her broom as evidence that she came.

If your children are older, face it: They'll do what they want. You can try dropping hints about the ill effects of too much sugar. Or you can all enjoy a good debauch and get back to salad in November. I vote for the latter, it is probably needless to say. And I vote for everyone's handing out something with caramel, my favorite. That way, when my children feel sorry for me and give me something, I'll get something good.

DECORATING YOUR HOUSE

Consider putting scary masks in your windows with a flashlight providing an eerie light below them. Make spiderwebs in the corners by stretching out cotton into thin tendrils. Use candy wrappers, or candy bars, to decorate your front door. Make a "candy man," a figure made entirely of miniature candy bars, and wearing funky clothes. (Use a doll as a base.) If he's big, sit him in a chair by your front door. If he's small, sit him on top of a pumpkin, or hang him over the doorbell.

Age-old Antidotes
Hold a button when you are afraid.
Wear garlic around your neck to
protect against vampires.

Ghosts are easy to make out of old white sheets—just crumple up newspapers for a head shape, wrap the sheet around it, and tie white string beneath it. You can make black eyes from construction paper, or paint them on. Then hang the ghost from your front door or from the outdoor light in your yard. I've seen sheets dropped over outside lamps, too, then tied beneath the light housing with black fabric. When the light is turned on, the ghost's face is lit up. Before you try this, make sure there's no risk of fire.

You can make an area of your house "haunted," and bring select trick-or-treaters through it. Have them come into the darkened room and stick their hands into bowls filled with "brains" (spaghetti), "eyes" (peeled grapes), "blood and guts" (Jell-O and warm water) or "teeth" (broken pieces of chalk). Let them feel a "dead man's hand" (a rubber glove filled with sand). Dried fruit can be ears, and a pickle can be a nose. Have the children plunge their hand into a bowl of pistachio nut shells and tell them it's toenails. Make creepy music by playing a record at the wrong speed, or use some spine-chilling organ music, turned up loud. Tickle the backs of necks with feathers.

THE JOY OF PUMPKINS

Don't miss the opportunity to go out and find a pumpkin for Halloween. In our family, everyone gets one of his or her own. It's amazing how much personality pumpkins develop after you look at them for a while. Perhaps you prefer the tall and skinny variety. Or maybe the fatter they are, the more appealing you find them. If you're like me, you take pity on the misshapen ones and instantly adopt them. The more their ugliness is criticized by the rest of

your family, the closer you press them to your breast. Whatever your choice, bring it to the table on carving night, and have a ball.

If your children aren't old enough to handle a knife, they can still draw designs on the pumpkin that adults can cut out for them. Pumpkins don't have to be carved, either—you can simply dress them up! Put on red construction paper cheeks, false eyelashes, a toothy smile, any manner of hat. Sometimes people decorate pumpkins with other vegetables, using lettuce for hair, a hot pepper for a nose, cucumber slices for eyes, a green bean with white bean "teeth" for a smile. You can also paint faces on pumpkins.

If you carve, remember that anything goes. You needn't make the standard face of triangle eyes and nose and gap-toothed grin. I always carve in long, long eyelashes, for example, and poke in a beauty mark. Also, you can make two faces—one on each side of the pumpkin.

Light pumpkins with the traditional candles, or use miniature flashlights. When you're all done carving, consider using the pumpkin flesh for bread or muffins, and try roasting the seeds.

A FAMILY HALLOWEEN PARTY

There may be reasons you don't want your children trick-or-treating: Perhaps you don't relish the idea of their stuffing themselves with candy for days on end. Perhaps they are too young, or too old. Maybe someone is recovering from an illness and can't go out at night in the cold. Or perhaps you live too far away from neighbors to make

Halloween Supper

You might want to make a tradition of serving a certain kind of dinner every Halloween. Since I know my children are about to go out and devour a ton of candy I feel two ways:

1. I should give them a junk food dinner of choice, just to set the tone. Or:

2. I should serve them the healthiest raw vegetables and fruits I can find, so that there's some help for the junk to follow.

I alternate between the two.

Old Witches Nut Cake

3 eggs
1 (1 pound) can pumpkin
3/4 c. oil
1/2 c. water
2 1/2 c. flour
2 1/4 c. sugar
1 1/2 tsp. baking soda
1 1/4 tsp. salt
3/4 tsp. nutmeg
3/4 tsp. cinnamon
1/2 c. nuts
1 c. raisins
1/2 c. chopped nuts

Frosting:
4 oz. pkg. cream cheese
3 T. butter or margarine
1 tsp. lemon juice
1 c. confectioners' sugar

Preheat oven to 350° F. Beat together eggs, pumpkin, oil, and water. Add remaining ingredients. Pour into well–greased Bundt pan. Bake 40-50 minutes. Combine frosting ingredients and spread over cooled cake. Top with nuts.

treat-collecting possible. Whatever the reason, if you're not celebrating Halloween in the usual way, consider a family party at home.

A HALLOWEEN DINNER Invest in some festive paper plates—orange and black, or decorated with witches or pumpkins. Put a little paper cup of candy corn by each plate and, if you're feeling mischievous, a plastic spider under every napkin. Use a carved pumpkin for the centerpiece. You can offer soup, served in very small, hollowed-out pumpkins. There is such a thing as pumpkin soup, or use something hearty such as bean with bacon or split pea. With the soup, serve crusty Italian or French bread. Include a nippy cheese spread. Also serve a crisp green salad. Dessert can be orange sherbet and thin chocolate wafers. You can also make a cake in the shape of a fierce cat.

SOME HALLOWEEN FAMILY GAMES Try bobbing for apples, with a preselected prize going to the winner. Grabbing hold of an apple with your teeth is actually difficult enough to be interesting!

"Pass the witch" by having the first family member draw the head of a witch, then fold the paper down over her work, and pass it to the next family member, who will draw the neck, fold *that* down and pass it on, etc., until someone draws the feet. Then reveal the entire stunning creature. You might like her so much you end up using her for a decoration every year.

Have a Halloween treasure hunt where participants must look in darkened rooms to find the prize.

Spiderweb is a game where the person follows a piece of yarn wrapped around objects here and there, high and low, to get to a scary prize—perhaps someone leaping out to say "BOO!"

HALLOWEEN ACTIVITIES   After dinner, watch a scary movie and eat bags of preselected candy—an assortment just like you'd have collected if you'd gone trick-or-treating. Or make popcorn balls or caramel apples to have while you shiver together under a blanket.

Read a scary story together. The library abounds with books for Halloween, for all age groups. (Also available are tapes, records, and plays to perform.)

Tell each other scary stories. Let one person start out the story. Then, at some random but very interesting point, he says, "And THEN..." and it's the next person's turn.

Remember that the point in making Halloween costumes, as well as in dressing up (and in eating treats, for that matter), is to have fun! If anything you do for Halloween feels like drudgery or makes you irritable, stop! Think of how you could do it another way, so that you enjoy it. The family conference is a great place to plan a Halloween that everyone can enjoy and be involved in.

Thanksgiving Day

There are a lot of things to like about Thanksgiving Day. Perhaps what most people would mention is that Thanksgiving is the one day a year when you are supposed to be a glutton. If you don't groan getting up from the table, your hostess is insulted. And if you don't reappear at the table for a sandwich a couple of hours after you vowed you'd never eat again, you're a party pooper.

Another thing people like about Thanksgiving Day is how unspoiled it is, how noncommercialized. Year after year, it is the same, pure holiday as always: a time for families to gather together to give thanks for their many blessings. (Even in the worst of years, there are always many blessings.) It is a kind of relief to have a holiday sanctioning our saying out loud that we're grateful for things in our lives. Enumerating our blessings gives a kind of cleansing lift we get from going to confession, but for the opposite reason—we feel great for saying out loud what's right in our lives.

No one has been able to tamper with the essential good-heartedness of Thanksgiving Day, or to trivialize it; and probably no one ever will. For that alone, we can be grateful!

I remember one year when my mother wanted to change our usual menu. I was stunned. When I managed to recover my voice, I begged her not to, as did everyone else, including my father, a latent master chef, who remembered all too well the year he tampered with the menu: People politely put a few crumbs of his oyster (can you imagine?) dressing on their plates, and then, relieved, stacked up high beside it the cornbread dressing we always have.

Now, I want to say right here and now that there is nothing wrong with oyster dressing, really. It is quite good. It is just not what we have. And that is all.

THE STORY OF THANKSGIVING

If you have been a hostess for Thanksgiving dinner, you may feel you've worked hard. And you have. However, next Thanksgiving when you are frantically making gravy

Learn About the Indians

Let this day be an opportunity to find out about today's Native Americans. Pick a tribe and answer these questions: Where do they live? Which of their customs have remained very much alive? How have they influenced our culture? What might we learn from them that could help us have a better world? A member of the family can find this information (and much more) at the library, then share it on Thanksgiving Day.

while trying to keep everything else hot, remember the first Thanksgiving. Ninety Native Americans showed up at the table—for three days. Try to find a turkey that big! (Or, for that matter, a table that big!) Of course, the Native Americans, being the good guests that they were, went out and shot five deer when the platters started emptying. I can just see the hostess, standing there and receiving such an offering: "Oh! More meat! Well, thank you very much, Mr. Massasoit. I'll just go [tiny sigh] cook it up right now."

That first Thanksgiving was in 1621, in Plimoth (original spelling) colony. William Bradford, the governor, set the time aside to give thanks for the bountiful harvest after the first hard year in the New World. In 1789, President Washington proclaimed November 26 Thanksgiving, but only the northern states celebrated it.

Sarah Hale, a writer and editor, wrote letters to governors and presidents for 35 years, suggesting that Thanksgiving be made a national holiday. In 1864, President Lincoln so proclaimed the fourth Thursday in November. (I think he also secretly decreed that since a woman was so hot on this idea, women could be responsible for the cooking in perpetuity.)

If you think our family overreacted to oyster dressing, listen to this: In 1939, President Roosevelt changed Thanksgiving Day from the fourth to the third Thursday in November. There was nationwide consternation: Everywhere people were running around saying, "What? What??" By 1941, Thanksgiving was back where it belonged. In the place people were used to. In the place where it should be. Just like the cornbread stuffing. Thanksgiving is a good time to remember what we often forget: to say that we are grateful to be together, and to acknowledge, with thanks, each other. Each member of the family makes a unique contribution to it. Use this holiday to say, "Thanks for being you, for making our family what it is."

DECORATING

FOR THE FRONT DOOR Find some lovely, twisting vines, and hang them in a swag over the door.

Tie or wire gourds, Indian corn, milkweed pods, or eucalyptus to a natural fiber wreath, or a length of rope.

Bittersweet is beautiful tied with ribbon and hung onto the door.

If you have an entryway or a porch, fill a huge basket with dried flowers, tie an orange and brown ribbon onto it, and place it to greet your guests. Rust-colored chrysanthemums are nice, if your climate will allow it.

Have family members draw pilgrims and Native Americans, and put them on the front door. Another option is to work together on a drawing, the size of your whole front door. Perhaps the first year a basic drawing can be made, with elements of the original big feast added every year thereafter. It can become a challenge, after many years, finding something to put in the drawing, but it can be done, even if it's small: another bead for a Native American's necklace, perhaps, or another turkey bone tossed overboard.

Cornstalks can be put around your lamppost. Put pumpkins and gourds on the ground around it.

Thank You
Send thanks to people who've made a difference in your life. While the turkey is cooking, send a note thanking a congressman who voted for something you believe in; to a writer for being a source of inspiration; to a movie star for doing such a good job in a movie you loved; and, of course, to the people you love for being—well, the people you love. "Thanks for being you," however put, is always nice to hear.

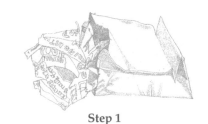

Step 1

Step 2

Step 3

For Indoors *Paper bag turkeys* are easy to make—simply stuff a paper bag with newspaper for the body, and use construction paper for the details. You can have every guest make one of these before dinner, and then put them all together in a chicken wire "corral" for admiring. You might even want to have a turkey beauty contest, with the children being the judges. Everybody makes a turkey; everybody takes home a different one. These paper turkeys can remind you to be grateful to the real bird that lost its life for your feast (a habit we should have learned from Native Americans).

Make Plymoth Village. Use a large piece of cardboard for a base. Then use brown paper or fabric for tepees, sticks and twigs for log cabins. Make thatched roofs from dried grass. Make little trees and bushes from branches you find outside. People can be made from construction paper, as can the food, which goes on a cardboard table. If you make a sturdy enough table, you can use clay or play dough to make food. Consider using bottle caps for pie plates, walnut shells for serving bowls. A circle of tin foil can be a frozen pond; shreds of cotton can be snow. Imagination goes a long way here. This is something a large group of children might want to work on together. Provide a lot of raw materials and a little adult supervision, and see what happens. If the village is not too big, it can be used as a centerpiece at dinnertime.

THE TABLE

Thanksgiving is the time of beautiful tables. People relish using their best dishes, linen tablecloths, cloth napkins, silver candlesticks, artfully overflowing cornucopias. For a charming homemade touch, younger children can draw "hand turkeys" to use as place cards. Older members of the family might like to exercise an artistic flair with other types of cards. The key, as always, is doing it together and making the most of the shared time.

THE CHILDREN'S TABLE

There are different points of view on where to seat children. Some people feel they should sit with the adults, and share in the general conversation. Others feel a children's table is a good idea. I prefer the latter, mostly because as a child I loved to sit with other children. (In fact, I still do. When I am seated at the adults' table and there is a children's table nearby, I stare longingly at it the whole time I'm supposed to be making worthy contributions to political discussions.) As a child, I found adult conversation boring. I also didn't like their general interference. Though we were seated close by the adults, we children at our own table felt wild and free. We giggled loudly at our jokes. We ate a lot of what we liked and none of what we didn't—no "Oh, just try this, honey!" coming at us from any mothers. Plus we got wonderful plastic dishes, which I adored—no stuffy china that you had to be careful of. Finally, the best part: When you were finished, you could take off and play—no sitting in a chair, swinging your legs for entertainment, waiting for Uncle Milton to finish his interminable story. You can make a children's table special by providing it with a centerpiece, a printed menu, their own serving dishes, and so on.

Reluctant Helpers
Occasionally a family member will say he doesn't want to do anything. My experience has been that whether the person is 5 or 50, he ends up really enjoying helping if you can just get him going. Make the effort— cheerfully insist that everyone help!

Word Game
As a group, hold a contest to see who can make the most words from HAPPY THANKSGIVING.

Potluck Thanksgiving
For large groups, consider having the host family provide the turkey, and draw other dishes from a hat so that each guest can bring something.

The Shopping

My grocery policy at Thanksgiving time is this: BUY EVERYTHING! This is the one time of year when all are allowed to get whatever they desire. White dinner rolls? Fine. Whole wheat? Fine. Both? Fine. Take the whole family, give each person who is able to push a cart a list, and turn everyone loose. Tell them that they can buy, in addition to what's on the list, at least one other thing of their choosing, no argument allowed.

THE COOKING

There are some people, myself included, who really love making Thanksgiving dinner. I like to get up very early, enjoy some coffee, and then get going on the stuffing; and have the bird in the oven long enough to start smelling good long before anyone else wakes up. It's nice to let everyone contribute to the menu, even if it's only lining up the radishes on the relish platter. You can make pies the day ahead, as well as the cranberry relish. That way, you can work at a leisurely pace, with everyone involved, and enjoy teaching your children the secret to your outstanding pie crust, instead of yanking your hair out because you're way behind time.

One family makes stuffing from scratch. Their traditional Thanksgiving eve involves gathering around a huge Dutch oven on the table and crumbling whole loaves of bread into it. I occasionally make homemade bread to use for stuffing. If you like the idea of homemade bread, but don't want to bother making it, try the frozen loaves of bread dough: just grease a bread pan and bake.

One family I know makes sure that everyone bastes the turkey at least once, for good luck. Another tradition is to hide a prize in the stuffing—wrap a piece of paper saying "WINNER!" in tin foil—small enough to hide, but big enough to not be swallowed. Present the finder with a Thanksgiving present—a chocolate turkey, perhaps.

On the day of cooking Thanksgiving dinner, a lot of people fall into the bad habit of not eating, wanting to save their appetites for the big meal. This does not work. Forty-five minutes before dinner is served, you are ready to faint from hunger, and you end up opening the oven door to "taste" the stuffing so often you're not hungry when it's time to eat. Better, I think, to eat a special breakfast early—pumpkin muffins or bread, perhaps, with some other breakfast foods, and then save your appetite. Despite the strong case I always make for having the same menu every year, it's nice to have something new, too, to serve not instead of the usual things, but besides them. We have added a spinach casserole to our "must have" menu as a result of doing that. My friend Dan always serves mashed rutabaga, because his mother always did. Who likes them? Nobody. Who eats them? Nobody. Would he do without them? Never. "It's how my mother still comes to Thanksgiving dinner," he says. "It's my tribute to her." (Then he shuddered and said, "Ugh! Does anyone like those things?" I had to admit I do.)

THANKSGIVING ACTIVITIES

So now you're all together, the feast is waiting, and the stomachs growling. There may be more to making the most of this traditional time than simply digging in. Within the big event you can create a bagful of small rituals that will add meaning, joy, and an ever-growing sense of how great it can be to be part of a family.

ALPHABET THANKS Going around the table to say what you're grateful for is a wonderful thing to do, but a lot of times people get stumped. Perhaps that's because most of us are, at the heart of it, shy beings, who have a hard time saying the things that mean the most to us. But it is a good thing to articulate your gratefulness, even if it does make you squirm. The Alphabet Thanks might help by adding a note of humor as well as narrowing the range of choice. Go

Massachusetts Pumpkin Muffins

1 c. sugar
1/4 c. light vegetable oil
2 eggs
3/4 c. canned pumpkin
1 1/2 c. flour
1 T. baking powder
1/2 tsp. baking soda
1/4 tsp. ground cloves
1/4 tsp. cinnamon
1/4 tsp. nutmeg
1/2 tsp. salt
3/4 c. raisins
1/2 c. chopped walnuts

Preheat oven to 400° F. Generously grease a 12-cup muffin tin. Mix sugar, oil, eggs, and pumpkin. Sift together flour, baking powder, baking soda, and spices. Quickly stir together both mixtures. Fold in raisins and walnuts. Fill cups two-thirds full and bake 18-20 minutes, until golden brown. Test muffins for doneness by sticking a toothpick in the center of one. Toothpick should come out clean. Let cool before serving with butter or honey butter.

Wine with Dinner

Many people who know about such things suggest zinfandel for a Thanksgiving dinner wine. It's American, for one thing, and has the hearty taste of berries and spices.

The End of the Bird

Stuck with a near-picked-clean carcass? It makes delicious turkey soup. Make it, freeze it, and serve it a month after Thanksgiving.

A Feast for the Pets

In our house we don't think it's fair for only the humans to eat well on Thanksgiving. Therefore, we make sure all the pets get something, too: After the turkey innards get cooked for their broth, the cats get them. The dogs get a few chunks of the dark turkey meat. The fish get shrimp brine and the bird gets an onion cracker. (If you do this before you sit down to dinner, you may have more peace.)

around the table, while everyone is eating, and have them say something about life they're grateful for, that thing starting with the letter in the alphabet they've worked up to. For example, "I'm grateful for the *apples* on the trees." "I'm grateful for the cool *beaches* in the hot summer." "I'm grateful for my best friend *Carol.*" This is particularly fun (and less embarrassing) if it's done quickly.

PRAYER Saying grace needn't make people uncomfortable. Appoint someone in your family who is comfortable with public speaking to say a few words. Also, simply observing a minute of silence can be a form of saying grace.

HELP OTHERS Guests for Thanksgiving are usually family members. But in the family I grew up in it was a bit of tradition to bring along someone who had nowhere to go. This could be a friend from school or work, or someone who just moved to town. In these times, it might be nice to invite a homeless family to your table. This may be a good topic for family conference time. How can we share what we have? To whom would it be most meaningful? This is a terrific opportunity for some soul-searching talks.

Helping make and/or serve Thanksgiving dinner at a shelter, or delivering Thanksgiving meals to those less fortunate than yourself, can go a long way toward making you appreciate the message of Thanksgiving. You can also help start a drive for shelters at your local supermarket: Ask to have an area at the front of the store set aside for people to make donations of canned goods, fresh fruit, paper products, goods in jars (like peanut butter) and boxes (like spaghetti). Then volunteer to drive those things to a shelter.

TAKE A HIKE A long walk is mandatory in our family on this holiday. I like to take one before we eat, so that when I walk in the door, I get hit with all the smells. And I like to lurch out the door afterward, groaning, because if I don't get moving I could sit down and never get up again.

SHARE THE WORK I know it's a ritual for many men to wander into the living room and sack out in front of the game after dinner. I actually don't mind this. I like hanging out with the women and making fun of all the snoring men. There's something about women wearing aprons that makes for great conversation. Of course, we could converse in the living room while the men did the dishes. In some families, men and women actually do work together, preparing dinner and cleaning up. I've heard this, anyway. Somewhere, it must be true. But I must confess I've never seen it close up. It might be fun to draw names for teams to work together: for setting the table, for clearing it, for washing, drying, and putting away the dishes.

JOBS FOR THE CHILDREN Kids' work need not be mundane tasks like clearing silverware and napkins, and counting how many people want decaf. For example, "assign" playing checkers with Grandpa to someone; hanging up and fetching coats to another. You can ask that a new member of the family be made to feel special; that someone be responsible for answering the door; that someone else be in charge of taking out all the trash. An older sibling might be responsible for getting a younger one ready for dinner—and hosing him off afterward. It is better to ask in advance for children to include all their cousins in play than to embarrass them later.

Cook's Privileges
Whoever cooked Thanksgiving dinner is absolved from cooking for one entire week.

The Paper Plate Break
While it is wonderful to eat off elegant china, it is a relief to the cleaners-up if dessert is offered on paper plates. There are beautiful and sturdy designs available. If you can't bring yourself to use paper plates on Thanksgiving, at least make sure that someone different from the one who washed the dinner dishes washes the ones for dessert. Perhaps the guys can do this while the gals retire to the den for conversation and cigars. Provide bubble gum and chocolate ones, as most guests will probably decline the real thing.

THANKSGIVING GAMES

Games are worth playing at almost any get-together. Why? Well, for one thing, they're fun! But they also get generations inter-relating, and help structure some of the youthful enthusiasm of children attending.

THE TURKEY GAME This is like a cross between Clue and a reverse version of hide-and-seek. It takes a large group of players, say six or more. Each player is given a list of around five side dishes. One child plays the turkey, and wears a construction paper wattle. He hides while the others count and then search for him. When someone finds the turkey, she must whisper into his ear what she will "serve" with him (e.g., mashed potatoes) and then scratch it from the turkey's list, unless it has already been suggested. If it has been suggested, the turkey shows the person the dish scratched out on the list, gobbles loudly, and the person must then hide with the turkey, as well as any other people he has captured. The fun is having several people hiding in one place together. The object, of course, is to be the last one to find the turkey(s). If the last person names something already guessed, the turkey wins, and doesn't get served for dinner.

TURKEY TREASURE HUNT Hide around the house pictures of turkeys the children have drawn or cut out of magazines. Set the timer for 15 or 20 minutes. The person who finds the most turkeys is the winner and gets to take home a double portion of his or her favorite dessert.

FEATHER GAME Make a construction paper headband and feathers. On each feather, write a stunt for a person to do, e.g.: Twirl around six times, then close your eyes and stand on one leg for the count of five. Spell your name

backwards and then pronounce it. Walk across the room with a book on your head. Each player picks a feather, then performs the feat.

AFTER THE FEAST

Did you know that turkey contains tryptophan, an amino acid that triggers the sleep mechanism in the brain? No wonder we feel so relaxed after Thanksgiving dinner! Perhaps this relaxed state of mind can make it easier for all of us to try to talk to everyone who comes to the dinner.

After Thanksgiving is over, think about ways you can carry the spirit of gratitude forward into your everyday family life. Perhaps you can add a moment of silence every night when you're all together, devoted to something that happened that day for which you are grateful.

Leftovers

Guests get sent home with fixings for a turkey, stuffing, and cranberry sauce sandwich. Put the stuffing, etc., between two generous slabs of turkey. Wrap in foil and add brown and orange ribbon and a "Thanks for coming" note.

Thanks to the Host Family

Guests, the day after the feast, pen a nice "Thank You" note to their host and/or hostess.

197

Hanukkah

There are those who call Hanukkah the "Jewish Christmas." Considering that the holiday falls near Christmas and that gifts are given, the comparison is probably inevitable. But Hanukkah has nothing to do with Christmas. It is its own quiet and lovely holiday: a historical, cultural, and religious celebration of light.

The Hanukkah celebration includes lighting the candles on the menorah each of the eight nights of the celebration, reflecting on the miracle that inspired the holy day, playing the dreidel, exchanging gifts, and eating fried foods such as potato latkes and jelly donuts. When the candles are lit and all the family members sit still before them, a unique kind of peace is felt: an unspoken appreciation of the joyousness of light, of the redemption that miracles bring, and of each other.

THE STORY OF HANUKKAH

In 168 B.C., Antiochus Epiphanes was the Greek king ruling Syria. In the interest of strengthening his empire, he decreed that all his subjects should worship the same Greek gods he did. Jews were not allowed to study their holy scriptures, the Torah, or practice their customs or celebrate their holy days. Those who refused to cooperate were to be killed. When the Syrian soldiers came to Jerusalem, they entered the Jewish temple and desecrated the altar by using it for pagan sacrifices. They also set up figures of Greek gods.

At first, the priest Mattathias led Jewish guerrilla fighters against the Syrians. Then his son, Judas Maccabaeus, became the leader of a three-year revolt, the first war for freedom of religion in history. Maccabaeus's small army (the Maccabees) took on the powerful Syrians, with their elephants, chariots, archers, and spear carriers, and emerged victorious. The revolt ended in 165 B.C. when the Jews drove the Syrians out from Palestine and reclaimed the temple in Jerusalem. Then they dragged out the idols and scrubbed clean the temple.

The Word
In Hebrew, Hanukkah means "dedication."

A Tradition
Some rabbis teach that during the eight days of Hanukkah there is to be no public fasting or mourning.

A Custom of Candles

In Turkey, there is a custom of weaving candlesticks with fibers in which the ethrog of Sukkoth was wrapped. (Ethrog is the fruit of the citron anciently used with the palm branch in the celebration of Sukkoth, the Jewish religious festival of Thanksgiving, and it is still used as a symbol of that occasion. Sukkoth was celebrated originally as an autumn harvest festival commemorative of the temporary shelters of the Jews during their wandering through the wilderness.) After the holiday, the candle remains are formed into another candle, which is then used for searching for leaven before Passover. This brings a continuity to holidays.

At the time of the rededication ceremony, a seven-branched candelabrum, the perpetual lamp, was set in place for the purification rite. But then it was discovered that the Syrians had also desecrated the oil. Only one small cruse still bearing the seal of the high priest existed, enough to last one day. Nonetheless, the lamp was lit, and continued to burn the miraculous length of eight days, enough time to allow for the preparation of more oil. Hanukkah celebrates this lasting of the light; the focus is not on a victory of humans over humans, but on recognition of a divine miracle.

LIGHTING THE MENORAH

A menorah is a nine-branch candelabrum designed to commemorate the eight days that the oil in the temple lamp burned. One holder anchors the shamas, the "worker" candle that lights the others. One candle is lit for the first night of Hanukkah, two for the second, three for the third, and so on. The candles are lit from the right to the left. A prayer is said while lighting the candles, and they are then allowed to burn themselves down to their bases. The menorah should be put in a place where the outside world will see, perhaps on a windowsill.

In some families, the head of the family lights the first candle and then leads three blessings and a prayer of thanks. Then the family sings a song together, and each child receives a small gift. On the following nights, the blessings are trimmed to two, and the children light the candles, with the oldest child going first. On the final night when all the candles are lit, the parents may give their children a bigger gift, as well as Hanukkah gelt—real money—or chocolate coins covered in gold foil.

There are good reasons for non-Jewish as well as Jewish families to develop Hanukkah traditions—appreciation of a beautiful celebration and the culture from which it comes; a time to consider the ever-present possibility of miracles, for example. At the very least, non-Jews can be encouraged to learn and understand (and thus appreciate) the ways of another religion.

SOME MENORAH TRADITIONS

A NEW MENORAH EVERY YEAR Every year, buy a new menorah of some kind. When Hanukkah comes, light them all, starting with the oldest one first. Your house will be filled with a glorious light all the nights of Hanukkah.

INDIVIDUAL MENORAHS In many families, each child has her or his own menorah, and loves picking out colors of candles to light each night.

MEDITATION In our house, we hold a long moment of silence after the candles are lit, in order to listen to the language of our hearts.

STORYTELLING Tell one installment of the Hanukkah story each night, ending it with a question for everyone to think about until the next installment. For example, if the first installment tells about Antiochus's decree, the question might be, "Does anyone ever have the right to decide religion for someone else? Why or why not?" or "Why did Antiochus think it would strengthen his kingdom to have everyone have the same beliefs?"

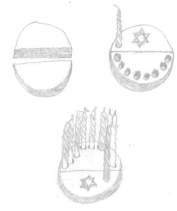

A Simple Menorah to Make

Flatten a hand–sized ball of clay into a circle about one inch thick. Cut it in half, and then join the halves gently back together, so that you can see a line running across. Poke eight holes in the bottom half with a birthday candle, one in the top for the shamas. Draw a star of David in the top half. Let dry, then paint if desired.

The Children's Candle In some families, the fifth candle is the children's candle. On the fifth night, the youngest child lights the candle, and all the children in the family get all their gifts.

The Dreidel

The word dreidel comes from the German drehen, *to turn. The symbols have these meanings:*

N=take nothing

G=take all the pot

H=take half the pot

SH=add to the pot

(Oftentimes, while the children play dreidel, the adults play cards.)

Hebrew ~

PLAYING DREIDEL

It is said that no work should be done by the light of the Hanukkah candles, so games are played instead. One of these is an ancient game of gambling called dreidel. Players spin a square top, marked on four sides with the Hebrew letters of Nun, Gimel, Hay, and Sh'in. These letters stand for the sentence Nes Gadol Haya Shom, "A great miracle happened there!" Players gamble pennies or pieces of candy. Depending on which letter comes up when you spin the top, you add to or take out of the pot. Decide on the number of rounds you will play before you begin— children won't want to stop!

GIFT-GIVING

It used to be that the nuts, chips, or the few pennies used in playing dreidel were the only presents of Hanukkah. This form of gift-giving is an old practice, and quite independent of the custom of giving presents at Christmastime. But giving presents at Hanukkah time has taken a different form in our culture, and now it is expected that one's gifts will be a little more lavish than peanuts. It's always fun to exchange gifts, but it seems important that this aspect of Hanukkah not take over the entire holiday, having it become a kind of substitute for Christmas. Here are some ways of giving gifts at Hanukkah that might help guard against that:

HERITAGE GIFTS   Have at least one of the gifts celebrate some aspect of Jewish life: a calendar, history books, a kit to make a dreidel or a menorah, a mezuzah (a piece of parchment, inscribed on one side with scriptural passages and on the other with the name Shaddai, rolled up in a scroll and placed in a small wooden, glass, or metal case and affixed to the doorpost of some Jewish homes as a symbol of Jewishness and a reminder of faith in God).

GIFTS GIVEN SPARINGLY   Give gifts only on one night of Hanukkah; first night or last or one in the middle—whichever makes the most sense for your family.

GIFTS OF YOURSELF   Give nontangible gifts, such as a little piano concert by one member of the family for the rest, a song, some act of labor, the inviting of friends to dinner, a lengthy call to a far-away friend or family member, a vow from parents not to nag for an entire day, a vow from children to put away their own clean laundry for a week.

GIFTS YOU MAKE   Let all presents be home/handmade: an original poem or story or song or play, a knitted scarf, a delicious dessert.

GIFTS FROM THE WHOLE FAMILY   Give gifts as a family to those outside the family: charities or people you all love.

FOOD

The most traditional and familiar food of Hanukkah is potato latkes, served with applesauce and sour cream. They can be made from many different recipes, but are almost always fried in oil to commemorate the history of this holiday. If you don't want to overdo the fat, make baked potatoes and eat them with sautéed onions, tradi-

Giving Love

One Jewish Community Center used Hanukkah as a time to give to the homeless. They brought together senior citizens and children, and had them decorate thousands of wooden and plastic spoons to sell at the First Annual Festival of Bread and Lights. They gave the money to Project Bread for use in 300 soup kitchens, food pantries, and shelters for the homeless. The project coordinator described it as creating a new Hanukkah tradition. Besides selling spoons, the event featured celebrity appearances, food, and entertainment by performing arts groups.

Latkes, or Potato Pancakes

These are a must for those who really like tradition.

*3 large potatoes, scrubbed (left
unpeeled) and grated
1/2 c. very finely chopped onion
2 eggs
3 T. flour
1 tsp. salt
1/2 tsp. baking powder
vegetable oil for frying the pancakes
pinch of powdered ginger
gingered applesauce
sour cream*

Put grated potatoes into a bowl of water to cover so they won't discolor and turn brown. In a large bowl, combine the onion, eggs, flour, salt, baking powder, and ginger. Remove the potatoes from the water in handfuls and squeeze dry. Place in a clean dishtowel and squeeze all remaining liquid out. Add potatoes to the egg and onion mixture. Mix well, and use the potato mixture immediately. (Eventually, the batter will become discolored, but this won't affect the taste.)

(Continued on page 205.)

tional applesauce, and a low-fat sour cream. Potato pancakes can be made ahead and frozen on a cookie sheet before being packed into freezer bags. Reheat on a baking sheet at 400° F until very hot and crisp.

A VICTORY MURAL

According to history, the Maccabees won by setting up a "dummy camp." When the Syrians attacked that camp, the Maccabees were hiding in the nearby hills. They descended and, having the enemy surrounded, conquered them. Draw a mural of this event. Use as many symbols as you can, such as an altar, an oil lamp, or a temple.

MIXED RELIGION HOUSEHOLDS

In our household, we celebrate both Hanukkah and Christmas to honor both my husband's and my backgrounds. One year, I tried to combine them, opening Christmas presents on nights we lit the Hanukkah candles. This was a disaster. The essence of each holiday disappeared.

The fact is, Christmas and Hanukkah are two separate holidays, different in every way, and each deserves to have its own traditions followed in the purest way possible. Beyond that, children of mixed traditions deserve the opportunity to understand and experience both "sides" in order to help them decide what traditions they would like to follow when they have their own households.

Whether we are honoring two religions' traditions, celebrating our own Jewish holiday, or reaching altogether outside the tradition of our own family, it can also be a way to communicate a wonderful truth: the world is made up of many diverse cultures and traditions, all of them important, none inherently better than any other, and all of them capable of contributing positively to the world in which we live. Each small step we take toward understanding one another brings us closer to a more compassionate world.

Latkes, or Potato Pancakes
(continued)

In a large sauté pan, put about 1/4 c. oil. When the oil is hot, put in a heaping tablespoon of batter for each pancake, and spread the batter very thin with the back of a spoon. Cook over medium heat until well browned and crisp, about three minutes on each side. Drain on paper towels and serve immediately, or keep warm, but never covered (they'll get soggy) in the oven. Add a few more tablespoons of oil as you fry the pancakes in batches. Serve hot with applesauce and sour cream. Serves 6.

Christmas

Why is it that the holiday that's supposed to be the biggest, the best, the most rewarding, the most fun, and the most beautiful often leads to terrible anxiety, disappointment, stress—nothing you would ask for if you were sitting on Santa's lap, right? It happens over and over again, too. We just don't learn our lessons, despite the tons of advice we're given in countless magazines ("Ask yourself 'Whom am I doing this for? If the answer is someone else too much of the time, don't do it!'" Ha! Or "Make a list of the presents you really want to or must give and then hold to it!" Ha!). Year after year, we knock ourselves out baking, buying presents, and decorating; we party too much; we put ourselves deep in debt; and all the while in the stillness of our hearts we know we are going about this all wrong.

W ell. I would be a fool if I were to suggest that I can change all that. I fall into many Christmas traps myself: I stand in the kitchen with flour all over myself, muttering and swearing, turning out more and more Russian tea cakes than I "need," when what I really need is to go to sleep; I spend way, way, way too much on gifts; I yell at the kids too easily because the rising level of tension makes me incapable of tolerating anything. But: I believe we are all capable of doing small things and taking some alternative approaches to Christmas that can make a big difference—and emphasize the true meaning of this holiday, which is beautiful.

THE STORY OF CHRISTMAS

The exact birth date of Jesus is unknown. The Apostles did not record the year of his birth, and when Dionysius Exiguus, a monk and a scholar, worked out the first Christian calendar in the sixth century, the date was miscalculated by at least four years. Later scholars put the date between 7 B.C. and 4 B.C. In A.D. 325, the church took December 25 as the day for the birthday of Jesus, as people were used to celebrating Saturnalia, the pagan feast celebrating the winter solstice, on that day anyway. Whatever the date, the story remains the same. A census of the world was being taken in the year that began the Christian Era. Joseph was of the house of David, and he and Mary went to Bethlehem to register. While there, Mary "brought forth her firstborn son, and wrapped him in swaddling clothes, and laid him in a manger; because there was no room for them in the inn." Shepherds in their fields, guided by a

Gifts of the Magi
Frankincense is a gum resin containing volatile oil obtained from various, chiefly East African or Arabian, trees. It was valued in ancient times for use in worship and for embalming and fumigation. Myrrh is also a resin that was used for incense and perfumes and medicine.

A Memory Tree

Use your Christmas tree to display reminders of special times together. You can use dried flowers from a bouquet you picked on a family hike last summer, the bride and groom from your wedding cake, seashells from visits to the ocean. Also use small souvenirs from places you've visited.

star, came to see the child. Twelve days later, Wise Men from the East arrived and presented their gifts of gold, frankincense, and myrrh. The custom of giving Christmas presents probably goes back to the Wise Men's offerings.

There is a legend that on the night Jesus was born, all the trees in the forest bloomed and bore fruit. The practice of decorating Christmas trees began in late 16th- or early 17th-century Germany. Martin Luther, the leader of the Reformation, came back from a Christmas Eve walk. To suggest the beauty of the night sky that he had just seen, he set up a candle-lighted tree. German-Americans brought the custom with them to this country in the 1700's. Paris had its first Christmas tree in 1840, and England in 1841. The greatest Christmas tradition of all, of course, is the message brought forth by the birth of Jesus: Peace on Earth, Good Will Toward Men. Year after year, if not day after day, it is worth reminding ourselves of that.

THE TREE

One year, the only tree we could afford was a truly pathetic looking thing, nearly bald, but I think I liked that tree the best of any we've ever had. It seemed to really need a home, it had a transcendent dignity when it was decorated, and I swear it *appreciated* us. Never mind that "outsiders" made fun of it—we loved it for all its shortcomings. I have always admired the tradition of choosing the ugliest tree on the lot. Here are some other ideas about Christmas trees you might want to use every year:

CHRISTMAS TREE FUND Save pennies all year. Every Sunday, put them into rolls. By the end of the year, spend what you've got on the best tree you can find.

SYMBOLIC ORNAMENTS   Let there be at least one thing on your tree to represent everyone in your family, pets too! My mother keeps a white poodle on her tree, made of white pom-poms, to represent her dog, Molly. My now 48-year-old sister is represented by a light-bulb Santa ornament she made when she was in kindergarten.

PRESENTS ON THE TREE   Hide small gifts for each member of the family amid the boughs of the tree, to be opened on December 26. This is "Boxing Day," a holiday in England, when alms boxes for the poor used to be distributed.

A FAMILY TRIM-THE-TREE PARTY   Using beautiful red ribbon, divide the tree into sections so that everyone gets his own place to work. This will eliminate the familiar "Hey! I was going to put something there! That was my spot! I *quit!*" When you're finished, sit back with a hot cup of cocoa, turn out all lights except the tree's, and admire your work. If you are severely myopic, like me, remove your contacts or your glasses and enjoy the romantic blurry effect, similar in tone to when Doris Day stared into Rock Hudson's eyes.

SERENADE IN GREEN   After you've finished decorating your tree, hold hands around or in front of your masterpiece and sing a carol to it. "Oh, Christmas Tree," will do fine, but feel free to sing any carol(s) you like.

DINE BY TREE LIGHT   Pick a night or two a week to have dinner before the tree—picnic style, or on a card table. This will ensure that you have time to admire what you worked so hard to do.

Fire-retard Your Tree

Saw off a few inches from the bottom of the tree. Then let the tree stand overnight in a bucket filled with this mixture:

2 gal. of hot water
2 c. Karo syrup
2 oz. liquid bleach
2 pinches Epsom salts
1/2 tsp. Boraxo

Also use this mixture in the bottom of the tree stand. In addition to fire-retarding the tree, it will keep the needles green.

Think Opposites
Give your big, burly husband some bubble bath, your wife a socket wrench.

TRADITIONS AROUND GIFTS

Sometimes, in our earnest effort to buy the "right" thing, we forget that gift-giving is, more than anything, a simple expression of caring. It should be fun on the part of the giver and the receiver. Try some of these ideas to help make that happen for you and yours:

DRAW NAMES Do this in your extended family. This saves on time and money, and the emphasis really isn't on the gifts; it's just on being with each other. Even if you can't be together, there's nothing wrong with drawing names. Appoint the senior member of the family to do this, and then let everyone know whom they "got."

SIBLING SITTERS If you or your siblings or friends have children of your own, form a December day-care co-op. A couple of days or nights a week, each of you takes turns watching the children while the others go out shopping. For a lot of children, you can hire high-schoolers to help.

THE MONTHLY PLAN Divide your list by 12 and buy Christmas presents monthly. Perhaps every April you buy your mother's present, and she looks forward to receiving a springlike gift.

SOMETHING FUNNY EVERY YEAR In our family, we always give one funny present to at least one person: a light-up bow tie, really silly underwear, one of those mirrors that screams when you look into it—the possibilities are gleefully endless!

GROSS GIFT It is probably because of my gross immaturity that I like this tradition so much. It all began with an unseemly purchase I made in a joke shop, an incredibly lifelike arrangement of ... well ... a dog's calling card. I wrapped this up in a beautiful box, with beautiful wrapping and ribbon, and gave it to our friends Jeff and Dan as one of their presents. "For your new home," I told them. "To give it that comfortable lived-in look." They were properly disgusted, as was I when they gave it back to me the next year! Never mind. I gave it back to them the next year, cleverly disguised in a very big box. Undeterred, they... Well, you get the idea.

THE HORRIBLE BOX THAT WILL NOT DIE One year, well over forty years ago, my father gave my mother a present in a beautiful box he got at a department store gift wrapping center. It was so pretty—red and gold foil-checked, with a big, red bow—that my mother saved it to use the next year. And the next. And the next. Today, the box is beautiful in spirit only. Each year, my mother decides who will "get" the box. It is quite an honor to be the one who receives it, and she is careful to be fair about giving turns to all of us—she knows we'd notice otherwise! It's quite a responsibility, too, to get The Box, since if you breathed too hard on it, it would probably disintegrate. And that would be truly awful, because Christmas would not be Christmas without The Box.

THE GIFT TAG TIP-OFF Write hints on the gift tag about what's inside the present. This not only increases anticipation, but helps explain why a certain gift was chosen just for that person. For example, "For Gretchen, the new cook."

MAKE A SANTA'S WORKSHOP Use a part of your house where a door can be closed. Decorate the door as you imagine Santa's would look—perhaps plenty of snow lodged in the corners of the windowpanes that you draw

Some Recycling Tips for Christmas

Re-use Wrap Save both gift wrap and ribbon. Ribbon can be ironed to look like new—paper, too!

Christmas Greetings Use Christmas postcards instead of regular cards.

Gift Wrap Make your own from newspaper (the Sunday comics are brightly colored), use pretty, reusable shopping bags, or give a canvas bag as part of a gift.

Decorating Presents Consider gluing on seashells, horse chestnuts, beautiful rocks, dried flowers, bits of lace, rhinestones, pearls and sequins, Christmas pictures from magazines.

Re-use Cards Use the Christmas cards you got last year to decorate packages you're wrapping.

Uses for Fabric Wrap big gifts in fabric that can then be used for other purposes. My mother has a Christmas-motif tablecloth that one of her gifts came in. After she opened the gift, I simply hemmed the wrapping. It could also have become napkins or an apron.

or put up with construction paper, perhaps notes from elves stuck on it. Keep all the wrapping supplies here. When "Santa" is wrapping, no one can enter!

THE CHRISTMAS THANK-YOU BOOK Buy a beautiful blank journal. Before you begin to open presents, get the book and the beautiful Christmas pen you use only to write in it. Enter the year, and the names of the people there. Then, as each person opens his gift, record what was given, to whom, and by whom. One person can be responsible for this year after year, or you can rotate by assigning a different person to be "gift secretary" annually. When it's time to write thank-you notes, there won't be any confusion about who gave what. The book is a good year-round source for when you're looking for gift ideas for other people. Also, it will help you remember what you got each year, especially those "what I always wanted!" gifts. If you're getting on in years, don't despair—you can still have one of those exciting Christmases. I gave my 70-year-old father a Red Ryder BB gun last year, and he said he'd been waiting 60 years for it!

THE PRESENT YOU CAN'T BUY IN A STORE

One woman I know has no young children, and Christmas was beginning to have an empty feel to it. She and her family decided to give each other small gifts in their stockings only, and to give the money they would have spent otherwise to charity. They make a list of all possible charities all year long; then, the few weeks before Christmas, they narrow it down to one for each family member. After a wonderful dinner on Christmas Day, they clear the table and write a check apiece. She says it feels *great*! This may be something you'd like to try. If you still have small children, make just one of your gifts to charity, from them. Here are some other ideas for nontraditional gifts:

CREATE SOMETHING Each year, have everyone come up with at least one gift that he or she creates in some way. It can be as little as a story or a poem, or as big as a quilt. But it must be original and hand-done.

MAKE A DONATION Make it in someone's name to an organization you know they'd like to support: AIDS, American Cancer Society, Greenpeace, the ballet, the symphony. Or buy your gifts at a shop or from a catalogue that carries products from countries and co-ops that are working against poverty (for example, Pueblo to People).

GIVE A SERVICE Offer to do grocery shopping for someone, or yard work, or baby-sitting, or making a fancy meal, or washing their car. Then make sure you follow through on your offer!

CHRISTMAS 'ROUND THE YEAR Continue a good thing. On the 25th of every month, give of yourself to someone else. Volunteer time in a soup kitchen, deliver goods to a homeless shelter, visit a lonely person at a nursing home, write a letter to someone.

GIVE "SOMETHING OLD" Once, during Christmas season, I saw a woman in a store admire another woman's earrings. That woman promptly took them off, and gave them to the woman who had admired them. I was moved, and I thought, "What a wonderful tradition that would be, to give someone something of yours that you love and

True Family Gifts

The Family Tree A gift everyone can relate to is a copy of the family tree, printed beautifully, rolled up, and tied with pretty ribbon.

A Trip Home If one family member lives far away and can't afford airfare home, chip in and give it to him—and then let being together be present enough for all of you. (If you just can't stand to be without gifts, give each other five things that cost under two dollars each. A challenge! But doable!)

Secret Santas Starting December 1 and continuing through Christmas, draw slips of paper from the Christmas jar. There is one slip of paper for each member of the family. One slip will have a tiny X on it. Whoever gets the X does not react, and all put their papers back into the jar. The person who drew the X is Santa for the day, and picks someone in the family to be exceptionally nice to. See if you can figure out who Santa is!

they've admired!" They'll know it's "used," of course, but in this case that's part of its charm: It's invested with good personal history, good vibes, and good luck.

TRANSFORM TOYS A few months before Christmas, collect some of your children's worn-down or broken toys. Bring them to your own Santa's workshop and refurbish them with loving care: Dolls get a bath and shampoo, new hair ribbons, a new outfit; stuffed animals get new eyes and big bows; an old sled gets a new layer of paint; bicycles get new wheels, a fancy basket, and streamers. This is a wonderful whole-family activity.

WHAT I WANT THAT YOU CAN'T BUY Ask each family member to tell you what that is. Children may ask that you play a game with them, read to them, let them go to the pet store and play with a puppy, stay up really late, wear your sweater to school—who knows? You may ask to have your hair brushed, the pot and pan cupboard straightened, your back scratched. This also is a fine thing for a couple to do with each other.

GIFTS FOR BABY JESUS Hang up a stocking, especially for gifts from the heart. A child may give one of his favorite toys; a craftsperson may make something, a father may put in a clock as a symbol of giving more time to his family; a mother may make a list of acts of kindness she wants to do. No one need explain any of this to anyone else.

COUNTDOWN TO CHRISTMAS It may be worthwhile to make a family pact, early in the season, that you all will try hard to reduce the stress that can so easily appear in this season. Agree that if someone seems to be getting overwhelmed, others will help. Help each other remember the point of everything you're doing. Don't forget that some-times it's the small, unplanned things that end up meaning the most—stop to smell the evergreens!

FINISH THE PUZZLE AND IT'S CHRISTMAS   The day after Thanksgiving, get to work on a huge jigsaw puzzle, Christmas theme-oriented if possible. The whole family can work on it during their spare time. It can't get finished before Christmas Eve but it must be finished before you open presents!

SANTA'S MAGIC ELF   Set out a tiny elf doll on the first of December. Every night, have a member of the family secretly move it to a new location. Every other member of the family should hunt for him when they wake up in the morning. On Christmas Eve the elf moves to somewhere on the Christmas tree where everyone will look for it on Christmas morning.

MAKE AN ORNAMENT A YEAR   On the first of December, visit a craft store and let everyone pick out things to make an ornament. Or use things you find around the house. Pretty soon your whole tree can be decorated with hand-made ornaments.

SANTA'S MAILBOX   Put one of those "country style" mailboxes in the house, perhaps under the tree. If you don't want to buy one, make one out of cardboard. Every time someone notices someone doing something nice, however small, he writes anonymously to Santa about it. On Christmas Eve, all the letters are read aloud and then forwarded to Santa to consider for next year.

AN ADVENT CANDLE WREATH   Buy or make a wreath into which you set four candles—twist the candles around to anchor firmly, or use candle holders glued into place, and

St. Lucia's Day

Incorporate an ethnic tradition into your family's holidays. Have children serve their parents breakfast in bed on December 13. This date is the beginning of Christmas celebrations in Scandinavia. It honors the legend that tells of a terrible famine during which St. Lucia appeared, with her head circled in light, to deliver food. Swedish children wear beautiful costumes to present their parents with sweet breads and hot coffee—the girls, long white gowns with red sashes and a wreath of lighted candles on their heads; the boys, white hats with gold stars.

An Advent Calendar

Supplies: a long strip of red or green material; 25 large, flat buttons, labeled with marker 1–25; a large needle; red or green yarn; and a picture of a Christmas scene, preferably drawn by someone in the family.

1. Glue the picture to the top of the fabric.

2. Sew on 25 pieces of yarn with which to tie buttons on in any pattern you desire: a bell, a Christmas tree, a candy cane, a star.

3. Glue a pocket to the back of the fabric to hold the buttons when you untie them.

4. Beginning December 1, untie one button a day.

add a large candle in the center. The greenery as well as the circular shape are meant to suggest life everlasting. The four candles, one pink and three purple, represent the Sundays before Christmas, "the Advent season," and Jesus, as the light of the world. The first purple candle is lighted with ceremony at dinner on the Saturday night before the first Sunday. Light the two purple candles for the second Sunday; the pink candle is lit for the third Sunday to remind all that the waiting is almost over. On Christmas (at the stroke of midnight if you all stay up that late) light the last purple candle and use it to light a taller candle placed in the center of the wreath, the white Christmas candle.

AN ADVENT GIFT RIBBON This is a long piece of ribbon for each member of the family, hung on a door or mantel, onto which four gifts are stapled. Each Sunday everyone gets to open a present. These should be small gifts, so as not to take away from the Big Event.

COOKIE CONCERTS Every year, we make Christmas cookies the same way—to the strains of "The Nutcracker." We cannot begin until we hear it start, and we play it over and over until we're through. This is the only time of the year we're allowed to listen to it, so we don't get tired of it.

A WAY WITH THE MANGER If you set up a Nativity set, try leaving the crib empty. Nearby, leave a pile of straw. Every time anyone does a good deed of any kind, he is allowed to (secretly) put a piece of straw in the crib. By Christmas Eve, there will be a soft bed for Baby Jesus, who appears during the night and is there for all to see on Christmas Day.

ONE HANDMADE CARD Every year, each family member makes at least one handmade card. These can be given to anyone the maker chooses. Some children always give them to grandparents, who are experts at keeping such things in perpetuity.

I CAN'T WAIT FOR CHRISTMAS One week before Christmas, sit in a circle, each of you with a unisex present costing less than five dollars on your lap. Read a short Christmas story aloud. Each time you hear the word "and," pass your present to the left. When the story's over, everyone opens what he has, unless it's the one he bought—then he trades with the person to his left.

THE ANTI–STRESS CORNER

Now, I know I said I couldn't change the fact that we get stressed out at Christmas. But here are some hints that might help anyway:

DIVVY UP THE MUST-DOS Write down all the things you need to do and divide them up. Put on a Christmas calendar what needs to be done on what day. Don't be a martyr—solicit as much help as you can.

TURN THE PAGE INSTEAD OF THE CAR KEY Shop by catalogue. But remember to do this early!

SET UP A "WHINE TIME" Give one full minute to each member of the family every day after Thanksgiving until January 2. If you feel fine, whine anyway—this will be preventive medicine.

AIR YOURSELF OUT WHEN YOU WEAR YOURSELF OUT When things start getting to you, go for a quick walk. Even ten minutes will help. Or ask for, or give, a big hug.

Some Things to Use for Homemade Ornaments

Clothespins Draw faces on them, and dress them up. Use cotton to make a beard for a clothespin Santa. Or turn them into Christmas birds to sit on branches.

Sewing Spools Make gorgeous with glitter, and hang on the tree with silver or gold thread.

Tin Foil Use to make stars (make durable by wrapping around cardboard).

Egg Carton Sections Hang them upside down, spray paint them gold and silver, and they become Christmas bells.

Jar Lids Trace around the jar lid onto felt. Cut this out and glue it into the jar lid. Now glue in a picture of a Christmas scene, drawn or cut out; or a family photo; or some special memento. Line the edge of the lid with gold or silver rick–rack or yarn.

Play dough Make some or buy some and use it to make all manner of ornaments. A garlic press makes great "beard" material if you make Santa.

Tiny Touches

Let every room in the house feel Christmasy, even if it's just the smallest gesture: a towel in the bathroom with a Christmas motif, a Christmas candle in the bedroom, an ornament hung over the kitchen sink. Children can decorate little trees to keep in their room, and be in charge of hanging up years' worth of school Christmas art projects everywhere.

IN THE STILL OF THE NIGHT While the rest of the family is in bed, go quietly, all by yourself to sit and stare at the lighted Christmas tree; and remember what Christmas is all about, really.

WHEN PROCRASTINATION IS GOOD If you're overwhelmed, wait until after Christmas to see decorations and attend Christmas events such as "The Nutcracker."

THE POST-HOLIDAY REVIEW Have a family discussion every year about what was really fun and worth it, and what wasn't. Write these down and refer to the list when planning next year. It will help you set priorities.

FOR CHRISTMAS EVE AND DAY

THE MAGIC WALK On Christmas Eve, after the sun goes down, take a walk to look at all the beautiful decorations in your neighborhood. If you don't have many, you can go to a neighborhood that does. If it's too cold, consider a car ride to enjoy the sights. One of my favorite activities when I was a little girl was to go with my best friend to look at our neighborhood's Yuletide efforts. We had an added twist: We took turns closing our eyes and being led by our guide to a beautiful Christmas sight. The guide would line the person up with what she wanted her to see, then say grandly, "Okay, open!" No matter how many sights we were brought to, it was always a wonderful, breathless moment when we followed that command.

SANTA CLAUS Really, he must come. Even if everyone knows the terrible truth. Have him stamp up to the front door, ring the doorbell, and drop in for a visit on Christmas Day. He can rub his tired feet and enjoy a Christmas treat while he gives a dramatic account of the activities of the night before. The showier and louder the Claus, the better. Cast accordingly.

HANG A STOCKING FOR YOUR PET   We hang four, for our two cats and two dogs. One year our male dog couldn't contain himself and raided his stocking the first night it was up, leaving a fine mess on the living room floor. Since then, the stockings are hung high!

THE CHRISTMAS GIFT ANGEL   Let the youngest or the oldest child be responsible for passing out the presents. If you like, let him or her stand by while each gift is opened, before going to get the next. After all, it's fun to see a person open the gift you gave. Have all shout out what they think a gift is before it's opened, unless, of course, they know.

ALL OF US IN THE MORNING   When children grow up and marry, there's often a conflict about where to spend holidays. If you live in the same town, the immediate family might agree to have Christmas breakfast together—just like old times—and then go their separate ways.

THE CHRISTMAS MORNING GIFT SEARCH   Here is a way to delay the start of Christmas a little bit, allowing members of the family who wish to sleep later than 5:30 to do so. A gift for the early riser(s) is well–hidden, and must be found. The first hint will be provided by a clue left by Santa under that person's pillow. Then she must find other hints, and, ultimately, the gift, which will be very engrossing and very quiet. Or: Hang full Christmas stockings on the bedpost while the children are asleep. When they wake up, they can unwrap and play with these presents in bed. Put in interesting toys, books, some things to eat.

Luminaria

This decoration idea comes from Mexico, but I first saw it in Minnesota.

To make these Fill brown paper bags with at least four inches of sand, for weight and for safety. Stick a candle into the middle of the sand, and when it's dark out, light it. It will make a lovely glow, especially against snow.

These decorations are said to be put out to light the way for the Christ child and many people therefore only light them on Christmas Eve. In some neighborhoods, everyone does it. Perhaps you can start such a tradition in your own neighborhood.

The Christmas Tablecloth

This is used only once a year, at Christmas dinner. Make it out of red, white, or green felt, and go crazy decorating it. You can put on your favorite Christmas cards, covered with red or green netting (sew or glue them in place). Cut out other decorations from felt—round Christmas ornaments decorated with glitter and sewn-on beads, holly leaves, candy canes. Each family member can make one decoration each year. Soon it will be a challenge to find a spot, but do it, even if it's just a red sequin that you sew onto a green holly leaf.

DISPLAY OF GIFTS   After gifts are opened, leave them under the tree for everyone to look at the next day. Then they're all yours. I used to love the added anticipation of seeing my toys just lying there, unwrapped, waiting. One word of warning: One year we left our opened presents under the tree and set off for midnight Mass. When we returned, we discovered that our dog had, in our absence, had her own little Christmas party: She'd eaten the cheese assortment my father had received as a gift.

AFTER CHRISTMAS

RECYCLE YOUR TREE   After you've taken it down, decorate your Christmas tree again, only this time for the birds and squirrels. Put on peanut butter pinecones, popcorn, and suet cakes, and scatter sunflower seeds beneath it. You can also sink it into a deep pond or stream to form a refuge area for fish. Or cut up the branches and use them for mulch. You can burn fir, but mix it with hardwood logs—it will pop and hiss.

CHRISTMAS TWELFTH NIGHT   One woman told me her family has always felt bad about the idea of the 12 days of Christmas being nearly lost in our culture. They feel that even on New Year's Day they're not quite ready to part with their tree, that in fact after all the hustle and bustle of the holidays, they enjoy it more. So they wait until January 6. Then, in the early evening, they go from room to room taking down the decorations. Just before they undecorate the tree, they unwrap one small present that has been saved for that occasion. Dinner is always followed by a cake made in a Bundt pan to symbolize the crowns of the three kings, who tradition tells us came on Twelfth Night, or Epiphany, to see the Christ Child.

EPIPHANY CRÈCHE According to tradition, the Wise Men arrived on January 6, Epiphany. Many people do not add the camels and Wise Men to their manger scene until then. You can also place the Wise Men far away from the manger. Then, each day until Epiphany, move them a little closer.

There is a reason that we carry on with Christmas festivities, despite the problems we often have during the holiday season. It is that there is an essential goodness to it all, a way to find warmth and brightness in the dark of winter. Do all you can to make this holiday be what it should be—a time for family closeness, appreciation, and fun.

Goodbye-to-Christmas Party

Cope with post-Christmas blues by having a party January 25. If you'd like, have everyone wrap up a gift they couldn't use, and put them all in a big grab bag. Before going home, each person picks a present.

Going Out in a Burst of Glory

When you take down your tree, keep a branch from it to burn in your fireplace. Everyone touches it before it is burned and makes a silent wish for the world. Be careful—the branches really flare up.

Twelfth Night Traditions

Other traditions associated with Twelfth Night include drinking wassail and pouring cider on the apple trees to help bring in a good crop.

New Year's Eve and Day

January first is seen as a time for beginning anew not only a calendar year but also certain aspects of our lives. Many of us make resolutions feverishly, only to pout a week later when nearly all of them have been broken. It seems to me, though, that the idea of making resolutions is a good practice because it points out what needs improving. Even if we don't live up to all our resolutions, at least we've acknowledged that some things can use attention. And, in that noblest of human gestures, year after year, we try.

New Year's Eve for many years was celebrated by over-drinking, by going to or hosting some party where everyone behaved a little foolishly and sat glumly at the breakfast table the next morning reviewing their faux pas. As we become more aware of the dangers of alcohol, this practice is being moderated somewhat, at the very least by the use of "designated drivers." In addition to that, more and more cities are sponsoring "First Nights," indoor and outdoor celebrations on New Year's Eve presented by musicians, actors, mimes, puppeteers, and other artists. These events often last all day and into the night, climaxing with fireworks at midnight. They welcome and are appropriate for all ages, and may provide for many a wonderful alternative to traditional New Year's Eve parties. After all, how many times can you put lamp shades on your head before it gets really boring?

It seems only right that the people we live with throughout the year be the people we celebrate with when the New Year comes. But many of the traditional ways of celebrating New Year's are adult–oriented only. So our task is to try to find ways to make this a holiday we can share. Perhaps it will be a half-hour "mini party" before young ones go to sleep, using an alarm clock set to go off at "midnight," several hours early. Perhaps you will want to go all-out and plan several events from New Year's Eve straight through all New Year's Day that include all the members of your family as well as other friends and relatives. However you choose to do it, though, the coming of the New Year does seem worthy of celebration. It is an

The Original New Year's

The first known New Year's celebration lasted 11 days and was held in the temple of Babylon. The account of it, written with wedge-shaped characters on clay tablets, described praising native gods, who were identified with the sun and other heavenly bodies. The celebratory ritual served to purify Babylonian people for a new year to come.

Chinese Traditions

You need not be of Chinese descent to incorporate some of these ideas into your New Year's celebration:

• Wear red.
• Eat a fancy fish or chicken meal.
• Sleep on New Year's Eve with a lucky penny under your pillow.
• Make a Chinese New Year's Scroll to hang on the wall for good luck: Start with a long piece of red wrapping paper. In black magic marker, write: GUN HAY FAT CHOY. This means "Happy New Year." Decorate the background with whatever materials you can find that are red (threads, buttons, pictures from magazines, glitter). Then glue the ends of the paper around long cardboard tubes, and hang the scroll up.

acknowledgment that we've come through yet another cycle intact, so to speak; and it is good for us to look forward, with hope, to beginning another.

THE STORY OF NEW YEAR'S

New Year's Day hasn't always been January first. For a very long while, it was a spring holiday. Before time was reckoned by the movement of the earth around the sun, ancient Romans regarded a new cycle as beginning with the first green of spring. The year was 10 months long rather than 12, and the New Year fell on March first.

In 46 B.C., Julius Caesar introduced a new and better calendar, and January and February came into being. Because Roman senators took office on January 1, that became the beginning of the New Year. For various reasons, other days and months were used in Europe. Since 1752, our country and nearly all nations have used the first of January as the start of the calendar year.

January was named for the Roman god Janus, whose name comes from janua, the Latin word for door. This god was always pictured with two faces—one looking forward and one looking backward. All customs of New Year's Day have been connected to saying goodbye to the past and welcoming the future.

CHINESE NEW YEAR

Chinese New Year takes place in January or February and lasts for fifteen days. It provides Americans of Chinese descent a time to reassert old customs and traditions. One of these traditions is having a whole fish or chicken with the meal that starts the New Year. Having both the head and the tail signifies a good beginning and a good end.

Anything perceived as pertaining to good luck is quite important during the days that celebrate the Chinese New Year. Saying good things around the house is lucky; the color red is lucky. Chinese characters painted in gold paint on red paper are posted everywhere, especially over doorways, where luck and fortune are said to enter businesses and households.

INCORPORATE OLD BELIEFS

It's really worthwhile to create your family's own version of ancient traditions. You make for a sense of continuity, reach backward through time to pull something of the past into the present. You discover the joy of joint-invention, cooperation, exploration. And, as always, doing things together in one way brings you closer in all ways.

WEATHER PREDICTION   It was once believed that the weather for the twelve months of the year could be predicted by the first twelve days of the new year. As a family, keep a chart of the weather for the first twelve days. You can make this a real work of art, and have each member contribute to it at a certain time each day, say at sunset. Then transfer your information onto the yearly calendar. Make a date for the end of each month to see how the predictions matched up. Was February mostly cloudy and cold, as was January second? Every time you "predicted" accurately, give yourselves a weather-related treat: Umbrellas. Beach balls. Sun hats.

Where Old Customs Come From

Ringing in the New Year. It used to be believed that the New Year should be given real, physical help. People beat out the old year with sticks, and rang bells to usher in the new.

Today, many cities provide fireworks on New Year's; and it's a sad New Year's Eve party indeed that doesn't include silly noisemakers to use uninhibitedly at the stroke of midnight.

Wassail, a drink served on both New Year's Eve and New Year's Day, comes from an old Gallic word meaning "good health." All-day open house receptions were popular on New Year's Day, and this drink was served. The tradition of serving a drink continues, though today we often replace it with eggnog.

LUCK OF THE YEAR The New Year's luck was thought to be determined by who was the first person to cross over one's threshold. A dark man brought good luck; a fair man, bad. A woman signified that a death was coming! Because of this belief, "first foots" were hired to be the ones to cross people's thresholds first. They brought with them certain gifts: whiskey or a stone, to symbolize strength; or a green twig put on the hearth to symbolize new life.

"Hire" a member of your family to be the first to cross the threshold, dressed, of course, as a dark man. Make a costume that can be used year after year, decorated with New Year's paraphernalia. For example, use a man's shirt, and sew on noisemakers; further decorate with glitter and confetti. You may want the new year to be represented by the youngest member of the family, the old year by the oldest. Also, consider laying fresh greenery along window-sill or mantel to symbolize new life and a fresh start.

A FAMILY NEW YEAR'S EVE

When thinking of things to do on this holiday, it is helpful to remember an anecdote a friend told me. She let her then ten-year-old son stay up to watch the ball drop in Times Square on television. It was his first time, and for him it was a very big deal. When the ball finally signalled the beginning of the New Year, he got so excited he jumped up, cheered, and threw his arms around the other three family members. Watching something so seemingly simple was stupendous for him! It is often true that when it comes to children, less is more.

OLD-FASHIONED GAME NIGHT   Invite friends and neighbors and their children into your living room, where you've set up card tables for different kinds of games, board and/or card. Serve chips and dip and other kinds of finger food. The idea here is to have something to do on New Year's Eve, but people do not have to stay until midnight unless they want to.

AN OLD AND NEW PARTY   Invite old and young people—children and grandparents, older and younger friends. Have them wear a combination of old and new—a new blouse, an old skirt or an antique pin. Serve a brand-new recipe and an old reliable one. Encourage guests to bring in something old—a book they've read, some objet d'art they're tired of, costume jewelry that has lost its appeal, even some favorite recipes. Put these in paper bags and, grab-bag style, exchange with other guests so that each goes home with something "new."

A NEW YEAR'S PREDICTION PARTY   There are many "fortune tellers" who are willing to come to parties to predict what the future holds for you and your guests. Some read palms, some read Tarot cards. All are entertaining, and sometimes spookily accurate.

One of my friends throws the I Ching coins every New Year's Eve, asking what he might expect in the year ahead.

LEAP INTO THE NEW YEAR   All family members stand on chairs just before midnight. On the stroke of twelve, each jumps into the New Year. Be careful!

At the Dinner Table

- Decide what was the best thing the family did together during the past year, and make suggestions for what might be good for this year.
- Talk about some things you learned during the past year, and things you'd like to learn in the new one.
- Consider the distant future: What might transportation be like? Housing? Clothes? Family units? Food? Jobs? Child care?
- Go around the table and have each person share a fond memory of the old year, and express a hope for the new one.
- Try to think whether "old business" is completed: any arguments to be settled, debts to be paid, thanks to be expressed?

A Massachusetts Recipe for Wassail Bowl

1 gal. cider
1/2 lb. dark brown sugar
1 T. whole allspice
1 T. whole cloves
2 sticks cinnamon
2 blades mace
1/4 tsp. salt
2 c. dark rum
2 lemons, halved lengthwise and cut into thin slices
3 oranges, halved and cut into thin slices

1. Place cider and brown sugar in a large kettle. Tie the allspice, cloves, cinnamon, and mace in a muslin bag and add to the kettle with salt. Bring to a boil and simmer fifteen minutes.

2. Remove spice bag and add the rum, lemons, and oranges just before serving. Serve hot. (Yield: About three dozen servings)

LET THE NEW YEAR IN   Even if the temperature is 20 below, open the doors and windows wide to welcome the New Year. Hold a moment of silence, and just listen; and make a silent wish for all humanity. Then quickly close up everything, and drink something hot!

SHARE THE NEW YEAR   When children are too little to stay up until midnight, they are often very disappointed. Make them feel better by promising that you will wake them up at midnight, and then don't forget to do it! Say a soft, "It's midnight, Happy New Year," and then tuck them in again. You might want to offer a small glass of apple juice, to toast the New Year, before they go back to their dreaming.

A MIDNIGHT CHURCH SERVICE   Many people like to go to church to welcome in the year, then go home for a very late supper, prepared ahead of time.

"WATCHNIGHT SUPPER"   One family has a big spread of homemade and bought appetizers, some simple, some gourmet. They invite another family with whom they are very close and spend time really reviewing the high points of the past year—laughing and remembering together while they "watch" for the new year to arrive. For some, it's also a family time of prayer for grace and growth in the coming year.

ON NEW YEAR'S DAY

New Year's Day is a great time to be together. Lie low, recall the good times you had this holiday season, celebrate the fact that you are together.

THE BIG, BIG BREAKFAST It is a rare thing for the family to be able to be together for a leisurely breakfast. Consider finishing off the holiday season by going all-out for a dream breakfast. Serve all your favorites—eggs Benedict; huge and "terrible" sweet rolls (you know, the kind with six pounds of butter in them); French toast, mile-high stacks of pancakes; bacon, sausage, ham. Decorate the table beautifully, using all your best dishes.

ASSESS YOUR LIFE Are you, as much as possible, doing what you want to do? Make a list of what you like about your life-style, and what you don't like. Then make a list of changes you'd like to see happen. Are there steps you can take to make the changes possible? Do the same with your relationships, your house, your family interactions. New Year's is a great time for standing back and taking stock.

FAMILY PREDICTIONS Have everyone in the family make five predictions about each other person. Store these in a safe place—a large envelope in your desk, a jar in your cupboard. On the next New Year's Day, read them together to see how well you did.

CALL A NEW FRIEND AND AN OLD ONE Time often sneaks by busy people. Let this slower day remind you to make some plans to get together with people you love, perhaps all at once.

CHRISTMAS THANK-YOU NOTES Have some special blank cards or stationery set aside for this. Make it a family activity, and sit around the kitchen table writing thank-you notes for the presents you received.

TAKING DOWN THE TREE Make some fun out of this by having a progressive party. Go from one house to the next, undecorating the trees at each.

Renew Your Refrigerator

One of housekeeping's most dreaded tasks is cleaning out the refrigerator. But if it's really thoroughly done only once a year, it's not so bad. When you're done, celebrate by buying one (or more) new gourmet items you've always wanted to try. Put them in the place where you removed the "science experiment."

Resolutions to Keep On Keeping On

1. *I will continue eating light during the week so I can eat more on the weekend.*
2. *I will continue to praise my children lavishly for work well done.*
3. *I will keep on doing the best that I can at work.*
4. *I will keep on taking adult education courses.*

REDECORATE A ROOM Have the whole family in on this one. Decide together how an old room might look new, and then rearrange furniture for a different look.

TOY EXCHANGE It's easy for kids' rooms to start getting out of control with great numbers of books, toys, and stuffed animals. Make the first of the year the day to take out everything but the essentials, and store the rest in a place where your children can get to. Settle on a reasonable number of things, and then bring those back to the room. Rotate loads of toys every so often, keeping the number of items the same. When kids don't see things for a while, it's almost like getting something new—they feel like they're going shopping in their own house.

NEW YEAR'S RESOLUTIONS

One of the problems with resolutions is their unique kind of overeagerness. In our desire to use the New Year as catalyst for change, we aim pretty high: Lose 25 pounds. Don't argue with our spouses. Get along with our exes. Find a new, fulfilling, and higher–paying job. Perhaps a good resolution would be to make realistic resolutions, ones that we have a chance of living up to. Thus, instead of vowing to lose 25 pounds, we could promise ourselves to call a weight-loss clinic to check out their program, and/or to do 15 sit-ups a day. We could promise to count to ten—or five—before responding to our spouses angrily. We could look in the paper at the job market four Sundays in a row, to see what's out there.

In addition to making resolutions more realistic, we could make them more "user friendly." Why must resolutions be so self–critical, so punitive? Why not make a few vows to keep on with what we're doing right? Perhaps one of the reasons New Year's resolutions are so hard to keep is that they are too self-centered. Perhaps if we made them about other things, and other people, they might be easier to honor. For example, you can make a resolution to call a lonely relative once a week, or to send him a card. You can resolve to donate one hour a month to a soup kitchen. You can promise to take the dog for a long walk every Sunday.

Human nature being what it is, it may happen that we don't live up to our resolutions very well no matter what their orientation. But it's important to have a desire to improve life for yourself and those you care about and to make an annual commitment to do that. The specifics may not always happen the way that you'd like them to, but loving intentions shape our lives and make a difference, even if we can't readily see it. Resolutions point us in the right direction, give us something to work toward. They make us understand the worth and importance in trying hard. And sometimes we actually lose five pounds.

Let New Year's serve as a reminder that in beginnings lie all hope. Try, whatever your experiences in the old year, to look forward with optimism and excitement to all the gifts the new year may bring.

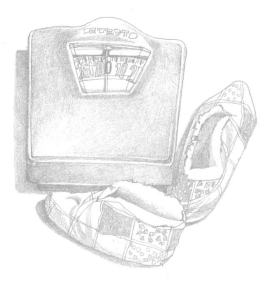

Your Big Day
Welcoming a New Baby
Birthdays
Milestones in School
A Family Reunion

Our lives are filled with everyday events worthy of celebration. Too often, we let them fly by, crowded out by the business of our lives. Yet those times are made richer by building traditions around them. What can we do, for example, to mark a baby's entrance into the world, to honor him not only as a unique individual but as an integral part of a well-established group of people?

And we don't have to stop with the arrival of each family member! There is every reason in the world to make a big fuss over every birthday. It is a person's own, whole day, and she should be told, in every way possible, that all around her are people who are glad she is here.

School, too, makes up a big part of every child's life, for many years. How can we involve the whole family, and become more aware and appreciative of school's many offerings? Though our children go off somewhere else to be in school, and collect more and more experiences uniquely their own, the whole family can share in that major piece of their lives.

There are regular opportunities to celebrate together in the confines of our rather small families. But it can bind us closer to each other to get together with the extended family as well. When we are together with a large group of relatives, we see walking, breathing evidence that some things are shared and endure, and set us off as the bound-together and unequivocally related family that we are. That remarkable evidence is worth witnessing on a regular basis, as are all "big days" in our lives. Make it happen!

Welcoming a New Baby

There may be no family event that so uniquely and individually affects each member as the birth of a new baby. A woman becomes a mother, a man a father, a sibling a brother or sister, a sister an aunt, a mother a grandmother. For each one, the introduction of a new life into an already established clan means something different. While a grandmother may be ecstatic to hear about the birth of a long-awaited granddaughter, that granddaughter's brother may be feeling something quite ... well, dissimilar.

Whatever the individual family member's reaction, however, the reality is the same: Here is a new life, a miracle, full of promise and ready to make his or her own mark. That mark may be as large as a cure for cancer, or it may be relatively small. Whatever it is, though, it will be felt by the world into which the child is born, and it will count. The birth of a baby is, more than anything, a reminder that in this most basic and common of things, the propagation of the species, lies, always, the extraordinary.

Well, so much for the fanfare. What can be done in practical terms to welcome a new baby? What will mark the occasion, celebrate the fact of this important arrival? What will create fond memories for the whole family? This is a time to create an atmosphere where honest expressions of all kinds of feelings are shared and welcomed. It is also a time to look for ways to pay attention to—and save parts of—all the events happening.

Here are some ideas not only for welcoming the newest member of the family but for congratulating the whole family into which it arrives.

BEFORE THE BABY ARRIVES

There are some people who believe it is bad luck to prepare a baby's room before he or she arrives. Not me. Forty-five seconds after I learned I was pregnant, I was out looking at wallpaper, comparing the relative merits of teddy bears, rocking in rocking chairs to evaluate their sleep-inducing potential, rifling through racks of tiny outfits. Getting the baby's room ready was a way of channeling some of my

Family Wishes
You may want to provide each family member with a brand-new, shiny penny to make his wish on. Then put the pennies into a clear, sealed container to keep in the baby's room.

maternal energy. Maybe I couldn't hold my baby yet, but I could select the cloth diapers she'd wear, wash and fold them and have them ready for action. For Mom, Dad, and whoever else makes up your "family," making a place for baby is a great and productive way of preparing emotionally. Here are some unique touches you may wish to add to your baby's room:

WALLPAPER SECRETS If you are putting up new wallpaper, hide things on pieces of paper behind it: good wishes, a poem you like, a paragraph about babies from a favorite writer, a copy of your favorite lullaby, photographs of wonderful or peaceful or meaningful things. Hide anything whose spirit you wish to be ever-present in the room.

"JUST FROM ME" Let each member of the immediate family contribute something of his own inspiration and choosing to the baby's room. Perhaps a sibling would like to pick out a stuffed animal, and the father would like to choose the night-light. Or perhaps their tastes are more, uh, unusual: tie-dyed Frisbees or fluorescent-green baby socks. One earnest sibling I heard about insisted on placing a dried-out sea horse on top of the baby's dresser. Whatever their proclivities, all family members should feel free to pick whatever they'd like, no matter how unlikely the suggestion may seem to others. As long as it's not dangerous, anything goes!

PHOTOS Everyone who lives with the baby can be represented in the nursery. Include group shots as well as individual members. Don't forget pets! Leave one frame empty, and when the baby comes home, take his photo to go into that frame.

FROM ALL OF US Work on something together that you can give the baby after her arrival. Consider a small quilt (simple 6-inch squares will suit a baby just fine), a collage, a painting on or for the wall, a piece of furniture or a toy box made in your basement workroom. The library is filled with books on crafts—needlework, art, and carpentry—to guide you and inspire you. My husband made a beautiful hand-painted rocking horse for our daughter that was in her room waiting for her when she came home from the hospital. I still remember, as though it were yesterday, the first day she sat on it. She was so excited, she screamed at the top of her lungs for at least a full minute. I don't mean cried—I mean screamed in delight. Now that's some gratitude for you!

D-DAY

Labor and delivery is unique for being the only time in your life you look forward to having pain. It's a little like an Olympic event, with you as guaranteed gold medal winner. If you'll be leaving behind siblings to go to the hospital to deliver, make plans for them well in advance. Leave them with someone they know well and trust, and have someone call home frequently to report on Mom's progress. Here are some things to consider for the group in the delivery room.

PRE-SELECTED TAPES Listen to these in labor. Anything from Mozart up to and including the latest top-40 artist can be used and then brought home to be played again for the baby.

The Father Cuts the Cord

When my first daughter was born, my doctor had my husband cut the cord. This seemed a great honor, and quite fitting, too. The doctor also had my husband, rather than himself, tell me what the sex of the baby was. Therefore, my memory of that moment will always be hearing my husband, as awestruck as I was, saying, "It looks like a girl!" My husband also was the first to hold both of our girls, and I firmly believe the few minutes he had with each of them helped form an important and lasting bond. We had already picked their names, and it was my husband who first called them by those names. Ask in advance that your mate be given these same privileges. From the doctor's point of view, they are little things; but I can promise that they will be huge to you, and they will linger long and importantly in your memories.

Collage

Consider "The Year I Was Born" or "My Birthday" as themes. Then include headlines, fashions, technology and science, prices of food, TV-show characters, movies, and so on.

FOCUS PHOTOS   A neighbor of mine who works on an obstetrics unit told me she's seen many women bring a photograph of themselves or their husbands as babies to focus on when the pains come. This reminds them of the wonderful arrival that will be the product of their labor. And often, of course, the new baby greatly resembles the one the mother's been looking at. You can also use a photo of the sibling.

THE BIRTH-DAY PARTY   Many people bring a celebration cake, dishes, and champagne to the hospital with them. Then, as soon as the delivery is over, they have a party, including singing "Happy Birthday" to the new baby. The staff and the doctor are included—though they may have to pass on the champagne, they will certainly enjoy the cake. Half the cake may be sent home to be frozen, then brought out again on the baby's first birthday (when this now seemingly helpless infant will enjoy putting a little in his mouth and the rest all over everything he can reach!).

If there are siblings who are not in attendance at the time of birth, have another party when they come to see their new sister or brother; or defer the party altogether until that time. One woman wrote to me: "Our oldest daughter was two and a half when our son was born. She arrived at the hospital with my husband, complete with a fancy bakery cake and candles. We had a birthday party there in the hospital room for the new baby. It was a great way for a toddler to welcome home a new sibling. After all, how can you resent a new baby who, just by being born, gave you a reason for a family party?"

A Written Account   A mother's own story of her labor and delivery can be something both she and her child will cherish. Write it as soon after the experience as possible. You needn't be a great writer to create this wonderful keepsake—you need only speak in your words, saying whatever you wish. Include what the day was like before you went to the hospital: even mundane things like the weather will be attended to with great interest years from now. My first daughter loves hearing about the cows in the pasture we drove by on the way to hospital when she was born; my second finds it very interesting that we saw a movie while I was in the early stages of labor and that I had not one but two ice cream sodas before she arrived.

Keepsakes from the Hospital   Bring home name cards made up for you and the baby, the wristbands you wore, even menus that you filled out during your stay. All of these things will be interesting later on. If in doubt, bring it home. It's easier to throw something out than to retrieve it later. You may ask for copies of the hospital record, too.

BABY COMES HOME

At last! The baby comes home and all is bliss, right? Well, probably not. This is a glorious moment, but a complicated one. Mom is tired, siblings are a little confused and jealous, the baby is making a rough adjustment to a very new environment, Mom's helpers may sometimes feel (or be) more of a hindrance. In the midst of great joy there is inevitable tension. It helps to expect this. Let yourself—and all around you—feel everything. If you want to cry, cry. If you want to laugh, laugh. Hold the good times close, and understand that the bad times will pass. And celebrate.

Tiny Contributions

Siblings who cannot yet write can nonetheless make journal entries, by drawing or by dictating to parents or others who will write for them.

The best way for toddlers or preschoolers to hold new babies is to sit Indian style.

241

Heirloom
If a ceremonial outfit gets too delicate to be worn any longer, consider framing it.

HOMECOMING OUTFIT   A friend of mine told me of a special tradition that is followed in her family. Each baby who comes home wears the outfit his father wore when he came home as a newborn. It is worn only for that purpose, then stored carefully away. When this family finishes having children, the outfit will be saved for their children's children to wear home.

DECORATING THE HOUSE   It's a fine sight for a new mother to come home and see her house festooned with balloons and crepe paper, all to welcome home her and her baby. The father, the neighbors, and the siblings can all work on this. Lampposts are a good place to anchor a whole bouquet of balloons. The front door can hold a giant "It's a girl!" announcement. A small bouquet adds a nice touch in both the baby's and the mother's bedrooms. A stuffed animal in the baby's bedroom can be holding a congratulatory note.

THE FAMILY CIRCLE   After the baby crosses the threshold into his house, have everyone in the family sit together quietly in one large room. Then pass the baby around to each family member, to be held and admired and to receive a silent wish or prayer. This should be a serious and special moment, with each person saying to the new arrival what's in his heart and on his mind—out loud or to himself. There's no guarantee that the honoree won't be crying, of course, but you can hope for the best. And if this special time does get interrupted by red-faced wails, assure everyone that their thoughts will still get through. Such is the magic of a silent wish.

PHOTO RECORD   Put a picture of the baby taken upon his arrival home into a frame you have bought for that purpose. Every week, at the same time, take another photo. Change the photos each week, keeping the old ones for the baby album.

PLANT A TREE   Start another new life. Plant a tree in honor of the baby on the day she arrives home. Every time she has a birthday, honor the tree, too: decorate it, and give it a gift—fertilizer, a wind chime, a bird feeder, eventually even a swing.

BABY'S BILL OF RIGHTS   When my first baby was about a week old, a visitor became upset that I wouldn't wake her up so that her face could be better seen. But I felt my baby had the right to undisturbed sleep. I wished then that I'd made a Baby's Bill of Rights that I could post on her nursery door for all to see. Number one would have been that the baby deserved to have uninterrupted sleep! You can make such a thing for your new baby, and have the whole family contribute. Siblings may be more apt to comply with rules that they help make.

RECORD THE SOUNDS   Capture the coos and cries your baby makes on a weekly basis. Only a minute or two is fine, until he starts laughing. Then you might not ever get enough.

TOASTING THE NEWBORN   Have a big extended family dinner. Make it a potluck to decrease the work load on everyone. After eating, toast the baby from a bottle of cognac. Then, lay down the rest of the bottle to keep for a major event: her wedding, for example, or her 21st birthday. At that time, toast "the baby" again. Make sure someone takes a group picture each time.

The Time Capsule

Why not put together a time capsule reflecting the day your baby was born—as well as the culture he was born into—to give to him on his 21st birthday? Include these and more:

- an entire newspaper
- many magazines that illustrate the times—a news magazine, a fashion magazine, a "woman's" magazine, a hobby or sports magazine, a computer magazine, a literary one
- postage stamps
- buttons (political and "attitude")
- an annotated grocery list (one that gives the item as well as the price)
- a TV guide
- the price sticker from a new car.

Enclose all of these in a clear, protective container. Years from now, the time capsule will be very much enjoyed by your child, and probably by you, too!

Journal Entries   These are wonderful to do for the baby's first year. Both parents and siblings will have much to contribute. A few sentences a day can go a long way toward illustrating just what life was like that first year. They may also give you some insights on the unique experience of the baby each family member is having—as well as clues to feelings that need attention. These journals can be given to the baby much later, or be kept by the authors as a very personal keepsake.

CONSIDERING THE SIBLINGS

It is of vital importance to pay attention to what other children feel at this time. It's a difficult time for them, having to share so much with someone who seemingly can do so little. All this fuss over a wailing, red–faced bundle! All those beautiful presents going to someone who doesn't even pick them up! All this waiting around for things because the baby seems to always come first! Even very small gestures from you—a loving stroke along the back of a little head, an inclusion in a minor activity—mean a lot at this time. Those gestures may also go a long way toward helping siblings get along later.

Sibling Gift Exchange   Imagine the surprise when the new brother or sister comes to the hospital with a gift, only to find one from the baby waiting for him or her! This beautifully wrapped gift is bought ahead by the parents, naturally, and brought to the hospital. There it is put into the baby's isolette to be found by the sibling, who just may decide, for the time being anyway, that this baby is all right after all!

BIG BROTHER'S (OR SISTER'S) BABY BOOK   Leave this out in an obvious place, such as on the coffee table. Not only will this remind the child that he too was a baby, but he will be oohed and aahed over again by sensitive visitors and parents, just as the baby is being admired now.

A BABY DOLL   This appropriate gift for a sibling allows him to care for "his" baby while his mother cares for hers. I have a happy memory of my daughter "nursing" her baby right beside me as I nursed mine. Hers always burped sooner, I must say, causing me much envy. I would ask my daughter for tips, and she would ever-so-patiently give them to me. A friend of mine tells me her son did the same!

CONSIDERING THE GRANDPARENTS

The storybook reaction to impending grandparenthood is incredible joyfulness. Here is what our parents have been waiting for—a chance to enjoy babies and children all over again, only this time being able to take frequent breaks, and not be where the buck stops. They get to be the ones to "spoil" while the new parents have to discipline. That response happens, it's true. But it also sometimes happens that people aren't ready to be a grandmother or grandfather, and the new role will take a lot of getting used to. Often, of course, there's a blend of both feelings. Regardless of initial response, it's nice to include grandparents in this very special time.

PROGRESS REPORTS   These are much appreciated by grandparents, who may relive the joy of having a baby through what you tell them. Phone calls are good, but

Birth Announcements

Why not let the sibling tell the news? When the birth announcement comes from siblings, it makes them feel more involved; and it establishes a kind of proprietary link that they seem to enjoy.

You can add some commentary to the announcements, if you'd like, perhaps something the sibling said about the baby:

"She's about the size of Daddy's shoe."
"She likes me best."

Gift Suggestions for New Parents

- Frozen homemade dinners.
- A "movie basket" complete with microwave popcorn, candy, and a guide to video rentals.
- Coupons for baby-sitting time.
- Coupons or a gift certificate for housecleaning.
- A coupon or gift certificate for a catered (and cleaned up after) meal in the parents' home.
- The All-Day Present: Fill a basket with things to brighten the day from start to finish. Mark each present with the time it should be opened. For example, the "First thing in the morning" gift could be a gorgeous—or humorous—coffee mug. "Midday" might be a satin pillowcase to use for a nap. "Bedtime" could be bubble bath. "The 3:00 A.M. Feeding", a night-light.
- A camera and film, especially Polaroids.
- Books on child care.

letters last longer. You probably cannot say too much or send too many pictures. This kind of correspondence reassures grandparents of their ongoing importance.

A CHARM BRACELET   Start a bracelet for a grandmother when her first grandchild is born. Engrave the baby's name and birth date on this first charm. Then add a charm for each new baby. My own grandmother had a bracelet with well over 100 charms (grandchildren, great-grandchildren, and great-great-grandchildren), and she had stories galore for each baby represented. I still say one of the reasons she lived so long was from the great aerobic exercise she got wearing that thing!

A PHOTO ALBUM   Grandfather deserves special treatment, too, and an album with the first photo of the newborn already in place may be just the gesture needed.

A WORD ABOUT "SPECIAL" SITUATIONS

THE BABY BORN HANDICAPPED   This is sometimes a terrible shock. But often, such a child proves to be an enormous blessing, teaching a family important lessons in recognizing true priorities, the meaning of faith, the power of love. Each new life, whether it conforms to arbitrary standards of normalcy or not, deserves recognition and respect. As parents of such a child, or as friends, you can set an example for others by your expressions of love and involvement.

THE BABY WHO DIES   Parents who endure this situation need very much to have the brief life of their baby acknowledged. It is awkward for most of us to think of what to say on such a sad occasion, but it is important that we try. Cards of sympathy and love may be far more appreciated than you know.

SHARED PARENTING I have a friend who fathered a child for a woman friend of his who prefers same-sex relationships. Though he of course did not have the baby, nor does he live with her, he nonetheless loves her and is very proud of and involved with her. When his baby was born, he longed for the congratulations and messages of love the mother received, but he received very few. He should have, though. He may be a father in absentia, but he is a father nonetheless.

SINGLE MOTHERS It takes a special kind of courage and love to have a baby on your own. Remember that these women profit as much—or more—from special treatment and acknowledgment as do mothers in more traditional situations.

AN ADOPTED BABY Many of the ideas suggested above are highly adaptable for the adopted child, regardless of his age when he arrives at his new home.

Having a new baby is a real event, monumental in importance. Every child and adult benefits not only from events and indications that he or she is special to particular people, but also from the mementos that can be referred to through a lifetime.

Birthdays

There are two ways to think about birthdays: like an adult, or like a kid. As an adult, you are not exactly thrilled when your birthday rolls around. For one thing, it's a reminder that you're even older. For another, it's a day when, if you're not careful, horrible things can happen. For example, there can be a surprise party at work. Even worse, a tiny choir of harried waitpersons might sing "Happy Birthday" to you while your dining partner looks away guiltily and the rest of the restaurant stares directly at you, smirking. Plus you usually have to buy your own presents.

I

f you ask me, it's much better to handle birthdays like a kid. Then, you leap out of bed on your birthday, full of chest-expanding excitement and general goodwill. You feel a zing every time you write the date. You look forward—rather maniacally, in fact—to opening your presents; and you don't give one thought to how many calories are in the cake and ice cream.

In a world that often feels too big and impersonal, it seems a good thing to honor one person's birth, to make, in that way, a statement that each individual counts a lot. All in your household deserve to have their birthday made special—even the pets. A birthday celebration is an opportunity to tell someone, "Hey—I'm really glad you're here." We owe it to ourselves and each other to take advantage of that opportunity.

THE BIRTH OF BIRTHDAYS

For thousands of years there was no calendar, and so naturally birthdays went unmarked. Gradually, though, by watching the movement of the sun, phases of the moon, and the changing seasons, the Egyptians of 6,000 years ago designed a calendar. The first birthday party in recorded history was given by an Egyptian pharaoh.

The calendar most of the world follows today is one Julius Caesar designed. At first, following this calendar, only well-known figures such as saints, nobles, generals, and national heroes celebrated birthdays. It is only in relatively recent times, in fact, that ordinary people have begun to celebrate birthdays. Even today, in many parts of

Birthday Customs

On a first birthday, it used to be the custom to place a piece of bread, a coin, and a Bible in front of a baby. What he reached for indicated whether he'd be healthy, wealthy, or wise.

The number of candles left burning on a birthday cake tells how many years it will take for your wish to come true.

In Thailand, on the birthday morning, there is a tradition of freeing animals. If the parents of a child can afford it, they buy as many birds or fish, or sometimes both, as their child is years old, plus one extra for the child to "grow on." After sprinkling each animal with blessed water, they let the birds fly free and return the fish to the rivers. This brings good luck.

Birthday Activities

- Visit a nursery to see babies born the same day you were.
- Call a nursing home to see if any residents there share your birthday. If so, send them a bouquet or small gift anonymously.
- Keep a birthday journal to write in each year about how it feels to be your age, and what you look forward to doing in the year ahead.

Superstar Birthday

Send an addressed, stamped birthday card to your birthday person's favorite movie star, asking him or her to sign it and put it in the mail. You don't have much to lose, and the birthday boy/girl would be thrilled to be remembered by an idol.

the world, individual birthdays go unnoticed. Instead, people have group birthdays, and "become" one year older on a given date such as a holiday or saint's birthday.

SOME BIRTHDAY TRADITIONS

Sometimes birthdays are so full of stress and anxiety that the birthday child ends up in tears and the birthday adult feels a vague disappointment that has him shrugging his shoulders and sighing, "Oh well. It's just a birthday." Often that is because expectations are too high on the part of both the birthday person and the birthday planner. Try to remember that the focus is on appreciating the birthday person, responding to her or him as a unique individual whom you are glad to have around. That does not mean spending a lot of money to provide the equivalent of Ringling Brothers for entertainment, mountains of fancy delicacies for food, and presents that make your credit card company have their own party. Rather it has to do with the birthday person feeling that he or she has been gratefully acknowledged. Here are some ideas for honoring the birthday person that you may want to turn into traditions at your house:

BIRTHDAY BANNERS Every year, hang outside a hand-made cloth announcing, "There's a birthday here today!" It can be tastefully simple or marvelously overdecorated. In many parts of the country, a bouquet of balloons is fastened to an outdoor lamp or fence post to announce a birthday at that house.

BIRTHDAY WAKE-UP Sneak in while the birthday person is asleep to decorate her room with balloons, streamers, confetti. Hide a present in a drawer she's sure to open in the morning. Or do as one family I know does, and serve breakfast in bed to the birthday person, followed by presents in bed.

BIRTHDAY MENUS   Let the honored person dictate exactly what will be for breakfast, lunch, and/or dinner. No arguments—on this one day a year, anything goes!

BIRTHDAY TABLECLOTH   Give each family member a sheet to be used as his/her birthday tablecloth every year. Have any guests who attend a birthday celebration autograph it in permanent ink. Hand (and paw) prints are fine here, too.

NOSTALGIA COUNTDOWN   At a family party, go around the table having family members tell about some memory they have of the birthday person. If, for example, the person is ten, start by saying, "When you were one, you learned to walk." "When you were two, you shredded one of my favorite books." At the end, say together, "And now you are ten!"

BABY BOOK RECOLLECTIONS   Pull out the birthday person's baby book, and read aloud certain passages.

BIRTHDAY LETTER   Let everyone in the family contribute to a letter to the birthday person, recalling certain events that happened to her this past year. Pass the letter around to be read aloud. Keep these letters in a birthday scrapbook.

THANKS FOR THE MEMORIES   This is something parents might want to do when their children are young. A few days after the party, write down in a journal or scrapbook a few notes about what happened, how it went. "You had a cake in the shape of a clown, and you immediately ate the nose. The next-door neighbors gave you a doll that you insisted on carrying upside down. Your favorite gift was a yellow teddy bear sporting a red vest."

Treasure Hunt Poem

Give clues to hiding places of presents. For example:

You will find
A little treat
If you go look
Below where you sleep.

Hide the next clue with the present that's found each time. With the last present, leave the final stanza:

I hope you've had
A lot of fun
Your birthday search
Is now all done.

(If making up poems is not to your liking, a simple prose hint will do.)

High-tech Birthday Greetings

If the birthday person has an answering machine, have everyone you can think of call and sing "Happy Birthday."

Gifts for Babies and Toddlers

Bath Kit Fill a plastic tub with a hooded towel, a washcloth, soap, shampoo, and a few toys, such as sponges cut into different shapes.

Beach Kit Give an open-weave plastic tote filled with shovel, sand toys, sunglasses, hat, and a bottle of sunscreen made for babies.

Hat Kit Consider a collection of fanciful hats, and provide a mug rack to tie them on.

Eating Kit Provide a few novelty bottles, a collection of spoons, matching mugs and plates. Include gourmet baby crackers, and don't forget a bib!

Book Kit Even the youngest children enjoy books. Consider a nonbreak-able container to hold a sampling of the cloth variety that is not only looked at but often tasted and happily mauled as well. You can also "mix and match" by using some cloth and some of the heavier cardboard models.

GIFT FOR THE SIBLINGS When children are young, it's nearly unbearable for them to witness someone else getting a pile of presents while they get nothing. Soften the blow by routinely supplying a small gift for those siblings whose birthday it isn't. Sign it from the birthday boy/girl.

JUST-ME BIRTHDAYS This idea works especially well in families with a lot of children. The birthday child goes out to dinner at a restaurant of his choosing, dressed exactly as she chooses, with parent(s). She is, for this time, an "only child." She should be appropriately fussed over—in fact, go to extremes and "spoil her rotten."

A GIFT AN HOUR Spread presents out, to be given throughout the course of the day. This makes a fun part of the birthday last a long time.

ONLY HOMEMADE The birthday person receives only homemade cards from every family member. Both the artwork and the message should be totally original. These cards are keepers!

ONE LITTLE CANDLE Buy a large candle for each family member. When it's someone's birthday, light that candle every year for as many minutes as the birthday person has years.

YOUR SONG OF SONGS At birth, the mother chooses a piece of music to be that child's birthday song. Then, every birthday, when the child awakens, he or she hears that special song.

HALF BIRTHDAYS At the six-month mark, make half a cake, give half a card, and a small gift (half as nice as a regular gift.) This works well once for a surprise party—people never expect it!

BIRTHDAY PARTIES FOR KIDS

Ideas for birthday party themes, decorations, games, and food abound. There are books and magazine articles filled with detailed instructions for almost every kind of party imaginable. There are backyard beach parties, doll tea parties, circus parties, pirate parties, "backward" parties—the list goes on and on. The idea is to think about what the birthday person really likes, and try to build a theme around that. The decorations, the food, and the activities all relate in some way to that theme. If, for example, you have a backyard beach party, have the guests wear swimsuits and bring a towel, and let them play water games. Give a beach ball as a party favor, or sunglasses. Serve "beach food" like hot dogs and ice cream bars.

Of course, it is not mandatory for a child to have a birthday party every year—there is much to be said for a quiet, family party. If you do decide to have a party, though, it may help to keep some things in mind.

How Many Children to Invite   Try the child's age plus one. This seems to work well except at one- and two-year-olds' parties. Then most of the guests are relatives who want to come and bear witness to the birthday child's playing with boxes and wrappings in favor of the gifts they held. In that case, invite as many as you please. Plan on the guest of honor's falling asleep just before the festivities begin, though.

Invitations   Send these out at least a week in advance, asking for an RSVP. Indicate when the party will start, and, more important, when it will end. An hour and a half or

A Recycled Gift

Here's something for youngsters to use to play house. Next time you start to throw away a box that frozen food came in, don't. Instead, stuff it with wadded–up newspaper to help it keep its shape, and tape it shut. Also, save cracker and brown sugar boxes, as well as any other container that would work as groceries in a play kitchen. "Wrap" these in a grocery bag. Then, in addition, give a dishpan, a dishcloth, a decorated kitchen towel, plastic dishes, a pot holder, and paper towels. You can also add plastic spoons and cups.

For Preschoolers

Toothbrushing Kit Give a fanciful toothbrush and cup, with the child's name put on it, if possible. Add a travel-size tube of toothpaste (try a child's variety!), a hand mirror that kids can use to see their good work, an egg timer so they know how long to brush, and some floss. Finish with some gold stars and a small calendar to record each day they remember to brush their teeth well.

Building Kit Try a few sampler packs of different kinds of blocks: plastic blocks, Lincoln Logs, Bristle Blocks. Add a couple of inexpensive plastic people or trees or flowers.

Dress-up Kit Head on over to the local secondhand store. Here you can buy wonderful outfits, complete from hat to shoes. Add some costume jewelry for the deluxe present.

Hair Care Kit Put together a comb, brush, and a mirror. For girls, add a variety of ribbons, barrettes, and hair ties in a see-through cosmetics case. Older girls might like gels or hair sprays. Boys may also like gels and a mustache comb.

two is usually plenty of time for the usual party protocol: an activity on arrival, a couple of games, the opening of gifts, the eating of refreshments, and one more game.

The object of a birthday party is for the guest of honor and friends to have fun. Do not feel compelled to adhere to a rigid schedule of activities. Go with the flow. If the kids are having a great time lining up plastic forks on the tabletop, do not insist they play pin the tail on the donkey.

BIRTHDAY GIFT SUGGESTIONS

While there is a wealth of information on how to orchestrate birthday parties, there is not much about what to give for gifts. It has always been useful for me to think "kit" when considering gifts—and to then give a present of presents that all "go" together. This is easy to do for any age, and always seems to be appreciated. Here are some ideas you may want to use, or that may inspire you to create your own kit.

LAUNDRY KIT It is a peculiarity of young children that they really do love to "help." It is only when they get old enough to do it right that they begin to detest it. While they still find doing laundry glamorous, set them up with a large plastic pan, a tiny box of detergent, clothesline to string between trees, and the nonspring kind of clothespin. Later, make the job more appealing with a personal monogrammed laundry bag. By the time college rolls around, they'll be pros.

PURSE OR WALLET KIT Put in a brand-new dollar bill, quarter, dime, nickel, and penny for the older end of this bunch. A wallet might be enhanced with a picture of the receiver's hero and/or family members. A purse can be filled with a comb, mirror, facial tissues, a pretty pen, and notepad.

TRAVEL OR OVERNIGHT KIT Begin with a cosmetics case to hold a toothbrush, toothpaste, and a small bar of soap. (Hotel goodies from business trips work well here.) Add a hand towel and washcloth and put all into a duffel bag just big enough for pajamas and a change of clothes.

ART BOX KIT Use a 9" x 13" plastic container, so that the underside can be used to draw on. Inside the box put an assortment of art materials appropriate to age, ability, and interest: construction and plain white paper, crayons, markers, colored pencils, stickers, a paint box, scissors, stars, a glitter stick, watercolor pencils and paper, pastels, or oil crayons.

GOLDFISH KIT Assemble a bowl, some colored rocks, some fishfood, a plastic plant, a fish, and a book about how to care for it. If you're giving this to someone else's child, get the child's parents' permission first!

OFFICE KIT Try this combination: paper clips, a variety of pens and pencils, rubber bands, a desk blotter, and "While You Were Out" pads. Scotch tape is nice here, as is a stapler. An ink pad and stamp with the recipient's name and address will be greatly appreciated. You can also add typing paper and envelopes.

PLANT KIT Buy a pretty or interesting plant such as a Venus flytrap. Add some plant food and a watering can. Put the plant in a basket or novelty container.

BASEBALL KIT Give a baseball, a hat, a T-shirt, and a glove. Add a pack of baseball cards.

Gifts for Slightly Older Kids

Gum Ball Machine Toy Kit What is it about those cheap toys offered in gum ball machines that so enthralls kids? Consider buying a smorgasbord of those toys, and then putting them in a decorated tin—with a quarter and a dime taped to the top in case the recipient still didn't get the one he was hoping for.

Doll Supplies Buy sample packs of real diapers. Add a pacifier, baby cereal, and baby toys such as rattles. The smallest-size baby clothes fit many baby dolls and are higher quality for less money.

The Great Outdoors Kit Give a jump rope, jacks, balls of various sizes, colored chalk for hopscotch and sidewalk art, and a kite.

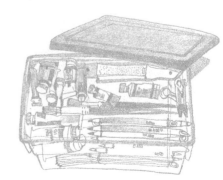

For the Teen in Your Life

If your teenager drives to school, fill his car with balloons and decorate it with streamers while he's in class. Add treats such as chocolate chip cookies for the birthday person and friends. In an envelope, give a coupon for a free tank of gas and a car wash. Hang the envelope from the rearview mirror with a ribbon.

When Your Pets Celebrate Birthdays

All pets enjoy treats to eat. A dog might like a good long walk, a cat a basket to lie in. Toys for dogs, cats, and birds are found in pet stores as well as in dime stores, as are fancy leashes and collars. And celebrating the event is one more time when your family can come together to make memories.

BOOK KIT Buy a paperback book or two, and include a bookmark and a pack of bookplates. There are many kinds of paper bookmarks available, as well as inexpensive metal ones with initials engraved on them. Reference books for children or adults can be given in kit form: consider a dictionary, a world atlas, and a map of the city or state in which you live.

PASSES KIT Everybody likes a day or night on the town. Give passes for two to a movie, a museum, or a ball game, or for roller-skating, bowling, or horseback riding. Include a pass for a free meal at an inexpensive restaurant.

COOKBOOK KIT There is a big variety of cookbooks available. Find one the birthday person would like and add an apron, measuring spoons, cups, cookie cutters, a mini-muffin pan, and a timer. You can throw in cake decorating supplies and a mix or two.

GARDENING KIT Give a variety of seeds and bulbs and the appropriate tools. Add some potting soil and gardening gloves. A little book on gardening is a nice addition, too.

PLAY-GIVING KIT Buy a few copies of a play you like (a children's play, if the recipient is a child). Add a roll of tickets, often available at dime stores. Then add costumes and props from the secondhand store. Consider fake furs, hats, plastic wine glasses, and the famous glasses- and-mustache combination. Complete with some stage makeup (dime store variety).

MAGAZINE KIT Give a few copies of magazines appropriate for the person's age. Add a gift subscription to one of them. Then add a basket to store them in.

VIDEO KIT Give a favorite movie, a box of popcorn, and a large plastic bowl. Complete the package with fancy paper napkins.

Consider a more expensive version of many of the above for the extra-special adults in your life. For example, an evening out is a welcome gift for many parents of young children, especially if you supply the baby-sitter. Also, adults might like a basket filled with exotic groceries such as mustards and sauces, anchovies and capers, etc., for their "kitchen" kit.

Older people might like some help with house or yard maintenance, or a promise to be driven somewhere, perhaps on a monthly basis.

Try to leave enough time for all aspects of birthday celebration—planning the party, buying gifts, making food, and so on. Birthdays should be fun for all, and communicate to the person whose special day it is that all around are people eager and willing to celebrate it with him or her. Ultimately, birthdays need to do only one thing: make people feel grateful for the day they were born.

For the Venerable

If you know someone who's going to be 80 or older, contact :
Greeting Office
The White House
Washington, D.C. 20500
Do this six weeks before the birthday arrives. They'll send a congratulatory message from the President.

Farewell Favors

Give out party bags as guests leave. Booty can relate to the theme of the party: for example, if it was a beach party, give a sand bucket holding a shovel, a deflated beach ball, sunglasses.

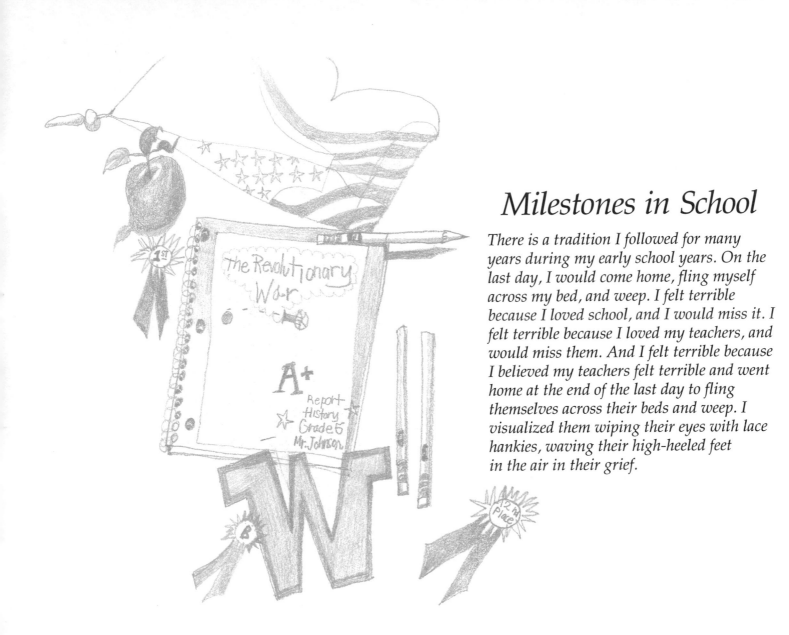

Milestones in School

There is a tradition I followed for many years during my early school years. On the last day, I would come home, fling myself across my bed, and weep. I felt terrible because I loved school, and I would miss it. I felt terrible because I loved my teachers, and would miss them. And I felt terrible because I believed my teachers felt terrible and went home at the end of the last day to fling themselves across their beds and weep. I visualized them wiping their eyes with lace hankies, waving their high-heeled feet in the air in their grief.

I do not recommend this tradition. There is too much anguish involved, and too much embarrassment when, in later years, you learn the truth: Although teachers may like their jobs and be quite fond of their students, they are closer to ecstatic than elegiac on the last day of school. It is as much a rite of passage for them as for the students.

There are other traditions I enjoyed, however, that I do recommend, and happily pass on to you. Other memories, too. (Ah, the smell of saddle shoes that have yet to leave their tissue paper layette, the perfect point of the brand-new number two pencil, the culinary promise of the virginal lunchbox.) I will also pass on things I did not experience personally, but wish I had. Because school is a big deal in one's life—not only for the annual, chest-inflating progress into higher and higher grades, but for the events that occur in a single year, sometimes even in a single day. A school year is rich with possibilities for celebration and for the creation of lasting traditions the family can enjoy.

It is worthwhile to think about how you can contribute to a student's (and your own) sense of anticipation toward school starting. For each year is a fresh start, full of new possibilities for friends and adventures and memories.

THE FIRST DAY OF SCHOOL

A School Tour If this is your child's first year at a school, try to arrange for a tour before the first day. Usually teachers are there a week or so ahead of time for meetings and classroom preparation, so the building is open; and principals are happy to show a new student around. Even if your child is a high school student, it's comforting for her

The Learning Jar
Start a "Learning Jar" at the beginning of every year. After every school day, your child writes down one thing she learned. This can be anything: the year Shakespeare was born; the singular possessive form of "I"; 2+2=4; where Vietnam is; the fact that if you twist the swings on the playground around too hard, you throw up. At the end of the year, take out all the pieces of paper and take turns reading them aloud.

Supplies

Giant office stores carry nearly every school supply you'll need, often at reduced prices. Things are available in bulk, but can usually be purchased in small quantities, too.

First Day Specials

Keep everything that will be worn on the first day in a garment bag labeled: DO NOT OPEN UNTIL THE FIRST DAY OF SCHOOL!

to see ahead of time where she will be on the first day. My daughter and I once had a picnic on the playground of a new school she was to begin that year.

A PRE-SCHOOL PARTY   If you know the names and addresses of children who will be in your child's class, invite them to a get-to-know-you party. Give school supplies such as personalized pencils as party favors, and play the "name game." Everyone sits in a circle. The first person says his name. The second person says the name of the first person, then his own, and so on. This game is guaranteed to help kids learn names fast! But keep an adult nearby, so that if a shyer member of the group has trouble with remembering names, he can get some help. Sometimes just standing or kneeling by someone offers some friendly reassurance.

BREAKFAST EXTRAVAGANZA   Have everyone in the family come for this early morning send-off. The food here should be something really special—eggs Benedict, Belgian waffles, fabulous blueberry pancakes. Let someone other than the usual meal-maker cook. Supply special napkins that are used only on this annual occasion.

THE SEND-OFF   In our neighborhood, children walk to the elementary school. On the first day, most parents accompany their children, especially in the lower grades. Outside the school doors, old friends greet each other, and parents share memories of their own first days. When the bell rings, there seem to be a million hands waving, a million hugs, a million shouted "Goodbyes!" If your child rides a bus and is young enough, make a tradition of waiting for it with them on the first day. For older school-goers, your calming presence and certainty of coming adventures, as well as an enthusiastic, "Have a great first day!" will send them off with good heart.

GOOD LUCK   When my daughter first started nursery school, I gave her a shiny new penny as I was saying goodbye, leaving her in the classroom. "If you miss me," I told her, "just put your hand in your pocket and feel for this penny. It will stay with you all day and remind you that I'm thinking of you; and bring you good luck, too!"

FIRST-DAY LUNCH   If your student carries lunch, this should be an "anything goes" meal—the one day a year when a child can pick anything he wants. It's nice to include a "thinking of you" note, or a funny cartoon, in your children's lunch on the first day. They'll know that they're being thought of while they're away.

STUFFED ANIMAL VIGIL   When my children went off to school in the early years, I set up their favorite stuffed animal in the window to watch for them to come home. This can be carried out forever, a quiet signal between your children and you that you're always happy to welcome them back after they've been gone. There's nothing wrong with a college student (or a 40-year-old married woman home for a visit) looking up to a window to see the ancient teddy bear seeming to say, "Welcome back! I missed you!"

FIRST-DAY SHOPPING SPREE   I'll bet I know how you shop for school supplies: Hoping to beat the crowds, you hit the stores a few days (or even weeks) early. Then, after school starts, you find out you got all the wrong stuff, and you're back there with the crowds anyway. Better, I've found, to hold off until you receive a list from the teacher. Then,

Stay-at-home Shopping
If you or your child hate going shopping, consider looking for clothes in catalogues. Take an evening to sit down together at the kitchen table and pick things out.

Made-at-home Clothes
If you or your child sews, go together to the fabric store to pick out a pattern for an outfit as well as the fabric she'd like to make it out of. Also, let her contribute as much as she's able in making it—cutting out a pattern piece, inserting some straight pins, sewing on a button.

On Buying Name Brands

Nine times out of ten, a copy of a status object will not be accepted by your child, even if you are sure "it's the same thing!" It's not the same thing, and your child will know it.

make a night of it: Have an early dinner out, then hit the stores. In addition to buying what's required, tell your child he may have one thing extra.

STUDY-AREA SET-UP   This is important. Every year, provide a clean, well-lighted and well-supplied area for your child to do homework. Provide an age-appropriate dictionary, atlas, and perhaps thesaurus, even a globe and wall maps. Add paper clips, a stapler, a tape dispenser. Set up this study area with seriousness and ceremony. Don't worry if your child prefers his floor or the bed for study— kids need or like to spread out. But a desk holds supplies, and shows that you take your child's work seriously.

CLOTHES SHOPPING   What would the first day of school be without a new outfit? Buy one up to a few weeks before school starts, but (here's the hard part) don't let the outfit get worn until the first day! If you can, take each of your children alone, so that the focus is strictly on them individually. My husband and I have two children, so we split up, and take one child apiece. Then we meet later for a fancy dessert.

FIRST DAY PREDICTION   The night before the new school year begins, have each child make a wish and a prediction (or several). For example, "I wish for a friend to sit next to me." "I wish for a big part in the school play." Or "I predict I'll get an A in math this year." "I predict that there will be six blond kids in my class." Seal these in an envelope and save to open until the evening of the last day. Did anything come true?

THROUGH THE YEAR

Remember that your child, whatever his age, has a very real need for you to travel alongside him as he goes through school. Every year has its ecstasies and its agonies. Your loving support helps minimize the hard times and amplify the good ones. Through all of these ups and downs, home can be a wonderful refuge, a place where people are interested and invested in him, and love him whether he brings home A's or F's.

PARENTS' NIGHT Get all dressed up, as though you had a very important appointment, because you do! When you get home, have another meeting, this time with your child, wherein you relate at length all the good things you talked about with your child's teacher, as well as everything in the classroom that you noticed.

REPORT CARD DAY This is the night to have a consolation/congratulation cake for dessert. Make it half one kind, and half another, to represent the triumphs and the regrets that report cards bring. About regrets: The person most invested in the child's doing well is the child herself. Your task is to emphasize what your child did right. That is not to say that you ignore bad grades. Children want to know how you feel when they bring home their report cards. But try to comment on "bad" grades in a positive way: acknowledge them, but say that you believe your child has learned something nonetheless and can do better next time. Good grades are their own reward.

SCHOOL PLAYS AND CONCERTS It's truly important that these events be attended. Invite grandparents and others you think might enjoy the event. Dress up. Videotape or photograph the event until your child's embarrassment

Turnabout Report Cards

Report card day might be a good occasion for you to receive a progress report from your children. If you think your ego can take it, tell them to prepare a report card that grades you as a parent. Let them come up with the categories.

Teaching Compassion at School

Request that an area in the lunchroom be set aside for donations to shelters for the homeless. Send in extra food in your child's lunchbox so that he can contribute. Along with canned goods and other nonperishables, consider batteries, discount coupons, sponges, socks, soaps, shampoos (parents who travel can supply a wealth of this kind of stuff), etc. Also, food that is perfectly good but not eaten out of your child's lunch box might be donated: sealed packages of chips or cookies, canned goods, etc.

Sun Pinata

You can make your own "sun" pinata:

1. Blow up as big a balloon as you can find, or purchase a big helium balloon.

2. Make a paste of flour and water, the consistency of watery glue.

3. Cut or tear approximately 2-inch-wide strips of newspaper, and dip these into the flour mixture.

4. Wrap strips around the balloon, leaving an area large enough to insert prizes you've selected.

5. Let dry. (Overnight is usually plenty. You can hang the balloon by its "tag"—insert the end of a wire hanger through this.)

6. Pop the balloon.

(Continued on page 265.)

level prohibits this (and even then, it might be worth sneaking in a little of the action). Keep the programs in a scrapbook or frame them to hang in your child's room.

THE GREAT HOMEWORK TURNABOUT   One day a year, you do your child's homework. Then have him check it. While you're doing his work, let your child do some of yours—balance the checkbook, plan an outline for a presentation. Chances are you'll both end up doing your own work. But it's good to walk in another person's shoes. Also, if your child wants to do his work at the kitchen table, consider sitting with him to do your "homework": paying bills, writing letters, making out menus or a shopping list, reading.

LAST DAY CELEBRATIONS

As there is ceremony in first days, so should there be in last ones. Make this a time to reflect on all the positive things that happened this year, which will help you all look forward to the next.

ICE CREAM SUNDAE NIGHT   An extravagant dessert after dinner on the last day of school seems well-deserved. Provide several kinds of ice cream and as many different toppings as you can come up with: caramel topping, hot fudge, whipped cream, nuts, fresh fruit, crushed candies. No dieters allowed anywhere in sight.

LAST DAY PICNIC   Doing this for your child and class-mates can be fun if you have a big yard and lots of energy. In addition to the food, provide a pinata you've filled with summer doodads: suntan lotion samples, inexpensive sunglasses, sand shovels, a coupon for a free ice cream cone or dip in a pool, little address books so that classmates can write to each other in the summer. Go all-out and add a slumber party.

TEACHER APPRECIATION   In many people's lives, teachers are second in importance only to parents. A fair number of children, in fact, are frankly in love with their teachers and will readily tell you so. Encourage your children to bring a thank-you gift to their teachers at the end of the year. If your school is touchy about this sort of thing, a homemade card will be fine. According to surveys, teachers appreciate these most.

DINNER OUT   This is a great family treat on the last day of school. Pick as nice a restaurant as you can afford, and dress accordingly. At dessert, present your children with a gift for their good work. It should reflect some aspect of their academic year.

ONGOING MINI TRADITIONS

DAILY REPORT   It's a common complaint that when you ask your kids what they did in school, the answer is always the same: "Nothing." That's what happens when you're foolish enough to ask your children something directly. It works a lot better to simply make time available every day after school. Something as simple as 15 minutes daily can yield a wealth of information. Share a snack—kids invariably are riding on empty by the time they get home. If you work away from home, make a telephone appointment for 10 or 15 minutes every day after school—just to check in with each other. Once kids get in the habit of sharing daily, they're more likely to open up. If they don't, though, don't

Sun Pinata (continued)

7. Color with yellow poster paint, and use Magic Marker for features: blue eyes, black eyelashes, pink cheeks, a red mouth, for example. You can glue construction paper sunglasses over the sun's eyes or onto its forehead. Make construction paper "rays," or use gold or silver foil. Bend the straight edges to anchor them onto the body of the sun.

8. Fill the pinata with prizes, then cover the hole with masking tape. If you can't bear to break your artwork, simply pull off the tape.

SAT Anxiety

There are many books and classes available to help your child prepare for the SATs. Be sure you start to use them well in advance, so that they allay rather than contribute to anxiety. Some prep courses last ten weeks!

feel too bad. Sometimes not sharing with parents is a necessary part of growing up and learning a healthy level of independence.

THE TEST ANXIETY TALK DOWN   There arise occasions throughout the year when a test matters a great deal. Both my children have had worrisome times because of this. Something that always seems to help is the same old "talk down" my husband or I give them. Basically, the message is this: Your job is to do the best you can. Study hard as you go along, and then let thoughts of the test go. We follow this with the famous "And then?" exercise: If the child's worst fears happen and he does poorly on his test, what will happen? He will get a bad grade. And then? He might have it affect his GPA. And then? He might get a bad grade on his report card. And then? Obviously, the point is to talk out all the child's fears, and also to remind him that one's goal in life need not be to make straight A's, graduate from Harvard, and make a lot of money. That is no guarantee of happiness, which seems to me to be the real goal. What matters is to be with those you love, and to say so; to honor your responsibilities toward people and the planet you live on; to try to make your life's work something you care about; to work to be the best person you can be. None of this has much to do with a test score.

The last time I did a "talk down" with my 16-year-old daughter, at the end of the talk, she sighed and said, "You're a good mom." Of such events are wonderful memories made.

WEEKLY LIBRARY TRIP   It is good to start going to the library regularly from the time your child starts school (or before). At first it may be only to check out a book for pleasure reading; then it may be a good place to do home-work; eventually, it will be used for writing sophisticated research papers. We always visit a pet store, then an ice cream store after the library.

FROM NURSERY SCHOOL TO COLLEGE
There are many major events throughout a child's school years. Starting and graduating from certain grades, attending certain social functions, even taking certain tests—all these are worth celebrating. What you decide to do, of course, does not particularly matter. What matters is that you are saying, "This is a big deal in your life, and you are a big deal in mine. So let's mark this occasion!"

YEARLY SCRAPBOOKS Each time a new school year starts, present your child with a journal or a scrapbook. Start it with a photograph of your child on the first day of school. Then fill the pages with anecdotes, work samplings, photos of their class or friends, report cards, awards. There are important things worth documenting that may have nothing to do with academics per se. For example, my children have learned about handicaps and musical genius; what prompts a "troublemaker" to act out, the arbitrary nature of popularity, what it's like to be gay.

NURSERY SCHOOL Beginning nursery school is a very exciting and scary thing. And there are ways you can help to make it more exciting, and less scary. Your positive attitude will go a long way to making the experience a happy one for your child.

Starting School Scrapbook One way to prepare for school is to take photographs of the classroom at the student's eye level so that she can, in the security of her own home,

PTA
Oftentimes, mothers and fathers of school-age children feel too time-stressed to serve on the PTA. But grandparents or aunts and uncles or godparents might like to.

Matching Clothes

For younger children who are just learning to dress themselves, use a piece of color-coordinated embroidery floss to identify what goes with what. (Sew a one-inch length onto labels and tie it off.) That way, any shirt with blue embroidery floss will go with any pants similarly tagged. When something will go with "anything" (blue jeans, for example) tag that in white.

inspect at length the new surroundings. You may want to mount these photos in a scrapbook. Most children are eager to show siblings, friends, and grandparents (to say nothing of drop-in guests like the telephone repairman) their school. This is best done before the first day of school, but it is helpful even after. Also, when she has photographs, she can show you the reading corner while she tells you about the story she heard there.

Plant a Seed On the first day of school, start growing something. Keep this in the child's room, telling him that both he and the seed are going to be doing a lot of growing this year. On the last day of nursery school, move the plant outdoors. (Select a hearty, fast-growing seed!)

KINDERGARTEN This may be your child's first school experience, or he may already be an old pro. Either way, each new year presents new fears and challenges. Your continued support will make a difference!

Make a School "Advent" Calendar Draw little pictures of symbols of school: rulers, pencils, books, etc., all with happy faces. Place them randomly on a sheet of paper. Cover with another sheet of paper that has "doors" over the drawings. Make this calendar for the first week, or the first month of school. Tell your child that by the time she has finished opening all the doors, she will have many new friends at school.

Keep Track of Attendance Paste a gold star on the calendar for each day of school attended. Count them up at the end of each month.

FIRST GRADE This is often the first year that children stay in school full days all week. It's also a time for new steps in independence.

Lunch Box Selection Lunch boxes are extremely important. Try to supply your child with a lunch box he adores. You may also want to tape a photo (of family, pet, or other comforting image) inside the top of the lid.

The Walking Test Children are often allowed to walk to school with friends at this age. Take your child out to pass a "walking test" similar to the driving test he will take when he's older. Check off skills as he demonstrates them: when to cross a street, both with and without a stoplight, how to look both ways. "Pass" him by presenting him with a certificate saying he is allowed to walk to school alone.

SEVENTH GRADE This is a prime time for kids to start "getting into trouble": smoking, drinking, using drugs. But this doesn't *have* to happen. Knowing you're on her side may be the telling difference for your young teenager.

Time to Grow Present your child with an alarm clock and tell him he is now responsible for getting himself up and ready for school. He is free of parental wake-ups.

Bring Home a Friend One way to combat peer trouble is by getting to know your child's friends and making them comfortable at your house. Make one night a week "bring home a friend" night: make stretchable meals such as spaghetti or stew or homemade soup on these nights, and set an extra place. Even if it goes unused, it will serve as a reminder that this is a night when guests are welcome.

SENIOR YEAR Like it or not, this is the year when your child is nearly ready to leave home. Help him and yourself by preparing for the near future and enjoying the present. Assign your child a chore that he will soon be doing himself: balancing the family checkbook, for example. Or planning, shopping for, and preparing a family dinner once

Crossing the Street
A Japanese custom is to have little children hold their hands up over their heads when they cross the street. This makes them "taller," thus more visible to drivers.

Budget Training

Let older children help budget for school clothes. Tell them you have X number of dollars to spend, and then let them decide: do they want one pair of expensive pants, or three pairs of inexpensive pants? Then make sure they understand they'll have to live with their decision— that's part of the learning process.

a month. Or being responsible for his own laundry. Though he may resist more "work," he will appreciate being prepared to live in the real, adult world. This also might be the year to do away with curfews.

Prom Night Record, with photographs and/or video camera, as much of this event as you can. Get some "before" and "after" shots—your child in jeans, and then resplendent in prom garb. Let your child borrow something he or she has always admired: jewelry, clothing, or even your fancy car. Before she leaves, a daughter has a "first dance" with her father, a son with his mother.

SAT Day It is a sad fact that much attention (perhaps too much) is paid to SATs, and therefore they make for a great deal of anxiety. When your child starts fretting about SATs, give him a box of "worry dolls." These are tiny figures kept in a box that are brought out, lined up, and assigned a worry each, leaving your child free to think about other things. Particularly effective if used before sleep. This may sound corny, but it can work!

In the weeks before the exam, play "Trivial Pursuit" using SAT question books as sources.

On the day your child takes the test, you take one too: try something for the first time, enter a contest. If there's nothing you can think of to "pass," try questions from SAT prep books. This will make you truly empathetic.

GRADUATION Your child is through with high school! What can be done to mark this very special time?

Say It All Celebration Have a graduation party that includes adults and friends who have been important to your child during her high school years. Provide music, good food, and a time for the sharing on both sides: your child says something, perhaps in a prepared speech, to all who have gathered in her honor. Each guest says something to your child. You as a parent can stand up and say some of what your child has meant to you.

A Graduation Scrapbook In a nice-looking scrapbook, document your child's graduation. Include plenty of photos, artwork, and cards. You can also keep a "secret" scrapbook for all your child's school years; then present it to her at graduation.

OFF TO COLLEGE Send along a quilt you've made over the years from scraps of fabric that have come from your child's school clothes. This is fun to keep secret from your children until the day they leave home. (Warning: prepare for tears from either side upon presentation.)

Send a "care package" to be waiting for them upon their arrival at the dorm. You can send a gift to be opened each day, as well as practical items.

There is a proven advantage, on every level, that children have when their parents are truly involved in the school years. Do all you can to share in this important part of your child's life. It will feel good to them and you.

The College Care Package

- Pajamas
- Stationery
- Bath oils, soaps, shampoos
- Perfumes and after-shaves
- A three-cup electric coffeepot and packages of instant foods such as cocoa, soup, oatmeal
- A few rolls of quarters for the phone and the laundry
- Film
- Coupons for discounts on products your child uses
- Candy, snacks, and gum
- A deck of cards

A Family Reunion

When I was a little girl, one of my favorite things to do was hang out on my Aunt Lala's porch with my cousins. Our parents were having a good time with one another and seemingly oblivious to the hour, and we weren't about to remind them that it was past our bedtimes. The women talked in the kitchen and drank coffee; the men drank beer in the living room and watched the "fights" on the tiny black and white television. We kids crowded together onto one suffering piece of porch furniture, punching each other and taking turns getting another doughnut inside, even though we'd been told over and over that we'd had enough. My cousins Bill and Tim were my heroes. They were smart, and funny, and my age, and they had great crew cuts. My idea of bliss was to grow up and live in a house right between them.

Now, of course, we are all grown up, and although Bill and Tim still live near each other in Minnesota, I live in Massachusetts. And my brother lives in Hawaii! In the way of most modern families, my relatives have scattered here, there, and everywhere. The distance can all too easily become emotional as well as physical.

What can we do to make sure we don't lose contact with our larger family, the one that extends beyond the borders of our mates and our children? How can we keep each other in mind, learn about what we're all up to, feeling, even looking like? Well, one way is to have a real family reunion. Yes, it means a lot of work and planning and commitment. People are short on time these days, and it may take a lot of convincing to get them to put in the hours they'll need to help arrange and attend such a thing. And with the great distances separating relatives, it can be a real financial hardship for everyone to show up. But: IT CAN BE DONE. And it will be worth it!

Real satisfaction and a unique kind of centering can grow out of remembering where you come from, and seeing what you thought were your unique mannerisms echoed elsewhere. One man who attended his wife's family reunion said he understood a lot more about his mate after meeting all her relatives—it actually helped their marriage significantly. Another woman said she found that the experience of sitting at an elongated picnic table with lots of other mothers widened her perspective and comforted her. "I found out I wasn't the only one who had the feelings—good and bad—that I do," she said. "It was great to swap mom-talk with people I'd been a kid with."

A Sample First Letter

To All Davis Family Members:

Do you realize how long it's been since we've all been in the same place together? In fact, some of us have never met each other! What would you say to a big family reunion? If you're interested, could you please indicate which of the following dates and places sound best to you? Mark your choices 1 through 4, in your priority.

Places:

> *Our house here in Texas*
> *A campground in New Hampshire*
> *A cruise to the Bahamas*
> *A dude ranch in Colorado*

Dates (we're shooting for a long weekend):

> *Memorial Day*
> *Fourth of July*
> *Thanksgiving*
> *Labor Day*

Please try hard to come. We'll have great food, activities for all the kids—and adults!—and it will be wonderful for everyone to see everyone!

You can plan a reunion for a day, a weekend, or a week. You can hold it in someone's home or at a resort, even on board a ship. Figuring out how to arrange for a family reunion, from beginning to end can be a real part of the fun. Start with genuine enthusiasm, and the rest will follow.

THE PLANNING

Family reunions usually involve those people of the family name, plus the mother and father of the senior Mrs. (All Davises, plus the senior Mrs. Davis's mother and father.) If the family is small, you can certainly consider inviting both sides. There is no law that says friends may not be invited as well. Don't set yourself up for disappointment by expecting every single person you invite to come. The fact is, no matter what date you choose, it will not work for everyone. And, despite your enthusiasm, not everyone's idea of a good time is a family reunion. So, rather than feel bad about those who can't or won't come, feel terrific about those who do.

In almost every family, there is one member who knows every other. It may be a grandparent or simply someone who feels it's important to keep in touch. That is the person to contact when you begin your planning—which should start, by the way, from a few months to a year ahead of the event! Begin a file of names, addresses, phone numbers, and names and ages of children, as well as specifics for plans as they develop.

Decide if you want to have a reunion for its own sake, or if you want to combine it with another special event. Is someone having an important anniversary? Would you like a Thanksgiving reunion? How about a gigantic picnic on the Fourth of July?

THE FIRST LETTER   Once you've come up with some options (note plural here!), it's time to send out announcements. Stock up on stamps and paper, and send out a form telling everyone of your intention and asking what dates would be best for them.

Once you hear back from people (and be advised that you may need to send reminders or call—perhaps more than once), pick a date and place, then DON'T CHANGE IT! If you do, you will only create confusion and more conflicts.

THE FOLLOW-UP LETTER   When most people have responded, and you've given up on the ones who haven't (not without a warning postcard, please), it's time to send another letter.

Or have participants write a "Do You Know Me?" letter, describing themselves: "I am 40 years old and work as a nurse in the intensive care unit. I have very red hair. I'm terrific at baseball. I have a husband who's in marketing and four-year-old twins who are into everything. I make the best chocolate cake in the world, and I'm bringing plenty of it to the reunion. Guess who I am and win a prize. Write your guess on this paper, with your name on it, and send it to our contact person. See you soon!"

KEEPING TRACK   After you know who's coming, and when, make a chart with arrival times and places. Later, you can decide who will give rides to whom. Also, if you

A Sample Follow-up Letter

Dear Davis Family Member,

We did it! The responses are in, and the time and place that was best for everyone was —. Please let me know via the enclosed postcard if that will work for you, and please try hard to make it work! Let me know when—and how—you'll be arriving. We'll try to coordinate things to combine rides from the airport.

Everybody's presence is so important. It won't be the same without you! [If you are planning a weekend or week-long event, it may be helpful to say here that even if people can come for only part of the reunion, it's better than not coming at all.]

I'll be in touch with you several times before the big event to set up committees, to make plans, and to let you know how things are going. In the meantime, thanks for caring about the family and, again, I can't wait to see all of you!

Come-ons

Once people have accepted the invitation, a series of "come-ons" will help maintain enthusiasm. For example, photocopy several copies of a photograph of a family member. Let's say in this case it's a little girl. Write a description of her: This young lady is five years old. She loves dogs and wants to be a ballerina. She can do splits, and she collects seashells. She has never met many of her relatives. What relation are you to her? Cousin? Great-aunt? Write your guess and return this letter to me. The winners will receive a prize.

are going to be using local motels, make reservations now, and let the families who will be using them know the rates and their room numbers, as well as the names and ages of other family members who will be staying there. Often you can get special rates for booking in advance, or for booking multiple rooms.

In planning where the reunion will be held, you'll need to consider time of year, location, and cost. If money is not a problem, a cruise might be a wonderful idea. If your family's interests lean toward the out-of-doors, a campground might be perfect. If someone has a huge house, you could possibly have everyone stay there—or at least meet there for activities.

It may help to have everyone send a contribution of $5.00 to the person in charge to help cover the costs of postage and phone calls. Also, if a family wants very much to come and just can't afford it, a collection might be taken to help them.

ONGOING COMMUNICATION   The main thing in planning is to keep everyone informed and enthusiastic. Do this with frequent updates and teasers, and by planning lots of activities to make this reunion really fun. Though one person is in charge, committees should be set up for making those plans. The more people are involved in planning the reunion, the more enthusiastic they'll be about coming. Is there an artist in your family? Ask him to design a program for one of the activities you'll be having, or to design a T-shirt you'll be having made for a souvenir. Is there someone who writes? She might like to contribute a story about some aspect of history in the family: the life of Great-Grandma, for example; or some funny, fictional piece that uses everyone in the family as a character. Those good with children can plan and supervise activities for them. So ask for volunteers, make assignments, and then follow up periodically on what progress has been made.

Remember, though, not to organize so much you drive yourself and everyone else crazy. Leave room for quiet times and spontaneity. Above all, know that no matter how carefully you organize, something will "go wrong." Keep in mind the fact that this is all happening so that you can meet and enjoy each other, even if it's not "according to plan." AND: Keep your sense of humor!

WHAT TO DO

A good family reunion considers all age groups. Kids need to get acquainted on their own terms. Teens, for example, are likely to want to have time separate from the adults and might greatly appreciate a day at an amusement park or a night listening to music in separate quarters. Babies can sit in circles close by their parents and chew on each other's toys. Toddlers can mix at a playground; and elementary school ages might enjoy working on a craft project together. Provide for a "kids only" picnic or hike. Adults might want an evening out, too. It is often a real delight for grandparents to care for the little ones, but don't make assumptions! It may work better, for example, for the teens to gather together one night for a mass baby-sit. Following are some ideas for activities:

THE GREAT MEET After everyone has arrived, have each member of the family stand and introduce himself, saying his name, how he fits into the family, where he lives, and, unless he objects, his age. Ask participants to bring along a

Committees

Lodging Checks out accommodations. Makes reservations. Decorates rooms, if he or she desires.

Food Plans menus, buys supplies, orders food in advance if necessary.

Entertainment Decides on things to do and makes arrangements for same. This could involve buying tickets to something, or reserving something for the evening—a bowling alley, skating rink, movie theater. Also responsible for hiring any entertainment.

Finance Keeps track of all bills owed and paid. In charge of paying bills and then getting reimbursed.

Mailings: Writes, photocopies, and sends out notices.

The Family
Member Swap

Trade kids! For the duration of the reunion, let your son "live" with your cousin and his family. If you miss having a four-year-old or wonder what it will be like having a teenager, see if you can "borrow" one.

Places to Have
Family Reunions

- one's home
- guest (dude) ranches
- wilderness adventures, such as river rafting
- a recreational park or campground
- a community hall
- hotels
- aboard a cruise ship
- on a houseboat
- in a "vacation city" like New Orleans or San Francisco.

Use libraries and travel agents to help you make your choice. Also, ask a thousand questions of people who have gone to and/or helped plan reunions.

family memento to share with the rest at this time—a piece of jewelry, an old photograph, a book, or anything else that tells something about the person.

CONTESTS AND COMPETITIONS Have the in-laws versus the out-laws in a game of volleyball. Pit the seven- to ten-year-olds against each other in a tug-of-war. Have a sack race for the four- to seven-year-olds, or for those who are in their 40's. You can also have a fathers-and-daughters versus mothers-and-sons bicycle race, or fishing derby. Mix up all the ages to create teams for softball or freeze tag. Consider time-honored games like relay races, egg-on-a-spoon races. Have a gigantic squirt gun fight.

MUSIC NIGHT Have those who play instruments bring them. Then set aside part of a day for recitals. A program can be printed in advance. Or borrow multiple copies of music from the local high school band or chorus director, and have an impromptu mass concert.

FAMILY CASINO Set up multiple card tables, and gamble for toothpicks. Children who don't like or know card games can play age-appropriate board games.

THE GREAT FAMILY SLUMBER PARTY Just what it says—everyone from Great-Grandma to the newest baby shows up in pajamas. This might work in a gigantic living room, or outside under the stars, or in a rented hall.

GIRLS' NIGHT OUT All the women in the family go somewhere or do something together. This, of course, leaves all the menfolk to do the same. Consider seeing a movie, making a project together, going to the beach, simply hanging out and talking.

MAKE A FAMILY TREE   Create a giant-sized version of the family tree, with a leaf for everyone in the appropriate place. At the end of the reunion, this can be one of the prizes given away. The tree can be drawn on large pieces of poster board taped together, or on more flexible paper that can be rolled up. Have your best artist work on this one—make a beautiful tree, perhaps complete with birds and nests.

CLERICAL SERVICES   Ask a clergy member to conduct a service for just your family. Some people have christenings at family reunions. Maybe someone in the family would like his wedding to be part of a family reunion!

PHOTO TIME   Make sure you make arrangements for someone outside of the family to take a group shot, so no one will be left out. Then make sure everyone gets at least one copy. It could be fun to provide cameras to teens to circulate and take candids throughout.

TALENT NIGHT   All of us have something we can do, even if it's only telling a good joke. Groups may want to get together to plan skits for this, or you can make "assignments" for same.

CHILDREN'S ARTS FESTIVAL   For anyone 12 and under. Put out a gigantic smorgasbord of art materials: construction paper, blank white paper, glue, glitter, feathers, sequins, bits of ribbon and fabric, markers, crayons, etc. Set a time limit, say an hour, and have the children create a piece of art called "My Family."

Accommodations

- When a lot of people sleep in one house, improvising is half the fun. Use mattresses and sleeping bags on the floor and create instant dormitories.
- Rent-it centers can provide dishes, beds, tents.
- Committees are useful for deciding location for the reunion, meals, entertainment, finances, mailings, clean-up. All committees report to the "leader."

FAMILY FASHION SHOW   If your family is the kind to have trunks full of wonderful old clothes, bring them! This might be a good event for the teenagers. Let them put together outfits and parade them before the family one night after dinner.

HISTORY/STORYTELLING   Those age 50 and up tell a story about the family into a tape recorder. Later, all gather around to hear it. Make a time limit—you can say a lot in two or three minutes!

CANDY HUNT   This will be a favorite for the little guys. Hide candy inside or out, and then turn the tots loose with sandwich bags to collect their goodies. If the idea of candy doesn't make you happy, use stickers or pennies.

MEALS

PLANNING   Here is where a committee can really come in handy. Do you want everyone to eat every meal together, or just the evening meal? Do you want all meals to be homemade? Do you want them catered? Or would you like to do both? Some people like the idea of relaxing and not having to worry about food preparation at all. Others find the notion of cooking with others a lot of fun, and they relish the opportunity of exchanging recipes, tasting another person's version of potato salad. If you're going to prepare food, it may help to form teams (be sure to make them out of different families, so that people can get to know each other) for certain duties each meal: shopping (have everyone donate a preordained amount to a central fund beforehand), preparation of tables, cooking, and clean-up duties. Bear in mind that if you are serving hot or cold foods, you'll need something to keep them that way. It is easier to serve as many things as possible at room temperature. Finger foods are always welcome—from deviled eggs to carrot sticks to chocolate chip cookies.

SEATING Ask everyone attending to send a small photo of themselves. Attach this to an index card that has been folded in half so that it can stand up and become a place card. Then, when setting the table, use these for mixing and matching tablemates. The only rule is that no members of the same immediate family unit can sit next to each other (with the possible exception of little ones who want or need a parent's help).

You can rent huge, long tables, and seat large numbers of people together; or you can set up several card tables. Small children do well seated around a coffee table, with a pillow for a chair. Place high chairs between places at the adults' table.

You might consider, if you are having a longer-lasting reunion, having some nights when everyone eats together, and other nights when the kids eat first and then the adults linger over coffee for hours.

SERVING Buffet style works well, or you can put the middle-years children to work as waiters and waitresses. If you do use waiters, make sure that one of the jobs in meal preparation is writing out a few menus—one for each group of about four people.

WHAT SHALL WE EAT?

POTLUCK Have everyone coming bring a dish: assign salads to one group, main courses to another, desserts to yet another.

Souvenirs

It's nice to have something tangible to take away from a reunion. Consider:

Shirts Have T-shirts made up saying something as simple as DAVIS FAMILY REUNION, and the year on them.

Hats Baseball or straw variety, embroidered with the family name.

Photograph Albums to be used for reunion photos only.

Stationery to encourage keeping up with each other.

Address Books for the same reason.

Planning for the Unplanned

Keep a fully stocked first aid kit around. Include acetaminophen for adults and children, dressing supplies, smaller Band-Aids, etc. Know where the closest hospital is, and how long it takes to get there.

Plan for smaller emergencies, too. Have available diapers, umbrellas, extra blankets, extra food, extra toothbrushes, feminine hygiene supplies.

ETHNIC THEMES Have a Texas Barbecue with ribs, cole slaw, and king-sized french fries; or a New England Clam Bake with clam chowder and a variety of fish; or an Italian extravaganza from antipasto to cappuccino.

PIE NIGHT One of the best parties I ever went to was one for simply eating pie. There was a long, long table, laden with every kind of pie imaginable, and I believe I tasted every single one. If you do this, have everyone who wants to contribute bring a pie; serve it the first night. This can also be done with cakes, of course.

MAKE A FAMILY COOKBOOK Do this before the reunion, so that the cookbooks can be given out as souvenirs at the event; or do it afterward, so that when the event is all over, there's still something to look forward to. Here's how:

Ask everyone coming (EVERYONE!) to bring a recipe. It can be a family favorite, or a dish that someone is planning to bring to the reunion. (Often, of course, these are one and the same.) Have the contributor include any family history associated with the recipe.

Sort recipes into categories: appetizer, main dishes, salads, side dishes, desserts. Or organize according to the family: treats from the Tom Davis Family.

Write out the recipes. You can get these professionally typeset, or use someone's home computer. Even calligraphy or neat handwriting works well, and gives a special "homemade touch" besides.

Get the book printed. You can photocopy and tie together copies with colorful shoelaces or ribbon. You can go to a professional printer, too. A copy of a plastic, spiral–bound 100–page book runs in the neighborhood of $6.00 a copy— check with your local printer, and take orders and collect money before or at the end of the reunion, depending on when you're going to give out the cookbooks. Don't forget to include mailing costs.

PLANNING FOR THE NEXT REUNION

Before everyone goes home, have a general meeting about the next reunion. If you can, find someone to volunteer to be in charge, and make arrangements for that person to get this year's records of names, addresses, a time table for mailings. If you can get it together to have the first reunion, chances are people will want to do it again!

A family reunion, with all its extended family, is also a good way to discover much about your immediate family. You'll also have a lot to share after the reunion is over— memories of things that happened, as well as a deep sense of—and appreciation for—belonging. There is a kind of cozy comfort in hunkering down with your own after having spent a while with a really large group. And your family can take real pride in having organized together an event that meant so much to so many.

Afterword

These are, in many ways, difficult and alienating times. In spite of remarkable advances in technology, we seem to have regressed personally. We have lost our ties with each other, abandoned our ways of being family that truly meant something. This has created a sad and empty place inside many of us, a void that needs filling. What do we do about it?

I believe we need to intentionally re-create ourselves as family, replacing all the richness and comfort we seem to have lost with ways that fit and make sense to us as we live now. Our lives are vastly different from the way they used to be, but many of our needs remain the same: to belong; to be comforted; to express and receive love; to have some sense of stability, especially emotional. When we celebrate and create traditions together as families, we are doing all that—and more. We are providing ourselves with a kind of shared spirituality.

It might feel funny at first to try to make changes in your family life. Trying new things can make anyone feel a little uncomfortable. But it's worth the awkwardness, worth the investment. Because it works. When you learn to come together in joy and with regularity, to give to and receive from each other, you not only meet immediate needs but go on to tend to vital places in the heart for the rest of your life. And there's a bonus: When you have that kind of contentment in your family life, it's easier for you to go forth and be a better person to others you meet. Perhaps the way toward a saner and more compassionate world has less to do with whom we elect than with what we do in our own families, in our own living rooms.

I once received a letter from someone who told me about a time he went for a long walk with the family. His three-year-old daughter was beginning to tire seriously, and he asked if she wanted him to carry her. She looked at the setting sun, sighed, and said, "No, thanks. Every time I see a pink sky, I don't feel tired." I believe traditions and celebrations are a kind of pink sky. They renew me; they put something I need in place; and when I am enjoying them, I don't feel tired, either.

We can all be inspired to make our lives within our families full of fun and meaning and an essential kind of energy. And it can happen not only on special days like holidays but also on the regular days, those marching Mondays and Tuesdays and Wednesdays that make up the bulk of our time spent here on this planet.

Life is for nothing if not for celebrating. And if celebrating is shouting our joy from the rooftops, traditions are the houses we stand on to do it. It is never too early—or too late—to start having both firmly fixed in our lives.